REMEMBERING
LOVE

Wendy Portfors

BALBOA.
PRESS
A DIVISION OF HAY HOUSE

This is my story written as I remember living it.

Balboa Press books may be ordered through booksellers or by contacting:

Balboa Press
A Division of Hay House
1663 Liberty Drive
Bloomington, IN 47403
www.balboapress.com
1 (877) 407-4847

Because of the dynamic nature of the Internet, any web addresses or links contained in this book may have changed since publication and may no longer be valid. The views expressed in this work are solely those of the author and do not necessarily reflect the views of the publisher, and the publisher hereby disclaims any responsibility for them.

The author of this book does not dispense medical advice or prescribe the use of any technique as a form of treatment for physical, emotional, or medical problems without the advice of a physician, either directly or indirectly. The intent of the author is only to offer information of a general nature to help you in your quest for emotional and spiritual well-being. In the event you use any of the information in this book for yourself, which is your constitutional right, the author and the publisher assume no responsibility for your actions.

Print information available on the last page.

ISBN: 978-1-5043-6019-7 (sc)
ISBN: 978-1-5043-6021-0 (hc)
ISBN: 978-1-5043-6020-3 (e)

Library of Congress Control Number: 2016910192

Balboa Press rev. date: 08/12/2016

In Memory of Brian

No one saves us but ourselves
No one can and no one may
We ourselves must walk the path
Buddha

$\mathcal{I}$ sit outside the neurosurgeon's office and count the seconds as they tick by. I concentrate on my watch dial as I don't want to look up and make eye contact with any of the other people waiting in the lobby. My stomach is churning and every sip of coffee is adding gas to the fire that is raging. As is my nature, I am early for the appointment. The nurse opens the door and invites the people sitting to my right into the office. I look at the three of them as they stand and walk past me. I see tears in the eyes of the oldest woman who I assume is the mother. I wonder if it is her husband or one of her children that is the reason behind the appointment. I look down again at my watch. Tick, tick, tick. The minutes keep moving on. It is almost an hour before the nurse reappears and calls me into the office. When I stand I feel weak and all my worrying has made me anxious and on edge. I know that it will take all my fortitude not to cry. I glance at the list of neurosurgeons operating from this office as I walk through the glass door and follow the nurse.

Dr. W is welcoming, holding my hand in his and kissing me on the cheek - the Latin greeting even in these circumstances. He has a bedside manner that makes me feel like I am the only patient that he has and I know the waiting room is brimming with other families waiting for news, good and bad, about their loved ones. I sit in the arm chair and try to relax. Dr. W sits down in his desk chair and spins the chair so that he is facing me directly.

"I am afraid that I do not have good news," he says looking directly into my eyes.

I feel my heart start to race and my hands get clammy. I wipe my hands down my pants and pause with my hands on my knees. I am scared to grip the arm chair as I am certain I will leave a mark. I look down at the floor. I swallow, trying to hold back the emotion. I am not sure that I can speak. I want to erase his words. I want to turn back the hands on my watch. I look back up at Dr. W and the expression on his face tells me what I didn't need to hear in words. All I can do is cry.

PART I

The Beginning

ONE

I went to work directly from high school, following in the footsteps of my two older sisters. I never considered going to university, as I knew my parents could not afford it. My father worked hard to raise six children on his salary so that our mother did not have to work and would always be at home for us. We grew up in a loving home, but it was in the era where hugs were infrequent and you did not hear "I love you" every day. Despite that, I knew that our parents loved us.

My first full-time job was working at the local Credit Union in the neighborhood that our family had always lived in. I tried hard to know most of the customers by name, which was part of making people feel like valued clients.

Mel was a customer who came to the Credit Union every Friday afternoon like clockwork. If I was serving another customer, he would wait for me to finish. He enjoyed talking while I completed his banking transactions. Generally, he would talk about his son who was in the Canadian Navy. He was proud of his son's service to Canada. Mel joked that he would introduce me to his son once his son was done his commission. As all good bank tellers do, I smiled and listened to Mel's stories as I completed his banking transactions.

It was Friday and I glanced up and saw Mel waiting in the customer line. When he stepped up to my counter there was an excitement in his voice as he spoke.

"My son will be home next week, and I told him about you," Mel said. "He is looking forward to meeting you."

I was at a loss for words. I had always played along with Mel's comments about meeting his son someday. Of course I never expected that the day would ever arrive when I would be faced with the situation.

"I never realized he was getting out already," I said trying not to sound alarmed. "Is he done?" I asked, feeling a stab in my gut.

"Yes, he is done and will be coming back to Calgary. I will tell him to call you here."

My head was spinning and I didn't know what to say. All I could think about was how I was going to get out of this mess.

I smiled at Mel and replied "Sure have him call. I am sure he has some interesting stories." Silently I was thinking how much I didn't want to go out with a sailor, and especially one who had just been on a submarine for several months. I never even knew what this guy looked like.

The following week I was just finishing with a customer when I was called to take the phone.

"Hi. I'm Mel's son, Brian," the voice said. "Dad said you were waiting for my call. I hope I'm not bothering you. He can get kind of carried away sometimes."

"Yes he did say you would call, but I am working, so I can't talk right now," I replied.

"Can I call you at home tonight?"

I didn't know how to say no so I gave the caller my home phone number and trusted that he would be an okay guy. He had to be okay–right? Mel was a very polite man, so I guessed his son was raised right. On the drive home I tried to play the upcoming conversation in my mind. I had to come up with a rational reason to convince Brian that I couldn't go out with him. I could have kicked myself for getting into this situation. Being nice had gotten me backed into a corner.

I was anxious by the time the phone rang, and I was feeling guilty that I would be lying. All I could hope was that Brian would accept what I said and not push to meet. The phone rang, and I picked up the receiver. I felt a pang in my stomach, as the thought of lying was already making me anxious. I had been raised to always tell the truth, and as I ran over the lie in my mind, I felt guilty. But I was surprised how easy it was to talk to Brian. I told him how I came to know his dad and I had heard all about him. He chuckled and told me about his decision to enlist in the navy and how his dad had not really supported his decision.

I glanced at my watch and realized that we had been speaking for more than an hour. Because Brian was so easy to talk to, I opened up more than I had planned to. We even knew people in common. I paced as we talked, and I was embarrassed as I fantasized about what he looked like. I pushed away an urge to suggest we get together. Deep inside I wanted to meet Brian and hear more about his adventures in the navy. I really was not interested in getting into a relationship. I explained to him that I had already purchased a one way ticket to Australia. I would be leaving in two months to meet up with friends. Luckily Brian was not interested in any relationship either. My comment about Australia led him into telling me about his time there.

We agreed to go out on a blind date that weekend just so that he could tell his father that we had met. We agreed that we would develop a scenario about not liking each other that we would be able to tell Mel later. I felt like a teenager plotting to lie to a parent.

Brian called twice before the planned date, and again we chatted openly. He suggested rather than meeting at the restaurant that he pick me up and we meet the other couples at the restaurant. He thought the time driving to the restaurant might help to shake any nerves. I agreed.

I went shopping for a new outfit. Even though I wasn't interested in Brian beyond the one date, I wanted to look good. As I fingered through the rack I came across a tan-colored jumpsuit. It looked good on me, and my eyes sparkled a darker brown. I smiled as I walked up to the cashier thinking of the jewellery I would accessorize with. Four hours later I paced, looking out the window and waiting for Brian to arrive. I was happy when he was on time. I waited for the doorbell before I opened the door and invited him in. He looked at me and I could see that something was on his mind.

"Of all nights, my Uncle Johnny called, and he is in the city," Brian began. "He doesn't drive in Calgary, so he is at the Carriage House Hotel on Macleod Trail. I need to go get him and take him to my place. He is flying out tomorrow to visit his daughter. I'm really sorry, but I don't have much choice."

"It's okay," I said, as there really wasn't anything else I could say. Not a good start. I just hoped that this was not an indicator of how the evening was going to go.

I'm sure there are some women who would have run the other way. As we drove, I was wishing that I had. Brian talked all the way to the hotel, telling me about his uncle and the great adventures they had when Brian spent summers on Johnny's ranch in southern Alberta. The whole trip I wondered what was going to happen next.

"He's a real character. Wait until you meet him," Brian said as he pulled into the hotel parking lot. We walked into the lobby, and there sitting on a chair was a man strumming a banjo and a group of people standing around him. I knew before Brian said anything that his was Uncle Johnny. He had on worn pants and suspenders over a checkered shirt that had the top three buttons undone, revealing what looked like a button up undershirt. His hat, I guessed, had been a cowboy hat at some time in the past, but now looked like it had been through a tornado and a good stomping by a bull. It was tilted and bent and four shades darker than it should have been because of the dirt and grime. You could clearly see the finger prints on the brim where he lifted it on and off.

"There he is," Brian said pointing.

"I kind of guessed that," I replied.

Johnny stood up when he saw Brian and laid the banjo on the chair. They hugged and gave each other a good pat on the back.

"This is Wendy," Brian said by way of introduction.

"She's a pretty little thing," Johnny answered, holding out his hand to me.

I looked over at Brian and smiled. He tilted his head in that 'had I told you first you may not have come' expression.

Brian picked up Johnny's bag and they walked out to the car. I followed behind already wishing this night was over. Brian suggested I drive Johnny's car and follow Brian back to his house. I guess Brian assumed I could drive, which I could. I just didn't have a license. I had only ever gotten a learner's permit. Also, we never discussed the fact that I had no idea how to get to the district where Brian lived. In my mind, I was already worrying about what I would do if I had to stop at a red light and Brian kept driving. Brian all the while was walking and talking to his uncle and I just followed behind. My heart skipped a beat when they stopped and I realized that Johnny owned what we now term "a boat on wheels." I don't remember the make but it had big tail fins. Vintage 1950's I guessed. The glory days of this vehicle were gone. The bench seat was faded and I expected it was covered in dust like the dash was. I thought of my new outfit as I slid in behind the steering wheel. With Johnny in the passenger seat and his suitcase and banjo case in the back seat we were off. Even though I asked Brian not to lose us in traffic, my stomach was flipping as I drove. I was sure that by the time we reached the restaurant, which seemed more and more distant, I would no longer be in the mood to eat. Johnny kept talking as I drove and I smiled over at him through pursed lips. I thought, *God, could this night get worse!*

Thankfully Brian drove cautiously, so even when the traffic lights were not in our favour, he pulled to the curb and waited for me to catch up. We finally arrived at Brian's apartment. I looked around the living room, waiting while Brian showed Johnny around. I watched as Johnny unbuttoned his shirt revealing a large kilt pin attached to his undershirt. The pin held several twenty dollar bills in place in addition to his daughter's name and address. I looked at this man who was probably terrified to be making a trip to Chicago the next day to visit his daughter. I felt guilty for taking Brian away leaving Johnny alone. He waved as Brian and I left. We were finally on our way to meet my work colleagues.

In the end, the trip to pick up Johnny allowed us extra time to talk in the car. By the time we reached the restaurant, we were comfortable with each other. I already felt a real connection to Brian. Within a couple of weeks, I fell head over heels in love. Brian was exciting, mature and so very interesting. He had travelled to countries I had never heard of. He was worldly. I didn't know anyone like him. My friends were raised in the same district that they still lived in. No one had ventured away from the comfort of the neighbourhood. I had never been anywhere, and Brian impressed me with stories of his navy travels. Even though we both had claimed to not want to enter into a long-term relationship, we moved in together less than a month after that first date. I forgot about my upcoming adventure to Australia and cashed in the ticket.

We both had found what was missing in our lives–love and belonging. Before we committed even further we decided to take a road trip to Florida. I wanted to see the ocean, but we also wanted to escape the winter in Canada. This became our first big adventure, and when it concluded we had travelled over ten thousand kilometres on the three-week trip. We spent every minute on that trip together and talked for hours, sharing our lives, our hopes and dreams. Six months after getting back from this trip, we bought a house, and were married six months after that.

TWO

looked back and realized how easily we settled into married life. I was working for a bank and Brian was in advertising sales. As Brian's salary was based on commissions, we had months when we were flush with money and months when we needed to cut back spending in order to pay the bills. This required us to learn how to budget right from the outset. Our first years meant career changes for Brian as opportunities came along that provided a more stable salary.

After thirteen years living in Calgary, we were presented with the opportunity to follow my career with a position in Saskatoon, Saskatchewan. This would mean moving seven hours away to another province. Brian had no hesitation, since he had ventured away from his parent's home at the age of fifteen, and then enrolled in the Canadian Navy when he was just seventeen. For me however, it was a major decision. I saw my parents and siblings weekly when we gathered on Sundays. Now I would be leaving that all behind. We would also be leaving behind our friends. We would be alone and in unfamiliar territory. Brian promised that we would make frequent trips home to visit.

After saying goodbye to everyone, we drove to our new home. Brian took the lead and drove his vehicle with our dog and cat, and I followed in my car with the other dog. I have to say that the trip was full of mixed emotions. There was elation for the excitement that lay ahead, of a new home, a new community and a new job for both of us. There was also apprehension as we were moving from a city of eight hundred thousand people to a small rural town of twelve hundred.

We had purchased a home in the town of Dalmeny, just north of Saskatoon. It was charming and afforded us good access to Saskatoon on a divided highway. We arrived tired and hungry after an eight-hour drive. After feeding the dogs and getting them settled into the yard, we let the cat out of the carrier. Next we enjoyed a cold beer from the cooler. We sat on the living room floor and ate our take-out meal. We had just enough energy to unpack the sleeping bags and pillows and fell quickly to sleep after eating.

The next day there was a knock at our patio doors. Before we could open the door it was slid open and two people walked in, sliding the door closed behind them. Brian and I looked at each other.

"Welcome. We're Ron and Gail Jepson. We saw the lights on last night so we knew you had arrived." They carried on telling about the town, the familiarity of everyone and some rules like 'we don't lock our doors here' which was a shock to us big city people. Lastly Ron and Gail told us about their family. The oldest girls were twins, Karen and Jane, next came Sandy, then Alex and lastly David. They told us about the church they attended and the bible and youth activities that occupied their children.

The next day we were introduced to all the kids when they came by with a loaf of freshly baked bread. Karen told us that they were told to just drop off the bread and go back home. Brian however, got them talking and laughing and eating candy, and eventually Gail had to walk across the lane to retrieve them for dinner. This was the beginning of a wonderful relationship with these kids. Ron and Gail were genuine people, raising well mannered, giving children.

In the months that followed, the Jepson children went back and forth with regularity. Alex and David were at the age where they required good parenting skills, which we didn't have, so most of our outings to sports events included just Karen, Jane and Sandy. We loved those kids and I smile now when I write this, thinking back to those times. Memories of the Jepson clan and our three years in Dalmeny always held a special place in our hearts.

In 1991 we made the decision to move to the country. Ever since Brian was young and spent summers on his Uncle Johnny's ranch, he had always dreamt of owning his own piece of heaven in the country. He loved the country life and wanted to get up in the morning and walk in the fields and listen to the sounds of livestock.

After searching the newspaper advertisements, we set out one day to drive by properties for a preview before calling the listing realtor. Brian was sure he knew which road to take to find an acreage we had seen for sale. It was a small property that would allow us to live a rural lifestyle and still be close enough to the city for our work.

Brian and I both loved driving down country roads and looking at properties, wishing we lived that lifestyle. Now we were preparing to make a change to fulfill our dream.

When we left the house it was snowing lightly, however it picked up in intensity within an hour. Brian drove up and down the gravel roads, but we never saw the property we were looking for. Not wanting to admit defeat, Brian suggested we backtrack home down different roads. I suggested we stop and ask for directions.

"We're not lost."

"No. We just can't find where we want to go," I said.

As we continued to drive I saw a *For Sale* sign and encouraged Brian to stop.

"Look at this house. I don't think we can afford this," Brian said as we looked down the long driveway to the house.

"I know this isn't the one we're looking for, but maybe they can give us directions. I'm sure with their place up for sale they are used to people stopping," I said.

We drove slowly up the drive and I got out and knocked on the door. The woman invited me to step inside. After a few minutes of introductions and questions she suggested we come in for coffee and her husband would be able to help us with directions.

I walked out to our car. "We're going in for coffee."

"We're what?" Brian questioned.

"They've invited us in for a coffee. They will try to help us find the place we are looking for. She said her husband knows everyone in the area."

"I can't believe we're doing this," Brian said as he got out of the car.

It was two hours before we stepped back into our car. Over several cups of coffee and cookies we realized this kind couple were the parents of someone I knew who was employed at the same bank. It was as if fate had brought us together.

This chance meeting became our blessing. We purchased the one-hundred-sixty-acre farm which would become our cattle and horse ranch for the next twelve years.

Moving away from Calgary changed the close connection with our family. We had missed Christmas dinners, birthday celebrations and occasions like Mother's Day, Father's Day, Easter and Thanksgiving. We had gained, however, long weekend visits in May, July, August, September and October when family would pack up and leave the city life of Calgary and head to the ranch.

Trips to visit us were always exciting times with several families traveling together and descending upon us. There was always lots of laughter, activities and farm chores to share. Of course the cameras were always snapping photos to preserve those precious moments together. Those times spent together are some of my fondest memories. I closed my eyes and could see our nieces and nephews bottle feeding calves, riding on the tractor, learning to drive the farm truck, climbing into the loft of the barn, swimming in the river on a hot summer's day, having picnics, playing on the hay bales and so many more fun country activities that they just couldn't experience in the city.

Each new pursuit brought squeals of joy, and the look on their faces was something that has always stayed with me. When a new calf was born, we would name the calf after family members, and that got the kids excited to come visit 'their calf'.

Those weekends of course, had to come to an end, and I always dreaded saying goodbye. I would be wiping away tears as Brian and I waved at the rear of the cars as they pulled out of the driveway onto the highway heading home. As sad as I was every time to wave goodbye, Brian and I would look at each other and revel in the silence. We had our little piece of heaven back to ourselves.

In 2003 we made the decision to return to Alberta with another career opportunity for both of us. Life on the ranch had been full of good times and happy memories. We also had sad memories when we had lost livestock due to freezing temperatures during brutal winters, drought which pushed the cost of livestock feed soaring, frozen vehicles, power outages, and a host of other problems complicated by weather. Also there was never an end to the work required to keep the ranch functioning.

Moving meant we had to sell off our cattle. I walked amongst them, called them by name and said goodbye to them individually. As I looked at them I remembered the day they had been born or the calves they had birthed. I kept the good memories with me as I left the corral.

In Alberta we purchased a forty-acre property. This was large enough for the horses and it would still give us a country lifestyle without close neighbours. Without the cattle, we looked forward to enjoying weekends golfing rather than mending fences. We packed up and travelled in our vehicles with five horses, four dogs and four cats.

We were thrilled to be back close to family and to the new opportunities ahead of us.

During our years in Saskatchewan, and after we returned to Alberta, both Brian and I travelled for work. Brian would be gone to South America or Mexico. Sometimes I would leave on Monday morning and return on Friday night. This takes a strong, committed relationship. Some people viewed us as two ships passing in the night, but Brian and I were always close and it did not matter where our work took us-we were together. Not a single day passed that we would not speak by phone or through email. Phoning from Venezuela, when Brian was there on business, was impossible so we relied on emails. Leaving the comfort of family and friends when we made that first move actually made us closer as we had only each other to rely on and build a life in the new community. We talked for hours, and every day we discussed our mutual work day, shared the challenges we were faced with, and constantly provided support to each other. We took advantage of work assignments in Vancouver and Calgary to enjoy those cities. We would have a weekend at the farm and then spend the next weekend in downtown Vancouver enjoying all the city had to offer. We knew that time apart meant some sacrifices but there was also a financial gain that would bring us closer to our ultimate goal of financial independence and early retirement.

In 2010 we were presented with what Brian and I felt was the opportunity of a lifetime. It was to relocate to Panama. We had long dreamed of living outside of Canada, so this was truly a chance we could not overlook.

At the time I was sharing care giving duties with my siblings, for my father. My mother had passed away the year before. I told my dad that I wasn't sure I should leave him. He looked directly at me and said "You know what your mother would say. She would tell you to go."

"I know," I said, still hesitant about what my decision would mean for my father.

I left the following week for Panama, as it was necessary for me to formally accept the position. I returned to Canada to make arrangements for Brian and I to relocate. The decision had been made to move my father into a nursing home. On my last visit with my father I showed him photos I had taken of the Panama Canal. My dad passed away less than a month later. This was incredibly difficult as I was in Panama when my brother called. I wondered whether I had failed my father in leaving. It continues to bother me to this day.

I tried to remain positive. Throughout the years Brian and I had viewed every door opened as an opportunity and tried not to focus on what changed when a door was closed. We tried to always look forward. This came partly as a result of guidance from my aunt.

In 1981, my aunt was terminally ill with cancer. She was my mom's sister. I had an incredibly close relationship with my aunt and uncle, they were like second parents. They lived just a few houses from us when I was growing up and our families saw each other every day. My aunt was entering her final weeks after battling cancer for more than twelve years, and Brian and I were sitting at her bedside. We knew she no longer had the strength to fight; the cancer would soon take her life. We would sit and share stories about our life with her, my uncle and cousin. One day she said to us.

"Remember to plan for tomorrow but live for today. Don't be like me and wait for retirement to travel. Enjoy every day you have."

Brian and I never forgot that. We heeded her advice and lived life with no regrets. Now, however, as I faced the loss of my dad, I questioned our move to Panama. I was overwhelmed. The distance between me and my family felt even greater now. I felt alone and uncertain of the decisions that I had made. Once I spoke to Brian I realized that even if I were still in Canada it would not have changed the outcome. My dad would still have passed away. I tried to smile, thinking of my last visit with him.

THREE

We enjoyed a wonderful life in Panama. We were fortunate to have lived in a large thirty-fifth floor apartment in downtown Panama City, with ocean views, domestic help and not a care in the world. We spent weekends golfing, walking on the beach or visiting nearby countries for quick weekend vacations. We loved hosting family and friends on trips from Canada and were always excited to show everyone what made Panama so special.

Brian had always wanted to develop a recreation room complete with a formal bar, stools, and a brass foot rail in our homes, yet we had never done it. He envisioned sitting behind the bar and serving drinks to family and friends as they swivelled on bar stools. When we got the opportunity to relocate to Panama, I went ahead to find a place to live and Brian stayed in Canada to organize our farm to rent in our absence.

When I entered the apartment that was being shown for rent I knew that it was the one for us. Off of the formal living room was a family room complete with a cherry wood bar and a brass foot rail. I took this as a sign that we were meant to live in this apartment in downtown Panama.

I called Brian that evening and described the apartment, the incredible views, the large living space, the maid quarters, the office, but I held back on saying anything yet about the bar. Brian was already impressed with my description, and then I added "and it comes with a full bar, ice machine, brass foot rail and racks for hanging glasses."

"Are you kidding me?"

"No, for real. I thought that would get you."

"Did you take it?"

"I told the broker that we were definitely interested and that I would confirm tomorrow, but I think I will call him tonight to ensure they don't show it to anyone else," I said.

"I am going to hang up so that you can call him right now as no other place will match that I'm sure," Brian said.

We spent countless hours sitting at that bar with family, friends and even by ourselves. It brought Brian hours of enjoyment to sip a beer and look out at the ocean. Friday nights were always special. When I got home from work we would sit at the bar and discuss the week's events and plan what we would do on the weekend to take advantage of this wonderful opportunity to live in Panama.

I think we enjoyed New Year's the most as Panama is a country that loves fireworks. Throughout the city and countryside fireworks were set off for hours on New Year's Eve, and we had a bird's eye view from our thirty-fifth floor windows. We had three-hundred-and-sixty degree views by walking from room to room as we enjoyed the celebrations and I snapped photographs. I remember some booms were so loud that our golden retriever, Kona, got nervous. On the third year, we celebrated at Summit Golf Resort. We golfed in the afternoon and then sipped champagne and watched the fireworks out of our hotel window. We also discussed a vacation we had planned. In the past few months we had taken mini vacations to take advantage of Panama's close proximity to so many countries. In August we travelled to the Bahamas, in September we had celebrated my birthday with a weekend in Costa Rica and in October we had travelled back to Canada for our annual visit with family.

On January 11th, 2013 we had planned to fly on a regional airline to Bocas del Toro, off the coast of Panama near Costa Rica. It is an archipelago comprised of the mainland and nine islands. It boasts beautiful beaches, amazing snorkelling and untouched territory. We had planned this trip for months, waiting for the dry season to be upon us. We travelled to the regional airport and waited with great anticipation. It was a short flight across the country and I looked out the window at crystal clear aqua coloured seas. The mix of blues and greens is always breathtaking to me, and no matter how many times I flew over a Caribbean ocean I was always awestruck. It felt like we had landed in another world. We walked across the tarmac and talked about the upcoming days. Brian had planned to go scuba diving and he was excited for the opportunity. He had spent the past few months updating his knowledge on line and completing the examinations necessary to update his diving certification. I was excited just to be in Bocas to experience new adventures, create new memories and of course for the photography.

On the second day, Brian checked in with the dive shop and signed the necessary paper work to join a dive group scheduled for the following morning. We spent the day walking around the town and eating at the amazing ocean-front restaurants. The next morning, much to Brian's disappointment, the dive was cancelled. He was offered a chance to dive that night but he declined. Instead we went on an island tour which included snorkelling and lunch at a floating restaurant. I look back on this and thank God for intervening and cancelling the dive. Had Brian gone diving he most likely would have died from an embolism.

Transportation between the islands was on boats of varying sizes. There were larger boats with big docks that attracted crowds of people who were willing to wait for the next available boat. Brian noticed that there were several smaller boats that seemed to be individually owned tied to a smaller dock. The captains sat patiently waiting for customers. He walked up to a boat with an older gentlemen sitting in it.

"Are you for hire?"

"Si, señor. Where do you want to go? I can take you anywhere. Come, come, get in" he answered waving at us to board the small panga. We stepped into the boat and sat on the wooden bench. We noticed there was only a small twenty-five horsepower motor, so it would be slow travelling.

The old man told us that the fare was $3.00 per person each way to Red Frog Beach. The hotel staff had told us about the Red Frog Beach Resort. It was a popular destination to visit for lunch, to walk the pristine beaches and to search for the poisonous red frogs.

"We want to go to Red Frog Resort first, but we also would like to boat past some of the other islands on the return trip, so you can tell us how much at the end," Brian said.

We were the only passengers in the little boat as it set out across the water. We enjoyed a leisurely trip.

"You can stay as long as you like. I will wait here for you," the captain said as he lent me a hand to step up on the dock.

"Thanks. We will probably be a couple of hours," Brian answered.

"No problem señor. I will be here waiting."

We walked down a long sandy road that led to the resort. The beach was amazing, and we climbed up to a lookout and watched waves crash against the rock cliff. We enjoyed a beer in the tranquil setting and chatted with guests before we started the walk back down the road. We totally forgot about looking for the poisonous frogs.

True to his word, the little man was sitting in his boat waiting for us. As we stepped down into the boat and settled on the bench, Brian asked him to stop at two other islands on the way back so that we could jump off and enjoy a beverage at the floating restaurants. The little man accommodated us and was amazingly patient as we jumped on and off his boat. At the last stop we met three young guys who had been stranded on the small island when their boat had left without them. Brian told them to jump into our boat, but that they would need to pay the $3.00 fare for the ride to the mainland. The young guys readily agreed and paid the captain when we dropped them at their hotel dock. The boat pulled away and we went down the beach to the dock where we had started from. Brian and I jumped out onto the dock, thanking the little man as we disembarked.

"How much do we owe you?"

"Just $10.00 señor."

"What about for you waiting and the extra stops?"

"The young men paid for the return trip. Just $10.00 señor."

Brian handed the little man a $20 bill and thanked him again extending his hand. The man held Brian's hand between his and smiled. He tucked the bill into his pocket, and as he turned we saw tears in his eyes. Brian and I looked at each other in surprise realizing how much the $20.00 meant to this small boat owner. We suspected our money plus the $9.00 the young men had paid probably exceeded what the man made on most days. We felt good to have made his day.

Before returning to our hotel we stopped at a water front restaurant. We walked out on the dock where we sat and talked, enjoying a beer. I climbed into a hammock and swung as I sipped my beer. We talked about how lucky we were and how much we were enjoying life in Panama.

FOUR

*T*hat four-day weekend came to an end too soon and we boarded a plane back to Panama City, arriving in the evening. We had been in bed just a few hours when Brian woke me up.

"I have a really bad headache. A real bastard of a headache," he said as he got out of bed and went to the bathroom to get some Tylenol.

"Didn't you already take some Tylenol?"

"Yeah, but it hasn't seemed to help. This is crushing!"

As Brian climbed back into bed I looked at the clock. It was 2:15am.

"Wend, wake up," Brian said shaking me. "My head is killing me."

I sat up and rubbed my eyes to come awake. Brian was sitting on the end of the bed with his head in his hands.

"You still have your headache?"

"Yeah. Nothing seems to be working."

"Do you want to go to the hospital?"

"I think so. I need them to give me something for this pain."

It took me a minute to orient myself and get dressed. I drove the five minutes it took to reach the Emergency unit at the hospital. Brian walked in unassisted, and as there was no one else in Emergency we were seen within minutes. The attending physician asked Brian numerous questions and gave him a shot to dull the pain. Brian was rubbing his neck, but when asked if his neck hurt he said he didn't have any pain in his neck. The attending physician, called Dr. S, the physician Brian had been seeing since we arrived in Panama. After several minutes and more discussion, they summed up Brian's current pain to neck injuries he had received years earlier and for which he had a prescription for pain medicine. After another hour Brian was feeling better and wanted to go home. As there didn't appear to be anything significantly wrong with him, they released him and we returned home.

The next morning Brian was feeling better, so I went to work. Our domestic employee, Danya, would be at the apartment so I was confident that if Brian's headache got worse she would call me at work. By midmorning I called home and spoke to Brian. He sounded fine and everything seemed okay. At lunch I called home but no one answered. I assumed Danya was cleaning and hadn't heard the phone. I continued to call for almost two hours and all calls went unanswered. I was feeling anxious, so I left work and drove the few minutes back to our apartment. When I arrived I walked into the kitchen to talk with Danya, but she wasn't there. I called out to Brian but got no response. His car was in the parking spot, so I assumed he was out walking.

I walked from the kitchen through the living room and could hear the television in the family room. I found Brian in the family room. He was fumbling with the cordless telephone trying to change the television channels. He frowned as he looked up at me.

"Where is Danya?" I asked.

"I don't know."

I walked from room to room to see if she was cleaning down in the bedrooms and just had not heard me. Danya wasn't anywhere. I could only assume that Brian had sent her home, otherwise she wouldn't have left. She of course had no knowledge of Brian's trip to the hospital the night before. I walked back into the family room.

"I can't get this damn thing to work and it ain't the batteries," Brian said, sighing heavily. "I was trying to get things ready for tonight but I didn't know who was coming over" he continued, looking over at the bar. I turned. On the bar rested every bottle of liquor we had, all lined up with glasses and the ice bucket.

"What are you doing?" I asked hesitantly, wondering what the hell was going on. We weren't haven't any people over tonight. It was Tuesday night. I could feel pounding in my chest as my pulse quickened.

Brian didn't answer the question but continued to focus on the telephone handset, pointing it at the television and pushing buttons. I stood there glancing from the bar to Brian and trying to comprehend what was happening. I walked over and picked up the television remote and changed the channel.

"Great. Finally, this damn thing worked. I've been trying to change the channel all afternoon," Brian said, as if he had changed the channel.

"How are you feeling? How's your headache?" I asked.

"I don't have a headache," he said rubbing the back of his neck.

I don't know how long I stood there trying to understand what I was looking at. Brian sat contently watching the television. Finally, I went into the office and called Dr. S on his cell phone. It is a wonderful circumstance in Panama that you are provided with the direct phone number to reach the doctor. I know that this is in part due to the fact we had exceptional insurance coverage but at times like this it was nice to know I could reach the doctor directly. I was able to hear back from the doctor within minutes. I explained the situation and his immediate response was that the confusion could be related to a stroke.

"Can he walk?" Doctor S asked.

"I don't know. He hasn't moved from the couch," I answered. "He's not slurring his words or anything like that. I mean what he is saying doesn't make any sense, but the words are clear."

"I am just leaving the office to attend a function, but I can come by the apartment on my way home. I will call you in a couple of hours. Just keep your eyes on him and make sure he doesn't fall."

"Gracias," I said.

I walked back into the living room and looked at Brian who was still focussed on the telephone handset.

"Did you have lunch today?"

There was no reply, so I continued. "What time did you send Danya home?"

"I don't know," he said looking at me with a vacant look that scared me. His eyes darted around the room. I wondered if he even knew who Danya was.

"Let's go to the kitchen and make some supper," I said and waited for him to stand. He wasn't unsteady at all which I was relieved to see, thinking that at least he didn't have a stroke. What had happened I wasn't certain, but I was confident that it wasn't a stroke. From what I understood about a stroke, Brian should be slurring his words and in addition to speech problems there should be some facial changes. Brian looked the same. He was confused for sure, but nothing else. His face was not drooping, his arms seemed to be working fine, and there was no sign of any paralysis.

I got him to sit down on a stool at the end of the island. I put potatoes in front of him and gave him the peeler. "Can you peel those?"

"No problem," he said.

I turned my attention to cutting up a chicken breast. Once I got the chicken in the frying pan I turned around and saw that Brian had not peeled one potato. He held the peeler in his hand and was looking at the potatoes, but it was clear that he was not making a connection between the peeler and the potatoes.

"Here, I'll do that," I said as I moved beside him and started peeling.

"I think I'll go to bed," Brian said and moved off the stool.

"Aren't you hungry?"

"No, we ate earlier," he said.

"What did you eat?"

"I don't remember."

I turned down the stove burner and walked with Brian through the living room, down the hallway and into the bedroom. I waited until he was undressed and in bed before I left the room. It was 7:30 pm.

I went back to the kitchen and finished cooking the chicken and put it in the fridge. I no longer felt like eating. My stomach was churning and I was getting more and more nervous as the minutes passed. I stayed up watching TV and waiting for the doctor to call. At 9:40 the phone rang and I grabbed at the handset that was resting on the couch next to me.

"Good evening, Wendy. How is Brian?" Dr. S asked.

"Actually he is sleeping right now. He didn't eat anything, but he can walk fine and nothing really seems wrong with him when I look at him except he is confused," I said.

"Okay, that's a good sign. Would you like me to stop by anyway?"

"I don't think there is any point," I replied.

"Well, bring him in to see me tomorrow," he said.

"I will. Thanks for calling," I said before hanging up.

I was confused as to what had happened to Brian and wondered if it was a TIA (transient ischemic attack) or mini stroke. My father had experienced several of those and was fine within a few minutes. I couldn't get it out of my mind and wished I would have asked Doctor S about it.

I was worried and could feel it in my body. My stomach was flipping somersaults as it always does when I get nervous. I felt exhausted, but there was no reason for it. I shut out the lights in the family room and walked down the hall into our bedroom. Before I undressed I stood and looked down at Brian. He was sleeping peacefully. I walked around to my side of the bed and clicked on the table lamp. I undressed, washed, and brushed my teeth by instinct. I pulled the comforter back and climbed into bed next to Brian. Toes, our cat, jumped up and nestled on the comforter between us. I reached down and patted her and she sang a song for me. I lay for a long time watching the minutes on the clock tick by. I was worried, and trying to put things out of my mind just wasn't working. Despite that, I eventually nodded off.

I sat bolt upright as I heard Brian making noise in the bathroom.

I reached for the light on the night stand and tried to focus my eyes on the clock. "Are you okay?" I hollered.

"Yup. Just getting a Tylenol," he replied.

"Do you have a headache?"

"No. I feel fine."

His response made me wonder about the Tylenol comment, but I didn't say anything. Brian had always taken a lot of Tylenol, so I thought maybe it was a reflex reaction that he took the Tylenol because the bottle was on the counter. Brian got back into bed and rolled over draping his arm over me. I snuggled into his body and felt comforted.

Brian was restless and kicking his legs which woke me. I looked at the clock. Three hours had passed. I reached over and shook him.

"Bri, wake up. Are you okay?" I asked as I turned the light on and got out of bed. In the reflection of the light I realized that Brian was thrashing about as he was tangled in the sheet.

"My head hurts. Like it really hurts. It's fucking killing me."

"I think we should go to the hospital, Bri."

"Me too," he said as he sat up on the edge of the bed.

The clothes Brian had taken off were folded on the chair on his side of the bed. I walked over and picked up the pile.

"Just put these on," I said laying the clothes on the bed beside him. Then I walked into the closet to get dressed myself.

When I was dressed I grabbed my purse which held the car keys.

"Ready to go?"

Much to my surprise, Brian was still sitting on the edge of the bed in his underwear.

"Why aren't you dressed?" I asked as I walked around the bed.

He looked up at me. "I don't know."

I handed him his tee shirt and watched him as he stared at the shirt in his hand. My stomach started to spin. I realized Brian couldn't dress himself. I pulled the shirt over his head and slid the shorts up over his knees.

"You will have to stand up now to pull up your shorts," I said as I pulled him to his feet.

Since moving to Panama we rarely wore long pants as the humidity was oppressive. I was glad for that now, as pants would have been too difficult to get on him. Brian stood, pulled the shorts up, buttoned and finished by zippering his fly. Unlike when he went to bed, he was now unsteady on his feet. I held on to him as we walked down the hall from the bedroom and across the family room to our front door. Luckily the elevator was right there and our car was located near the elevator exit in the parking garage. I tried to talk to Brian on the way down to the car, more to steady my nerves than his, but his replies only served to increase my anxiety level. He stood leaning against the wall of the elevator and squinting his eyes from the pain. I watched as the elevator counted down from our thirty-fifth floor. Luckily at this hour we didn't have to stop for anyone. By the time we stepped off my heart was racing and a cloud of doubt fell over me.

Brian weighed two hundred and twenty pounds, so he was not easy to hang on to when he started to walk at a tilt. It took all my strength to keep him upright from the elevator to the car. He nearly fell stepping down just one step. Once I got him into the passenger seat he reclined the seat fully and I worried that he would pass out before we got to the hospital. He didn't say a word as I drove the short trip. Of course, I hit red lights and I was tempted to jump them to quicken the trip. I pulled up to the emergency entrance and shut off the car. Brian did not move. I walked around to open the door for him. The security guard from the previous night recognized me and saw me struggling to get Brian out of the car. He waved at me to wait and ran into the hospital, returning seconds later with a wheelchair. It took both of us to get Brian from the reclined position into the chair. We had him in the wheelchair by the time a hospital attendant came out to help.

As we rolled Brian through the wide glass doors I noticed the same physician from the previous visit.

"He needs a CT scan," I said as I walked beside the attendant pushing Brian down the hall.

"What happened?" the doctor asked.

"I'm not sure, but I think he had a stroke," I said as it was the only thing I could think to say. I really didn't know how to explain his actions from last night.

The doctor took hold of the wheelchair and exited down another hallway. The man who had helped me get Brian through the double doors was a nurse, and he now walked me over to the registration counter. A woman sat at the desk. The nurse talked to her quicker than my mind could interpret. I stood quietly looking at them, not wanting to interrupt. I was getting a headache trying to understand the medical conversation in Spanish. Even though I worked in Spanish, I had no idea of medical words. I finally grasped some words I could understand. They needed a deposit from me for the tests. I was glad I had brought my purse, as the thought of having to pay for anything had not crossed my mind.

I then followed the nurse through another set of doors to the front of the hospital and the Administration Department. The hospital required a deposit of $10,000.00. I walked into a booth and sat down across from a strikingly beautiful girl. She had amazing skin, little makeup and eyes that shone. Her beauty was enhanced when she smiled. She spoke very quickly in Spanish.

"Habla mas lento, por favor," I said, indicating I would like her to speak slower. She repeated her words but not at a much slower pace. Then she wrote $10,000.00 down on a piece of paper and turned the paper to show me. My headache was getting worse.

I opened my purse and removed my Visa from my wallet and passed it to her. I silently tried to remember if I had paid the Visa balance. After a couple of attempts, she was able to get preapproval for just over $8000.00. She spoke to a young man who was walking past the booth. He stopped and stepped in. I was relieved when he spoke clear English. He told me that in the morning I could fill out the insurance papers and then the deposit would be returned to me. He confirmed that the $8000.00 would be sufficient. I was so glad to hear English I wanted to hug him. He gave me his card which I tucked into my purse.

I knew at this point I should have called my good friend and colleague – Victoria. She would have comforted me and I would not now have a headache. Victoria would have intervened and handled everything at the hospital. I have a strong, controlling personality and I always think I can handle all situations. To me it was a sign of weakness to fold under the pressure in a crisis and this certainly qualified as a crisis. These traits had contributed to my career success but I should have reached out to get assistance.

I walked back into emergency unit still with my pounding headache. The nurse ushered me into a cubicle, and it was only a few minutes until Brian was wheeled in and the curtain pulled. I saw no one else in emergency.

I looked down at Brian. "How do you feel?" I asked.

"I have a bad headache. Where are we?"

"We're at the hospital. You just had a CT scan to see about your headache. We are waiting for the doctor," I explained.

"Okay. Did they give me something to get rid of this pain?"

"I don't know. I wasn't with you. Probably not until they get the results I would think."

Just then the doctor came in. "How are you feeling now?"

"I think I'm okay," Brian answered.

I looked from Brian to the doctor and interjected. "He has a really bad headache."

"We have the scan results. Can you follow me," the doctor said as he opened the curtain and stepped from the cubicle.

'I'll be right back, Bri," I said as I followed the doctor. He was standing only a few feet away. He showed me his phone which had an image on it.

"This is the CT scan result. I have just sent this off to the neurosurgeon. He will call here in a couple of minutes and you can talk to him. I will put the image on the computer. Come with me."

I could barely walk. My legs felt like rubber. A neurosurgeon, I thought. That can't be good. I made my way behind the counter and stood at the doctor's side. He was moving the mouse over images on the screen. I just stared at the screen. There was a mixture of shaded areas on the image, all of which meant nothing to me.

The phone rang, and after speaking the doctor handed the receiver to me.

"Hola. My name is Dr. W. I am the neurosurgeon on call. I have looked at the CT image. Are you able to see the image on the computer?"

"Yes."

"Your husband has suffered a stroke and has considerable bleeding into his brain. The dark shading is blood. This is the cause of the pain. I will get ready and come to the hospital. It will take me twenty minutes."

All I could squeak out was "Thanks." I stared at the screen and the large area of the image that appeared darker. I tried to grasp what he had said. *A stroke, considerable bleeding.* I looked at the doctor and then turned away from the image on the computer screen and went back and stood by Brian's side. I said nothing to Brian but I silently tried to correlate what the neurosurgeon had said with the fact that Brian showed no outward signs of a stroke. His arms were moving around as he rubbed his forehead.

I looked at my watch. It had been less than two hours since we arrived at the hospital. In that time the CT scan was completed, sent to the neurosurgeon and I spoke to the neurosurgeon on the phone. I couldn't help but think if we were in Canada - we would still be sitting in the emergency room waiting for someone to deal with us. We would probably be sitting in the emergency room for several hours, I reasoned. Right now I was glad we were in Panama, no matter what the cost.

I looked at Brian who was vigorously rubbing his forehead.

"My head's killing me. Can you get them to give me something so that we can go home?"

"I just talked to a doctor. He is on his way," I answered. I did not want to alarm Brian by saying that the doctor was in fact a neurosurgeon.

It seemed like only a few minutes before the curtain was pulled open. A tall distinguished looking man walked in with the attending doctor behind him. He reached out his hand to me. "I'm Dr. W, the neurosurgeon on call. I spoke to you on the phone. Can we speak in Spanish?" he asked.

"I'm not sure I would understand everything, but we can try," I replied.

He smiled back at me. "Then I will try to explain in English."

He leaned down and touched Brian's hand. "How are you?"

"I got a headache. Can you give me something to help that, Doc?" Brian asked.

Doctor W continued. "The CT scan shows that you have suffered a stroke and shows considerable bleeding on your brain." He paused, looking from Brian to me.

Brian had no response, and I wondered if Brian even heard what the neurosurgeon had just told him about the stroke.

"We are going to keep you here overnight if that is okay?" Dr. W asked.

"As long as you get rid of my headache, I'll do anything," Brian replied rubbing the back of his neck.

Doctor W spoke in Spanish to the attending doctor who walked out of the cubicle. He returned within a couple of minutes. "We're going to take care of the pain," the doctor said and gave Brian a couple of needles which immediately calmed him down.

Doctor W looked over at me. "Here is my card and my cell phone number. Brian will be admitted and I will talk with you later today. Don't worry. We will take good care of him."

I followed behind as they wheeled Brian into the elevator and into a unit which I clearly understood - ICU. I kissed him although he was already fast asleep.

The unit was uncomfortably quiet. I went down the elevator and walked out to the car. I stood for a few minutes taking in the beautiful warm night. I breathed in the sea air and closed my eyes. I was in paradise, but it didn't feel like it right now. I looked at my watch. It was 4:30 am. I opened the car door and slid inside. I put the key in the ignition, turned it on and started to back up without looking in the mirror and I almost hit a car pulling into the emergency parking. Luckily an accident was averted, and I drove the few blocks home without seeing another car on the road. I walked into our bedroom and fell fully clothed on the top of the bed. I closed my eyes and tried to rest.

Sleep evaded me. My mind was spinning and my thoughts were turning dark thinking of the image on the computer and the amount of bleeding it showed. I thought of how Brian could still move, and that to me was positive. He didn't seem to have any paralysis, no slurred speech, nothing. I convinced myself that I was being silly thinking negative thoughts. We were lucky. Maybe it was just a mild stroke. I was confident that he would fully recover. He was strong.

In less than two hours I was standing in the shower. I made coffee and then called my office. I didn't think I had the strength to talk to anyone. Victoria was the Operations Manager and a dear friend. I left her a message that I wouldn't be at work and would call later and explain. I was glad that it was Thursday and the weekend would give me some time to process what was happening.

PART II

An Unexpected

Journey

FIVE

I went back to the ICU at 7:30 am. Brian was eating breakfast. He had on the tee shirt and shorts he had worn the night before, and I wondered if he had slept in them. He smiled when he saw me.

"How are you feeling?"

"Okay, I think."

"Do you remember coming to the hospital?"

"Not really," he said, looking directly at me.

"Well, you had a bad headache." Before I could carry on, Brian cut me off.

"Yeah, I remember the headache."

I sat on the edge of his bed.

"Am I okay?" he asked.

"Well, they did a CT scan early this morning. It showed that you had a stroke. You have bleeding on your brain, and that is why you had such a bad headache. We met with a neurosurgeon. They are going to keep you here a few days until they can get the swelling to go down and do an MRI."

"Where are we now?"

"You are at the hospital."

"Oh! How come?"

I felt a stab in my stomach. I smiled at Brian but did not repeat the conversation. I wondered if this was normal. Hell, how would I know what normal was?

A nurse slid the glass door open and stepped inside. "He has been asking for you," she said in pretty clear English. She walked around to the IV bag and then checked a machine that must have been measuring something but at the time he wasn't even connected to it. I wondered what the IV was for. Brian smiled at her as she walked around the bed and then disappeared as quickly as she had appeared.

"Was the doctor here this morning?"

"I don't know. It would be nice to have something to read. Did you bring anything?"

"No, I didn't think about it. I only left at 4:30 this morning, so I thought you would be sleeping when I got here. I will bring something back later."

"Are you leaving?"

"No. I just mean when I leave later I will pick up something at home for you to read before I come back. I can go downstairs and see if I can get you a magazine," I said.

"No. I don't feel like reading. I think I'm going home this morning."

I breathed in deeply. Brian was really confused and it scared me. I could feel my pulse quicken. My hands felt clammy and I rubbed them on the sheets of the bed.

"A neurosurgeon came to see you before you were admitted. He was very nice. I'm just going to go out and check with the nurses to see when he will be here so that we can get more information," I said as I slipped from his room.

"Doctor W's office is in the tower attached to the hospital. You can go there and talk with him," the nurse said.

Well, this was something new to me. In Canada it would take a referral and an appointment before you could ever get to talk directly to a neurosurgeon.

I walked back into Brian's room. "I am just going to go call the doctor and then I will be back," I said. I stepped outside of the ICU and decided to call the number the neurosurgeon had given me.

"Buenas dias, Dr. W. It is Wendy Portfors. You saw my husband, Brian, this morning in emergency."

"Yes. I was just there to see him this morning as well. Are you there now?"

"Yes I am just outside the ICU."

"I will be there in ten minutes and we can talk."

The morning news was on the TV, and there were inviting chairs and couches in the waiting room. I decided to continue standing as I did not trust myself to sit down in case I fell asleep from exhaustion. With my finger I traced the circular pattern on the cloth chair.

True to his word, the neurosurgeon was there quickly.

"Miss Wendy, how are you this morning?"

"I am not sure yet."

"Let's sit here for a minute," he said pointing to the couch. "Your husband has considerable bleeding on his brain. We are giving him medication that will reduce the bleeding so that we can get better images and determine what is going on. Tell me what happened before you came here this morning."

I told him about our trip to Bocas del Toro and then Brian's headache when we returned, the first trip to the emergency department, and then what brought us back.

"I thought with a stroke you have some paralysis," I said.

"That is true most of the time. We will not know exactly what caused the stroke for a few days. Brian is a healthy strong man so that is important right now."

"He seems really confused," I said.

"That is normal. There has also been an impact on his short-term memory. When the swelling goes down the memory may improve. Sometimes it does. We will not know for several days. He is a lucky man."

I looked at him and smiled. "I know it could be a lot worse," I said.

He stood and pointed to the doors. "Let's go see how he is now."

I followed Dr. W through the glass doors into the ICU and then past the nursing station to the cubicle Brian was in. Brian was sitting on top of the covers. He looked up at us but did not speak.

"Hey honey, how are you?" I asked as I kissed him.

"I'm fine," he replied.

"Brian, my friend, how are you?" Dr. W asked as he took Brian's hand in his.

"I'm fine Doc. I don't know why they have me in here though. Maybe you can tell me that."

"Do you remember our conversation earlier this morning?" Dr. W asked Brian.

"No," Brian said looking at me.

"Well, you are a very lucky man. You have bleeding on your brain which has caused a stroke. We are giving you medication so that we can do more tests and see what's going on."

"Oh, okay," was all Brian said. He then turned his attention to look out at the nurse walking past the glass.

"I'll see you later Brian," Dr. W said. He motioned for me to walk with him.

"I'll be right back Bri," I said, as I stepped outside of his room.

"I will check back on him later today. Call me if there is any change; you have my number. Call me whenever you want. We should know more in a couple of days. Until then we will keep a close eye on him. Like I said, his short-term memory has been impacted and that is why he doesn't remember that I was here already today. That may improve once we get the bleeding under control. My concern is that he is very confused."

I didn't tell Dr. W how concerned I was. Hell, I was scared to death. I went back into Brian's room and talked with him until he closed his eyes and fell asleep. I was thrilled that he looked so good. I was thankful that he could move and had no paralysis. I felt like we had dodged a bullet.

SIX

While Brian slept I decided to make the short trip home and bring back something for him to read. I knew I should make phone calls to family in Canada, but I was uncertain what to tell them at this point. I was operating on only a couple of hours of sleep and my nerves were jangled. I reasoned that by the end of the day I may have more information and emotionally I would be in a better state. I was back at Brian's bedside within an hour. He was still sleeping, so I stood and stared at him. I didn't know what else to do. The ICU was very quiet and you could hear every movement of the nurses as they checked on the other patients - the clicking of their shoes, the whispered conversations, the wheeled sound of IV stands.

Brian opened his eyes, and seeing me, tried to sit up.

"Why don't you keep sleeping. I brought you a couple of magazines and the paperbacks that were beside the bed. I don't know if you have read them or not. Also I brought you this little note book. It has a pen attached to it. I thought you could write in here when you think of something you want me to bring. Then you wouldn't forget. I could read it when I come to visit."

Brian looked at the notebook. I placed it on top of the table that swung over his bed. "It is right here when you want it," I said.

"Thanks."

I left the unit to go get a cup of coffee and when I exited the doors I was surprised to see Alicia sitting there. Alicia was one of my team members. She had come across from the office so that I would not be alone. I almost broke down in tears.

I stayed at the hospital until after Brian had supper and then I left to go home and face the calls I knew were necessary back to family in Canada.

I called Brian's sister, Katie, first and asked her to go over and sit with her mother, my mother in law. Katie only lived five minutes away, so this was a good option. I did not want Brian's mother to be alone after I told her Brian was in the hospital. She was approaching ninety years of age. She had talked to Brian only a few days before when we were getting ready to go on vacation. He had told her about our plans and his excitement to be getting the chance to scuba dive again. She, of course, had told him to be careful.

"Hi Mom. Is Katie there?" I asked.

"Yes, she has the extension. What is wrong?"

I took a big breath before I continued. I was standing, looking out to the city of Panama. My heart was racing.

"Brian is in the hospital. He had a stroke. He is going to be okay though. He has no paralysis and is able to talk and walk so I think it is just a mild stroke," I said cautiously. I tried to be as honest as I could without alarming them.

"What happened?" they asked simultaneously.

"When we flew home Monday night Brian complained of a bad headache. He took Tylenol through the night but it just did not let up, so early Tuesday morning I took him in to the Emergency at the hospital. Because he could talk and walk they just gave him something for the pain. They called the doctor Bri sees here for his blood pressure medicine. They assumed maybe his pain was related to his neck which bothers him from time to time," I said.

"But today is Thursday," his mother said.

"I know. So anyway he went home on Tuesday and was fine for the rest of the day. Yesterday there didn't appear to be any change so I went to work. Danya was working yesterday, so I knew if anything happened with Brian she would call me. Anyways, last night the headache came back and early this morning I took him to the hospital and they gave him a CT scan which showed the stroke."

"How long will he be in the hospital?" Brian's mother asked.

"We don't know that yet. They will do more tests and I will know more after the weekend. He is being seen by a top neurosurgeon. I will email every couple of days and give you an update. Don't worry about him. He will be okay."

"Give him a hug for me," his mother said.

"I will."

I walked to the family room and poured myself a drink. I needed something to steady my nerves. I could feel the emotion was just below the surface and continuing to talk about Brian being in the hospital was going to break me. I stood in the office and dialed my brother Wayne. I repeated the same information I had just shared with Brian's mother.

Wayne was shocked, but elated that Brian had no paralysis. I know he could hear the quiver in my voice.

"Do you want me to come down?"

"Thanks, but not now. They will be running more tests. Bri can walk but is a bit unsteady. He talks fine and then it is like he has a brain fart and can't think of a word, and then he gets off track with his thoughts talking about something totally unrelated. His short-term memory has been impacted, but the doctor said that is to be expected. I will call you in a couple of days when I know more," I said before saying goodbye. I asked my brother to advise my other siblings as I just didn't have the strength to repeat the story four more times. I was certain that I would break down and scare everyone, including myself. The distance between Panama and Canada felt magnified. In Canada the family would be with me at the hospital and we would be comforting each other. Now I stood alone to face what lay ahead.

I breathed in deeply. I had gotten through the conversations with Brian's mother and Wayne without crying. I took a sip of my drink and then dialed the phone for the last call to Brian's best friend, Larry. I repeated the story of what had happened over the past couple of days again.

"I'm going to hop on a plane and come down," Larry said.

"No, I would prefer that you wait," I said. Before I could continue Larry cut me off.

"You can't keep me from my best friend."

"I'm not trying to keep you from him, but Brian is in intensive care and so even if you came down you probably can only see him for a few minutes each day. In a few days, after the MRI, we will know more and then we can plan your visit. I hope that they let him out in a week or so, and then he will be at home when you come," I added. "I'm trying to adjust to this news as well and trying to do the best I can. You know Brian. He would prefer to see you at home and not in the hospital."

Larry was quiet. I could hear him breathing, but he said nothing. He and Brian had been friends for thirty years. They had met at a company Christmas party as Larry's wife and I worked for the same bank. The husbands were so bored not knowing anyone at the party that they spent their time up at the bar getting drinks, and over the course of the evening they uncovered all the similar interests they had. Since that party in 1983 we had developed a unique and close friendship sharing many vacations and visits in each other's homes. We had so much history between us, and I knew the pain Larry was feeling as I was feeling it as well.

We agreed to talk the next night and plan Larry's trip to Panama based on Brian's progress.

SEVEN

I arrived at ICU the next day and was locked out of the unit. The nurses told me that visiting is restricted to one hour in the morning and one hour at night. The previous day they had let me in when I rang the buzzer, and frankly I hadn't even read the sign about visiting hours. I was frustrated. Unlike the other patients in the ICU, Brian was alert and needed me at his side. He was confused and I knew he would not understand why I was not there with him. The nurses said they could do nothing to allow me more visiting time. I didn't know what else to do so I left the unit, and walked back into the hospital and headed for the neurosurgeon's office. I knew that I needed to get authorization to be allowed to spend more time with Brian. As I stood in the elevator I got concerned that I wouldn't get a change to the visiting hours, and that hadn't crossed my mind until then.

I sat in the waiting room and watched people stream one by one into the various offices. The longer I waited the more anxious I became. I wanted to be professional, and I practiced going over in my mind what I would say to the doctor. Unfortunately, by the time I got called into his office I was blubbering and could get no logical thoughts to spill from my lips. I started crying uncontrollably. The neurosurgeon picked up his cell phone and dialed. I barely listened to his words as he spoke rapidly in Spanish.

"Mi esposa," he said handing me the phone.

I placed the phone to my ears. "Hello, Miss Wendy. I'm Doctor L. My husband wants to know why you are crying. He has called me as I am fluent English."

"I'm sorry to bother you, but no one understands that I must be allowed to see my husband. The nurses at ICU say they can't allow me in except for an hour in the morning and another hour at night. All we have in Panama is each other. There is no other family. We can't be separated. He needs me and I need him" I said shakily.

"Is that all?" she asked.

"Yes. I just want to be able to come and go whenever I want."

"No problem. Pass the phone back to my husband."

"Gracias," I said before I passed back the phone. As Dr. W concluded the conversation with his wife, I wiped away my tears and quietly blew my nose.

"Don't be upset. I will arrange to move Brian today. It will be okay for you to visit. I will go with you now to the ICU and tell the nurses it is fine to let you in," Dr. W said, as he stood and motioned to the door.

We walked in silence to the elevator. I couldn't help but think how I would ever get this much personal attention from a doctor in Canada.

Brian had been asking the nurses every few minutes where I was and asked to use the phone. The phone number he gave them was our phone from when we lived in Saskatchewan, ten years earlier. The nurses of course, could not dial the number. They were glad when they saw me walk in with Dr. W.

The following day Brian was moved to the semi-intensive care unit where I was allowed to visit him at all hours. This was good for me and the nursing staff, as it kept Brian from asking the nurses to contact me.

I walked into his new room and was pleased to see Brian sitting at a small table. He did not look like any of the people I have known that suffered a stroke. He had no paralysis and was about to get himself dressed. He still wore a tee shirt and his shorts every day, refusing to put on a hospital gown. The hospital was very accommodating. The only real noticeable change was that his memory was impacted and to me that was something we could deal with. Brian was alive and moving, and I thanked God for that.

There was no real change that day or the next. On the third day I arrived and sat down on the edge of his bed. I told him about all the emails from family in Canada and then chatted about nothing in particular. He asked questions that did not relate to our life in Panama, and I wondered if perhaps he had just dreamed of being in Canada.

"Were you dreaming about being back at the farm?" I asked.

"I don't think so," Brian said, looking down at the notebook.

"You were just talking about the farm so I thought maybe...." My words drifted off as the neurosurgeon walked in.

Dr. W was a good-looking man with kind eyes and a pleasant smile. He had an amazing bedside manner. When he stepped into the room he placed his hand on Brian's shoulder and told him how great it was to see him sitting up. Brian smiled.

"How are you feeling today?" he asked.

"I'm fine."

Dr. W looked across at me and his face changed to one of concern. The smile was gone and his eyes now looked apologetic.

I turned my glance away not wanting to make eye contact. I felt a pain in my stomach and my heart rate quickened. I knew instinctively that the words the doctor was about to speak would not be what I hoped to hear. I looked at Brian who was content sitting on the top of his bed. I thought of him sitting fully dressed and wondered how he could possibly be a patient in the Intensive Care Unit. I looked back at the neurosurgeon.

Dr. W looked down at Brian, but his words were directed at me.

"I have some real concerns as your husband seems to be having difficulty getting his mind to advance. He is stuck on one thought. See what he has written in his book today."

What the hell was he telling me? Was it that Brian's memory was more impacted than originally thought? Wasn't this something we could deal with? I noticed that the neurosurgeon held his facial expression, and that worried me. There was no way to put into words how I felt. I listened to his words and tried to concentrate.

I looked at the little yellow note book, not wanting to turn the cover. On the page was written:

- *my cats name is toes. She is grey and has green eyes.*
- *my cats name is toes. She is grey and has green eyes.*

I glanced down the page and counted the statement repeated five times in less and less clear script. I gulped. We did have a cat named Toes, but she was black and white.

I held the memo book in my hand. I did not know what this meant, but I had a gut feeling that it was not good. I smiled at Brian whose eyes were darting back and forth from me to Dr. W.

"You really wrote a lot today. Good for you," I said trying not to sound concerned.

"I couldn't think of anything to say," he replied.

"You talked about Toes," I told him smiling. We had shipped Toes from Canada to Panama and she was clearly Brian's cat. One night while we were driving home on a rural road near our acreage in Canada, Brian caught a glimpse of something in the headlights and pulled to the side of the road. Walking along the grass were kittens. Brian had stopped the truck and he caught the little black and white kitten, but the rest scurried into the ditch. We could hear the kittens crying as they searched for their mother. It was clear that someone had dumped the litter and we knew they would most surely die. The next day we had driven back to see if any of the litter had survived the night, but we could not see or hear them. Brian felt better knowing that we had at least tried to save them. From that moment on, the kitten he named Toes was a part of him. Even though we had two other house cats at the time, Toes had stolen his heart.

"Brian, I would like to ask you some questions about today and how you are feeling," the neurosurgeon said.

"Do you know who this is?" Dr. W asked pointing to me.

"Yes, it's Wendy, my wife," Brian replied.

"How long have you been married?"

Brian looked at me and I knew he was searching for the answer. Finally, he said "Twenty-five years I think."

I looked first at the doctor and then at Brian. "We've been married thirty-seven years, Bri."

"That's a long time," Brian replied. We all laughed.

Dr. W asked Brian several more questions and with each question Brian looked at me before he answered as if he was uncertain of what the correct answer was.

"You are doing very well physically, but I have to tell you that we have concerns as you are repeating your thoughts and the nurses tell me that you are doing the same when they speak to you," Dr. W said.

I didn't know what to say to make the situation any better. I looked at Dr. W. "Will that improve with the medication?" I asked.

Brian and I both looked at the doctor.

"It is hard to say. We will have to do more tests. Could you stop by my office today?"

I felt anxious. I knew the request to go to his office probably meant that there was bad news to deliver. I looked at him and shook my head up and down so that he would know I would come by the office. Dr. W said goodbye to Brian and walked out of the room. I wanted to cry, but I bit my lip so that I did not break down and alarm Brian. As soon as Dr. W walked out, Brian started talking about the weather. Brian had already forgotten what the doctor said.

I sat with Brian and flipped through the yellow note book.

"Why don't we practice writing your name," I said, turning the book around for Brian.

He took the pen in his right hand and held the book.

"Do you want to write your name?" I asked again.

"Not really," Brian replied.

"Okay. Well, write whatever you want. It's good practice," I said.

Brian laid the pen down and turned his attention to the television. He watched it for an hour and then, still lying on the top of the bed, he fell asleep. When he woke up we chatted briefly, but he was not interested in having a discussion.

"I'm going to leave Bri, and go over to talk with the neurosurgeon. I will see you tomorrow."

"Okay, I'm going to sleep anyways", he said, not taking his eyes off the television.

"Do you want me to change the channel before I go?"

"No."

I kissed Brian and told him that I loved him. Then I went down the elevator and crossed the hospital main floor to the professional tower that was attached. I arrived at Dr. W's office and only had to wait twenty minutes before he stepped out to greet me.

"We will complete another MRI tomorrow and hopefully it will give us more information about what caused Brian's stroke," he said. "There is a possibility that the stroke was caused by a tumor. I don't want to think of that now. We will stay positive, but I want you to know that I am very concerned over Brian's thoughts repeating. We will watch closely every day and hopefully we will see change."

"I thought maybe it was normal that he couldn't write or think clearly," I replied.

"There should be some confusion, but Brian is not able to get his thoughts to advance, and that is not normal. Let's just wait for the next MRI. I will speak to you once we have the results," he said and stood.

I took that as a cue our meeting was over, so I stood and thanked him before I walked out. I felt weak with his words ringing in my head. I smiled at the receptionist as I passed her desk. I walked down the concourse and around the corner until I was in the waiting area for other doctors. I sat down trying to gather my thoughts. The tears flooded in before I could get control of myself. People seated look at me. I reached in my purse for a tissue and wiped at my eyes before I stood and walked to the elevator. I was glad that no one else stepped inside. I rode down alone.

When I got home I tried to focus on being positive, but Dr. W's words kept flooding my mind. A tumor. What will that mean, I wondered. Eventually I drifted off to sleep, but it was a restless night.

EIGHT

The next morning I logged into Brian's email account. There were several emails from his business associates in Canada. I send a quick email to say that Brian is just not feeling well and will not be sending emails for a few days. I know this will generate questions but I don't know what to tell them at this point. After I was done I went to my office as it was too early to visit Brian. My mind was not on my work. I walked into Victoria's office and we talked. She made me feel loved and encouraged me that all would be okay. I walked back to my office and closed off my computer. As I turned to leave, Maria walked in. She told me that she was praying for Brian every day and that a special prayer was shared in her church. She knew that it would help. I hugged her. I was so encouraged by the faith and compassion. I felt like there were guiding arms around me as I walked across to the hospital. My feelings were deflated as Brian was not the happy-go-lucky man he usually is. He did not want to talk or watch the television. He had no interest in the books that were on the night stand. He was laying under the covers, completely dressed. This was the first day I had arrived that he had not been sitting up in the chair. I offered him candy, and he said no. For Brian this was a first. He ate candy no matter how sick he was. He did not know if he'd had breakfast, but I assumed this was just his memory. He rolled over and dozed off to sleep.

I picked up his yellow note-book. Some of what he had written was indiscernible.

I turned the page and he had written:

- *how do I turn on the television*
- *how do I turn off the TV*

I counted down and the statements were repeated eleven times. Seeing the statements over and over made me anxious. I felt my hands start to sweat. I looked over at Brian sleeping and wondered what the days ahead would be like. I rested my face in my hands and closed my eyes. I wanted to stay positive, but I felt a dark cloud looming overhead. I felt tears building and kept my face covered. I stood and went into the bathroom and washed my face to hide the redness in my cheeks. I stared at myself in the mirror and tried to smile. I heard Brian moving in the bed, so I walked back into the room.

I was disheartened as he was not awake and the movement I heard was just him rolling over. I stood beside the bed and ran my hands through his hair.

It was a long day as Brian's mood didn't improve much. I watched the television and talked to him, but it was a one-sided conversation. He ate most of his supper, but then drifted off to sleep again. I wondered if they had changed his medication and that was why he was so sleepy. I kissed him goodbye, but he did not wake. I walked out to the elevator and rode down to the lobby. I walked across the street into the parking garage for my office building. Within ten minutes I was home.

When I walked into our apartment our cat Toes started meowing. I wondered if I had fed her this morning. I walked to the fridge and pulled out the cat food as she purred at my feet. Tagua, the kitten we had gotten just weeks before, was sleeping in her bed.

I filled the cat dishes and Toes was silent as she ate. I realized as I looked in the fridge that I had not had anything to eat that day but a chocolate bar. All I'd had to drink was coffee. I was too tired to even eat. I grabbed a beer and cracked it open. I guessed that the hops and yeast in the beer could be counted as a meal. I walked into the family room and flipped on the television. I got lost in a program as I drank the beer. Like a robot I walked down the hall and went to bed. As had been my pattern since Brian went in the hospital, I set the alarm for 4:00 am. That allowed me to catch up on work emails from the previous day before I returned to the hospital.

It was a restless night and the alarm went off way too soon. I dragged myself up and headed to the kitchen to start the coffee. I sat down at my computer and signed on to my work emails. I quickly spun through messages. In less than two hours I had shut it down. I felt good having accomplished more than I'd expected. I finished off the fourth cup of coffee before I showered. By 6:30 I was in my office. At 9:00 I walked across the street to the hospital. I thought about the previous day and prayed that Brian would have improved.

When I arrived I was pleasantly surprised. Brian was carrying on a conversation with the nurse in Spanish. He was dressed and sitting at the table with his book open.

"How are you today?" I asked.

"Great. How about you?"

"I'm glad to see you so awake. Yesterday you were kind of tired all day."

"Really. How come?"

"I don't know. Maybe you just weren't feeling very good."

"Maybe. I feel great today," he said.

"Would you like to go for a walk?"

"Sure."

I held Brian's hand as we walked around the ward three times. Each time we passed his room I watched to see if he made a motion to enter the door, but he just walked by. I realized he did not recognize where his room was. After the third round I stopped and turned into his room.

We spent the day talking as if nothing was wrong. Brian was content, and after lunch I walked back to work so that he could rest. I returned before supper and helped him with the meal. We talked, but it is like deja vu as Brian repeated what he had told me earlier.

I looked in his little yellow journal and saw that his writing had not improved. I read and tried to put meaning to the words.

- *I need contact lens solution*
- *also buy ice cream and hard candy*

I was hopeful that his thoughts were clearing as he knew he needed contact lens solution. Candy and ice cream were some of his favourite things. I continued reading and my hopes turned to fear as he wrote:

- *my name is Brian and I live in Saskatchewan*

We had not lived in Saskatchewan for more than ten years. Following these statements was scribble that I could not understand. I turned the page, which was blank, but a few pages later he has written:

- *good morning Wendy*

My heart pounded as I counted this statement scribbled seventeen times on the next three pages. I was worried. I wondered what if anything I could do to help him think clearly. I wondered what it would mean if his thoughts did not return to normal. I felt my stomach churn. I looked at more pages.

- *I wonder if Toes and Tagua will remember me*
- *I wonder if Toes and Tagua will remember me*
- *I miss Toes and Tagua*
- *Say hi to Mom*

Again these statements were written over and over, and he had gone off the page writing at an angle.

"Do you want to practice writing?" I asked.

"Not really," he replied. He looks out the window and because it is dark he thinks it is time to go to bed, so he starts to undress and crawl under the covers. I looked at the clock. It was 6:35 pm.

"Where are you going to sleep?" he asked.

"I'm going home. I'll come back in the morning" I said, but I did not make a move to leave.

"Oh. I thought you were staying here with me."

I looked into his eyes and saw that he did not want me to go. "I can stay for a while if you like, until you fall asleep."

"OK," he said and pulled the covers up. I turned out the light and in less than fifteen minutes he was asleep. I leaned over and kissed him. He did not stir. I ran my fingers through his hair. I wanted so much to lie down beside him and forget where we were. I wanted to feel his arms around me. I wanted to forget about tomorrow. I felt overwhelmed and tears filled my eyes. I closed my hands over my face, trying to stem the emotion. I turned and walked slowly to the elevator.

I paused when I exited the hospital. I stared up to the sky and asked God to please help Brian improve. I thanked God for the blessings that we had in our lives, but now I needed His help.

I drove home through misty eyes. I wished I could go anywhere else. I wished I had someone to talk with, someone who would share the burden of Brian's illness, but that was not to be. I carried it alone on my shoulders here in Panama.

NINE

hen I stepped around the corner from the elevator I heard a commotion coming from Brian's room, and my heart jumped a beat. I pushed open the door and stepped into a pool of water. The nurse advised me that Brian had turned on the bidet tap by mistake and had flooded the bathroom. When the water reached the hallway someone noticed and called for help. I just shook my head and tried not to chuckle. Brian was standing and watching everyone scurry to mop up the water, and he looked like a kid caught stealing from the cookie jar. He had such a look of innocence.

Someone had put a hospital gown on him. I wondered where his clothes were as he hadn't been wearing hospital gowns up until now. I wondered if his clothes had been soaked in the ordeal. I led him from the bathroom to the small table in his room and sat him down. I explained to him what happened.

"Who turned the water on?" he asked.

"You did."

"Really?"

"Well, I guess so. I wasn't here, but you need to make sure you don't do that again. There was really a lot of water on the floor."

Brian didn't acknowledge what I said. He started to talk about going to the beach.

"We will go to the beach once you get out of here," I said.

"Why don't we go today?" he asked.

"Because you are still in the hospital. When you get home we can go to the beach."

"I think I am going home today."

"That would be nice," I said. "Do you want to go for a walk?"

We were walking around the unit when the nurse came to locate us. Brian was scheduled for another CT scan and the attendants were waiting at his room. They put him in a wheelchair and pushed him down the hallway. I left and returned to work.

It was a blessing that the hospital was just across the road from my office as it allowed me to go back and forth with frequency. I returned to the hospital just before lunch. When I walked in, Brian was eating beef medallions, mashed potatoes and vegetable soup. With the exception of getting the lid off the soup, he was able to feed himself. He finished off Jello dessert and then neatly stacked everything back onto the tray.

When I returned at supper, Brian's mood had changed completely. He was struggling to write sentences in his notebook and was frustrated and angry, which was very unusual for him. I read what he had written:

- *tell Mom not to worry about me*
- *I have been gone a long time*
- *I wonder if Toes will remember me*
- *Say hi to Mom*

When I looked at this I wondered if that is what had frustrated him – thinking he had been gone a long time and would be forgotten. I took the notebook and laid it on the table. I tried to distract him with conversation, and it worked.

When I said I was going home Brian started to cry.

"Why do you have to leave? Why don't you stay here with me? There is lots of room."

I looked at him and my heart broke. I thought about curling up on the couch, and I wondered if the hospital staff would eventually send me home.

"I need to go home with you," he said, and stood to walk out with me.

"You have to stay here in the hospital, Bri. You can't leave until the doctor says it is okay," I said, trying with all I had to hold back the tears.

"I will get better faster at home. I want to see Toes and Tagua."

I hoped with all my heart that he would improve once he got home, but I knew I couldn't take him with me. I hugged him and told him that I would take him home as soon as the doctor approved it. That made him smile. I stayed until he was asleep. I shut out the light when I left and waited to see if he noticed me leaving. When he did not wake, I walked slowly to the elevator. I felt awful leaving him, and a sense of guilt washed over me. I hoped that he would not wake up during the night looking for me.

The following day was another day of confusion for Brian, and he would not leave his room to go for a walk. I went downstairs to get a coffee. When I returned it was as if Brian hadn't seen me. The loss of his short-term memory prevented him from knowing that I had just been there

"I've been waiting for you to arrive," he said.

"I was here. I just went down for coffee," I said.

I looked in his notebook and read what he had written.

- *I will do better if I am in my own place*
- *Can you talk to the doctor about going home*
- *I want to go home*

These statements were repeated over and over, but I was pleased to see that at least the words made sense.

Every night when I left the hospital I went home and tried to update family in Canada via email. The news of Brian's stroke had been a shock for everyone. They all knew that Brian was a strong and healthy man, so the expectation was that he would make a full recovery. It was important for me to hang on to this thought as well.

Every day well wishes and prayers arrived. Reading emails made me sad knowing that distance separated us from our family and friends and they could not go to the hospital to see Brian. I read an email from my sister Penny. She said that our mom intervened to ensure Brian did not go diving on vacation and thus saved his life. I too believed that heaven had something to do with it. She commented about how fragile and short life was. Her words reminded me of the neurosurgeon's comments about Brian's mind not advancing. I have not shared this information with anyone as I don't know what it means in terms of Brian's recovery. The thought sat in the back of my mind and haunted me.

I replied to Penny as well as my other sister, Janice and Aunt Maggie. I was honest with them about our having many challenging days ahead of us, but said that we were grateful for what mobility Brian had. I explained about his good days as well as those days when he was more confused. I shared the funny stories and chuckled out loud as I commented about Brian flooding the bathroom and also about the day I arrived when Brian was standing in the shower waiting for someone to shut off the taps.

When I walked into Brian's room the following morning, Dr. W was there talking with Brian. The CT scan was still not definitive, so they had made the decision to let Brian go home. We were both thrilled as our friends would arrive that night from Edmonton. The next day was January 25th and Brian would be released from the hospital after being there for nine days.

I went to the airport to meet Brian's best friend Larry and his wife, Sally. We went directly home as it was too late to go to the hospital. The following morning when we arrived at the hospital, Brian was sitting on the chair ready to go home. He was so happy to see Larry as he had forgotten they were arriving from Canada.

It was a short drive home from the hospital. When I opened the door to the apartment, Brian called our cats, Toes and Tagua and they ran to his feet. He started to cry as he bent down and picked up Toes.

After we had all settled in for a couple of hours, I dialed the phone so that Brian was able to speak with his mother and let her know he was home. He chatted on the phone as if nothing was wrong, smiling and laughing. I knew that his mom would be smiling on her end as well. Up until now I had only been able to update her by email, so I was thrilled that she could hear Brian's voice.

As the days passed it was hard for most people to notice any change in Brian. He was himself, at least outwardly. He had the same wit and desire to chat and enjoy a beer with friends.

Our friends had brought candy for Brian. Their daughters knew all the candy that Brian loved in Canada and had sent eight pounds of hard candy. Brian smiled from ear to ear. I laughed and told them that they were lucky they did not have to pay overweight charges for their suitcase.

I had scheduled a few days off work while our friends were visiting, but one day I had to go in to the office for meetings. Brian was confused because our friends were there and I was not, so eventually they had to call me at the office to talk to Brian as he asked repeatedly where I was. I explained that it was just his short-term memory loss that was causing this. Once I spoke to Brian he was fine, and the rest of the day passed. They all enjoyed being pampered by Danya, our domestic worker, who made them fresh lemonade and a spectacular lunch.

The following day I drove us all down to the beach, and Brian was able to walk on the beach with us as we picked sea shells. He remembered being on the same beach with Larry and Sally's daughter, Lauren, and her fiancé Trent when they were visiting us just three months earlier. Lauren is our goddaughter and we were thrilled when they visited. It was amazing that Brian remembered that as so many recent memories had been lost.

The next day we all sat down and watched the Super Bowl – Ravens vs 49'ers. Many years the four of us would be away on vacation watching the Super Bowl, so this was a great day of sharing old memories over football snacks and, of course, cold beer. We would normally be drinking Budweiser, but in Panama we drank a local beer called Balboa.

Brian was in good spirits with Larry around, and there was a lot of laughter in the apartment. When their visit ended I was sorry to see them leave and return to Canada.

TEN

could see the changes in Brian every day. Perhaps it was because I was looking for changes, or perhaps it was because I knew him so intimately. After more than thirty-eight years with someone, you pretty much know all their motions, their habits, the pattern to their life.

It was the daily tasks that no one else sees that were the most challenging. On some days Brian was unable to brush his teeth without guidance. He would start, but then stop and stare at the mirror as if he didn't know what he was doing. I moved his hand in the motion and some days it made him carry on brushing and other days he just looked at me with confusion. It is difficult to brush another person's teeth, for sure. I tried to stand behind him so that I could just move his hand, but even this was difficult some days as Brian would move around wondering what I was doing.

Shaving also presented a challenge, so I shaved him most days. I hide all his razors as well as the ones in my drawer of the bathroom vanity so that he would not shave when I was not around.

Brian continued to write in his journal. I looked at it every day and prayed for improvement. The day before he wrote:

- *I am having trouble understanding time*
- *I need to know what is real and what is not*
- *I have been reliving the same time over and over*
- *I have officially relived this day for the fortieth time*
- *same dream over and over. Groundhog day over and over*

I tried to make sense of it. When I asked him, he had no idea why he wrote it. I was pleased as he was writing sentences and I saw that as progress. I attributed the comments to his medicine and having hallucinations. The comment about Groundhog Day was, of course, from the movie that he loved.

It was February 6th. We had a meeting with the neurosurgeon. I helped Brian get dressed and got him into the car without any problem. When we arrived at the hospital he was confused and wanted to stay in the car and wait for me to come back. It took me a few minutes to get him to understand that he had to come with me.

Dr. W was so pleasant and welcoming. Brian smiled when he saw him, and I was happy that he recognized the doctor. A few minutes later, Brian was no longer smiling. He got frustrated because he did not pass the physical exams related to motor skills and peripheral vision. Dr. W told us that some things would come back but if they didn't then Brian and I would have to adjust to Brian not being exactly the way he was. Then Dr. W reinforced how lucky Brian was and that we should be very thankful, which we were.

Dr. W showed us two brain scans, neither of which were Brian's. He explained that the position and extent of edema were critical. Both patients had edema smaller than Brian's. One was in a coma, and the other had no movement on his right side. I stared at the scans remembering how large the edema in Brian's scan had been. I knew I should have felt better, but I didn't. I was now more worried that there was an underlying cause to Brian's situation that hadn't yet been discovered. Dr. W advised that he would be increasing Brian's medication, and therefore he had delayed the next CT scan for a couple of days until the medication could have an impact.

When we left Dr. W's office, Brian asked where we were going. He did not say anything about the visit and wondered if we were going out to meet friends. That only increased my anxiety.

People had always told me that I was strong but I didn't feel strong. I wanted so much for someone to put their arms around me and tell me that the doctors were wrong and Brian would be fine.

My friend Victoria was my rock in Panama. She was my right hand at the office. She listened to me and allowed me to cry. I was able to be honest and shared my fears with her. I knew that she was handling many of the matters at the office that would have been referred to me. She had stepped in and was making the decisions and updating me as a matter of protocol. I wanted to call her now and let all my emotions out, but I resisted. Back at our apartment I tried to be positive for Brian and didn't relive the neurosurgeon's comments.

Our good friends Belinda and Scott in Canada had been emailing almost daily asking to speak with us. They were anxious to hear our voices. I dialed the phone slowly, almost holding my breath and trying to control myself so that I didn't cry. I was grateful when Belinda answered the phone. I knew I could not talk to Scott. The sound of his voice would just be too overwhelming. Belinda was a registered nurse, so I could talk to her on a different level that allowed me to control my emotions. They offered to come to Panama to help. I was grateful for their concern and support, but I declined a visit until we knew more.

The date was February 15th and Brian's birthday. He was 60 years old. I had planned to take him out to lunch. When he stepped into the shower I went into the office to check emails. After replying to several emails, I shut off the computer and walked into the family room expecting to find Brian watching the television. He wasn't there, so I started down the hall to our bedroom. As I got closer I could hear the shower still running.

"What are you doing?" I asked. "You've been in there a long time."

"Really," Brian replied as he continued washing his hair. After he rinsed the soap he just stood in the shower. When he reached for the shampoo bottle again, I realized he didn't know how to turn off the taps and get out. I wondered how many times he had washed his hair.

I opened the shower door, took the shampoo bottle from his hand and shut off the water.

"Don't I need to do my hair?"

"You already have. More than once."

I was surprised that the water had not turned freezing cold after how long it had been on. From that point on I never left Brian in the shower without timing it.

With my help he got dressed and we finally left the apartment for lunch. I took him to the RIU Hotel in downtown Panama as we could sit outdoors by the pool and feel like we were a million miles away from the city. I ordered us both a beer, but Brian barely drank any of it. Normally Brian would enjoy several beers on his birthday. After we finished lunch, Brian was eager to go home.

Before he lay down I read him the birthday greetings that had come by email. He was grateful that everyone remembered him today. He laughed at all the comments about having a beer on his birthday. Brian had always been a Budweiser man, and everyone knew how much he liked his beer.

Over the next few days I replied to all the emails and told everyone that Brian had been well enough to celebrate and have a beer on his birthday. I did this because I knew that everyone would feel better, knowing that Brian was back to himself if he was drinking beer. I didn't want to tell them the truth, that he no longer had a taste for beer. I did not want to scare anyone as they were all so far away and there was no purpose served in telling them the truth.

My brother Wayne was the one family member with whom I shared the extent of Brian's condition. I had told him what the doctor's had told me, but I held back my fears. I am the older sister. The strong, Type A personality. I had never needed anyone to hold me up. I was unsure then how to ask for that help. I knew that I couldn't let Wayne know how uncertain about the future I was.

Wayne and Melissa arrived on February 19th. Brian had been out of the hospital for just over three weeks. They were surprised when Brian was with me to greet them at the airport. Most people equate a stroke with paralysis and visible changes, and of course on the outside Brian looked the same. He was his same jovial self and joked with them on the trip back to our apartment.

They had brought scholastic books from Canada at the grade seven level to help Brian. They had also brought lots of his favourite candy sent from other family members as well as themselves. Brian was thrilled, and I had to take away some of the candy for fear that he would eat it all in one sitting.

I wanted Wayne and Melissa to be able to experience Panama during their visit, so I planned trips to see the Panama Canal and other tourist attractions. I needed to watch Brian closely on each trip. I knew he would agree to go somewhere every day, and I knew he was not well enough for that. I had arranged for some of the sightseeing to be done with the help of Manuel, our friend and transportation driver.

On the Saturday I drove us out of the hectic city pace onto the highway leading to the beach. One hour later I pulled off the highway and onto the road that led to Punta Chame. It was a winding road lined with flowering trees that immediately made me feel more peaceful. I pulled the car off the road at a quaint little boutique hotel along the beach outside of the town. The beach was quiet, and when we went for a walk we didn't see another person. It allowed us to talk and enjoy the serenity of the moment. Wayne sat with Brian in the pool and drank beer with the Corona bucket nearby. I looked at them and thought of how many times we had enjoyed similar experiences, in the pool or at the beach laughing and reminiscing. I wished that I could freeze frame our life to always be able to enjoy times like this, to stop the passage of time forward. I just sat and watched them. I did not interrupt, allowing them to share this time alone.

After dinner we enjoyed a leisurely evening. The hotel had only fifteen rooms and it was not fully occupied. The few other guests had retired to their rooms, so it was just the four of us and the hotel staff. Melissa and I walked to the beach to capture the sun setting and watched the kite surfers. When we returned we all sat on the outdoor patio and watched a Bee Gees concert on a big screen. As we sat there it seemed like nothing in life had changed. It was just the four of us together like we had been on so many occasions. What lay ahead was forgotten and we enjoyed being in the moment.

When I went to bed that night I wondered how Wayne would get over the loss of Brian. They were close. There was a true bond beyond friendship. Wayne sparkled when he was around Brian. He laughed and let loose. The pressures of everyday life were put aside.

All too soon we had to return to reality in the city. It was a beautiful evening, so we decided to go for a walk down to the store. Brian wanted to go as well. On our way home, Brian tripped over a tree root and fell to the ground. Luckily he did not hurt himself other than scraping his shin. He was more worried about whether he had broken the contents of the bag he was carrying than if he hurt himself. Once we knew he was okay, we all laughed as Brian stood swearing at the sidewalk.

For the following day I had arranged a fishing trip. It was a truly remarkable experience to fish in the lake that supplied water for the Panama Canal, with monkeys in view and steamer ships passing as they traversed the canal. It was a spectacular day to be on the water. As we moved to another fishing spot we were all excited by the sound of the howler monkeys, and within minutes we were close enough that Melissa was able to video their movement in the mango groves above us. I could not have planned a better experience.

We all noticed the difference in Brian. He was unable to cast the fishing rod. He stood with the rod in his hand and the bait dangling, but he did not know what to do next to get the bait in the water. Wayne and I covered it up by one of us casting and then passing Brian the rod. Eventually Brian just sat down and didn't seem to have any interest in fishing. That saddened me.

When we got back to shore we had our catch fileted on the dock and that night Wayne fried up fish for supper and we had a feast.

On February 27th we said goodbye to Wayne and Melissa. I had a heavy heart saying goodbye and not knowing when we would see them again, but in the back of my mind was the day ahead of us. Brian was scheduled for another MRI.

Brian of course did not remember the appointment. He was in good spirits and feeling alert. He said goodbye to Wayne and Melissa and gave them both a big hug. He told them both to come back soon. I went down the elevator with them and immediately saw Manuel who was leaning against his car waiting to drive them to the airport. I hugged Melissa first and then hugged my brother tightly. I started to cry as I released my arms and let him go. I waved goodbye and walked back into the building.

I wiped my eyes before I entered the apartment. I took Brian's hand in mine and led him down the hall to our bedroom so that he could shower. He had become more and more unsteady, and even though I held his hand he ran his right hand down the wall to guide himself.

ELEVEN

*D*r. W called to discuss the results of the most recent MRI. I sat outside the neurosurgeon's office and watched the seconds tick by on my watch. I concentrated on the watch dial as I didn't want to look up and make eye contact with any of the other people waiting in the lobby. My stomach was churning and each sip of coffee was adding gas to the fire that was raging. As was my nature, I was early for the appointment. The nurse opened the door and ushered the people who sat to my right into the office. I looked at the three of them as they stood and walked past me. I saw tears in the eyes of the oldest woman who I assumed was the mother. I wondered if it was her husband or one of her children that was the reason for the appointment. I looked down again at my watch. Tick, tick, tick, the minutes kept moving on. It was almost an hour before the nurse reappeared and called me into the office. When I stood I felt weak, and all my worrying had made me anxious and on edge. I knew that it would take all my fortitude not to cry. I glanced at the list of neurosurgeons operating from the office as I walked through the glass door, following the nurse.

Dr. W was welcoming. He held my hand in his and kissed me on the cheek, the Latin greeting even in these circumstances. He had a bedside manner that made me feel like I was the only patient that he had, but I knew the reception area was brimming with other families waiting for news, good or bad, about their loved ones. I sat in the arm chair and tried to relax. He sat in his desk chair but spun the chair so that he was facing me directly.

"I am afraid that I do not have good news," he said, looking directly into my eyes. "The MRI has confirmed my suspicions. Brian has a brain tumor and that was what caused the stroke. We could not determine this at first because it was not clear because of the level of bleeding."

I gripped onto the arms of my chair. I looked down at the floor. My heart was pounding and I was not sure that I could speak. I wanted to erase his words. I wanted to turn back the hands on my watch. I looked back up at him and the expression on his face told me what I didn't need to hear in words. All I could do was cry.

"I will arrange for a biopsy as soon as possible. We can discuss treatment after the biopsy. For now, we need to stay positive," he added.

I stood and, because I didn't know what else to say, I thanked him and slowly walked out on rubbery legs that I wasn't sure would carry me.

I couldn't talk to anyone right then so I got in my car and tried to think while I drove around Panama City. I pulled into a parking lot and turned off the engine. I cried like a child, almost wailing out loud. I wanted to run and scream, but I knew that was not possible. I had parked a long way from the mall doors yet someone was pulled their vehicle in directly beside me. I wondered why they could not park somewhere else. I wanted to cry and scream inside my car without prying eyes. With dozens of other parking spots available, I was mad that this person had invaded my space. I sat for more than thirty minutes before I was able to gather the courage to carry on.

When I got home, Brian was reading and the television was on a Spanish channel. I sat down with him and picked up his yellow notebook. I read what he had written:

- *telephone Felipe and Leira*
- *how is Fernando and how is Saray. Perfect little mother*
- *I am thinking about you guys*
- *how are things at the new apartment*
- *hello to Fernando and Saray*
- *do not worry about me*
- *I am fine*

I was thrilled that Brian had written clearly about our Panama friends Felipe, Leira and their children. His mind had allowed him to think and articulate his thoughts which really made me smile. It took away some of the pain of the visit with Dr. W.

Further down the page he had written:

- *I am thinking about a glass of scotch with Jorge*
- *say hello to Victoria*

Again he was talking about our Panama friends. Brian had bought a bottle of scotch in Canada for Jorge, and it was still in our cabinet.

"What are you doing?" Brian asked.

"Just reading what you wrote. You were talking about Felipe, Leira and the kids plus Victoria and Jorge."

"That's good. How are they doing?"

"They are all good. They ask about you every day."

"That's nice of them. Did you tell them I am okay?"

I looked into Brian's eyes and saw the man that had been at my side for as long as I could remember. As I flipped through his book I wondered how best to tell him about the visit with Dr. W.

"I think I will have a drink," I said, and walked to the bar at the end of the room. "Would you like something?"

"What are you going to have?"

"Well I was thinking about a rum and Coke," I reply.

"That sounds nice."

I reached up onto the shelf and took down a favourite glass of Brian's. I took down an identical one for myself. I mixed a strong rum and Coke for myself and put less rum in Brian's.

"Would you like to sit up here at the bar?" I asked as I walked over and took his hands in mine. Brian always sat behind the bar when we had guests over. Now I led him to a stool on the other side of the bar so that I could sit beside him. I spun the stools so that we could look out to the ocean. I handed him the glass and I tipped mine to his in a toast.

"Here's to us, Bri," I said.

"Here's to us, Baby," Brian replied.

We sat in silence looking out to the ocean.

I steadied myself so that I did not get emotional and start to cry. I knew that then, more than ever, I had to stay strong.

"I went to see Dr. W today. You will need to go back in the hospital for a couple of days," I said.

"How come?"

"Well, the MRI showed a mass, and Dr. W wants to do more tests. He will explain it all to us when we get there." I was uncertain whether I should say more or not. Should I tell him it is a tumor, or wait? I didn't want to alarm him, and I decided that Dr. W would be the best one to explain it.

"Okay," Brian said, and continued to look out to the ocean.

TWELVE

The day I had dreaded had arrived. The biopsy was booked for that day, March 8. It had been fifty days since Brian was first admitted to the ICU. I knew from what Dr. W told me that the biopsy was a dangerous procedure but necessary, so there was no other option.

I did not sleep the night before. I got up, showered and dressed before I walked to the side of the bed and woke Brian. It took another hour to get him showered and dressed. I looked at the clock. It was 7:00 am. I had to have him at the hospital to be admitted at 7:30. I took his hands in mine and walked backwards, leading him out of the apartment to the elevator. I had his cane over my arm. We chatted about nothing on the ride down the elevator to the car. It was only a short drive to the hospital, and I was lucky there was a parking spot close to the door.

It was a small action, but being able to lift his leg to step up from the pavement onto the sidewalk was difficult for Brian. Eventually he did, and I put the cane in his right hand and held his left arm braced against me. It was a quick process having Brian admitted. I walked beside the stretcher as they wheeled him up to the unit. Brian sat on the edge of the bed. I stood and looked out the window. I passed the time by telling Brian about all the activity I saw down on the street. I looked at my watch. It was now 8:30.

I sat down on the bed beside Brian. I took his hand and held it as I explained that we were at the hospital and that he would be undergoing the biopsy today. While I was sitting there, Dr. W came in. He explained what the procedure would entail, more for my benefit than Brian's. After Dr. W left, Brian asked me why he was at the hospital. My heart broke.

When the attendants arrived with the stretcher, I kissed Brian and told him I loved him before he was wheeled away to surgery. Staying at the hospital would just increase my anxiety, so I decided to go to work for a few hours. The nurses agreed to call me once Brian was back in his room and awake.

I sat in a meeting with my manager's getting updates on department issues when my cell phone rang. I glanced at it and saw the neurosurgeon's name. I stood and motioned to my team. They walked out and closed the door to my office as I answered the call. I could feel my heart rate quicken. Dr. W requested I come to his office to discuss the biopsy results.

I walked across the street from the tower where my office was. It was a beautiful day, but then again all days in Panama are beautiful. I walked slowly and tried to calm myself so that I would not be too emotional when I arrived.

I was worried and desperately wished I was not alone. I turned my thoughts positive, suggesting to myself that all was well as Dr. W had called so quickly. They must have found that things are not as bad as expected. Yes, that's it I thought. I felt myself calm down as I stepped into the elevator. The power of positive thinking!

The receptionist was on the phone when I opened the glass door, but she stood and motioned with her hand for me to go in. I walked down a short hallway and saw Dr. W sitting at his computer. I stopped in the open doorway and knocked on the door frame. He stood and greeted me. Then the rug was pulled from under my feet.

"I wish I had better news," he said and hesitated. "It is easier to understand if I can show you the results. Let's go down to the radiology department." He motioned for us to leave. I cannot tell you what he said as we walked down the hall and got on the elevator. I wanted to run, but I wasn't sure that my legs would carry me. I felt flushed and my hands were sweaty. I wiped my palms on my pants hoping he would not notice. I stared at the floor and waited for the jerk of the elevator before I looked up. I bit my lower lip and looked at Dr. W, as he motioned for me to step out. I followed him as he walked into the radiology department and chattered greetings to the staff, who pushed a buzzer to unlock the door leading into the lab. I followed in his footsteps.

People in lab coats scurried around when they saw him, and it reinforced to me the important position he held at the hospital. A technician walked into a room with computers and sat down. I stood beside Dr. W. A couple of minutes later the technician stood up and left the room, shutting the door behind him.

"Here, sit down," Dr. W said as he pulled up another chair. I almost slipped onto the floor as the chair rolled before I sat down. Perfect, just perfect, I thought.

On the screen was a series of images of Brian's skull. With a pencil he pointed to the various images, explaining the shaded areas. I was hoping that I would not faint or puke. My stomach was churning.

"The biopsy has confirmed my suspicions." He pointed to another image.

"This shows the mass. It is very large and covers both cortexes. The tumor is called a Glioblastoma Multiforme, the most aggressive and fatal of all brain tumors."

Dr. W turned in his chair and looked directly into my eyes. "Brian is very, very sick." He waited for me to absorb those words before he carried on. "The tumor is inoperable. I am so sorry to tell you, but there is no chance that he will survive."

I could feel the bile climbing up my throat and I swallowed, hoping I could hold it down. I started to cry and felt such deep anguish. I repeated the neurosurgeon's words in my head – *"Inoperable! There is no chance that he will survive."*

Dr. W reached over and placed his hand on my shoulder. I looked up into his eyes.

"You should not be alone. Do you have any family here that we can call?"

"No. We are here by ourselves. All of our family is in Canada," I said as the tears ran down my face. I wiped away the sadness with the tissue, in my hand. For the first time in my life I wished that we were not alone. I wished I was surrounded by family that would hold me and comfort me.

"We will do what we can to get Brian well enough so you can take him home to your family. The brain is very powerful. It can work in Brian's favour, or if he becomes depressed over the diagnosis, his brain could become his enemy and no amount of treatment will help. We must remain positive, but I also want to be honest with you about Brian's chances."

I could not speak. I could not even acknowledge his words. I just sat in silence trying to erase the words.

"Let's go up now and tell Brian," he said. I saw the pain in his eyes and wondered how many times he had to tell families about a similar diagnosis. How many times had he destroyed lives with his words?

I followed him in silence as we left the lab and entered the elevator. He pushed the button and the doors closed. We were alone, but I knew I could not speak. I wiped away the tears and sniffled.

Another doctor was standing at reception when we exited the elevator. Dr. W spoke to him and he joined us as we walked down the hallway. Brian was sitting on the couch when we entered his room. He looked up at us. I saw the bandage at the back of his head.

Dr. W sat down on the couch next to Brian and put his arm around him. The other doctor stood leaning against the wall. I just stood there numb.

"I don't have good news for you," Dr. W started.

My husband looked up at me with inquiring eyes. I broke down in tears and sat on the edge of the bed across from him. I reached out and took his hand in mine.

"The biopsy has confirmed my initial suspicion. You have an aggressive brain tumor. A Glioblastoma Multiforme. It is very large and is inoperable, but there are treatments we can try. You are a healthy man and you and your wife have many vacations still to take, so you must fight your best fight. We will fight together," the neurosurgeon continued as he hugged my husband and reached out to touch my hand.

I looked at Brian and saw the fear. His eyes darted back and forth as he looked at me. I had seen that fear before in the eyes of a coyote that had gotten trapped in our barn. It was a bitter, cold winter night and the coyote had entered the barn to find relief from the winds. When Brian and I entered the barn to check on cows expecting calves we came upon the coyote. Brian was standing between the coyote and the escape route. The fear in the coyote's eyes was what I saw then in Brian. The news was a shock, and Brian was feeling trapped with the tumor blocking the escape route.

With the doctor's words, and in so few minutes, my husband's and my roles changed. I would no longer be able to lean on Brian. I was now the one who would need to take care of the two of us. I felt panic well up within me and my heart raced. God, how could this be happening? Brian was the protector, the travelled Navy man who I had always looked to for comfort. Now the responsibility had been shifted to my shoulders and I almost slumped under the pressure of Dr. W's words.

The neurosurgeon kept talking but I heard nothing. I moved beside Brian and held his hand as we both wept. I looked at Dr. W and saw a tear run down his cheek. In those few minutes my worst fears were confirmed. Life as we knew it would never be the same.

"You will need to discuss whether you want to undergo radiation and chemo treatments. I believe it is for the best, but the decision must be yours."

Brian said nothing. He looked at me for the answer.

"Yes, we want to do all that we can," I said.

"When I leave here I will go to the desk and sign the papers to release you. I will contact Dr. Y who will coordinate the radiation and chemo treatments. He will be in contact with you."

Dr. W had such compassion and I knew it was difficult for him to deliver this news. He squeezed Brian's shoulder. "Go home and enjoy your time together."

Dr. W walked out and the other doctor followed him. I looked at Brian and we hugged. We sat for a few minutes until we both stopped crying.

"I need a drink," I said as I stood and walked to the window. I stared down blankly at the traffic that was building on the street below. I thought of all the people bustling around without a care in the world and here we sat with our world crumbling.

"You need a drink. What about me! Let's get out of here," Brian said. "I want to go home."

"I think it will take a few minutes to get the release," I said without turning around. I knew if I looked at Brian I would break down. I wanted to call someone, anyone who could give us comfort, but we were alone. There was no family here. Just us.

Just then my Blackberry rang and I realized I had been holding it in my hand. I looked at the screen and then answered the call. It was from Ricardo, the most senior boss of my employer in Panama. I walked out into the hallway and listened as he started to ask me about a situation with a client. I was too polite to interrupt him. When he paused I said, "I'm at the hospital right now."

"Sorry. I didn't mean to bother you. How are things?"

And with that question I burst into tears.

"Wendy, are you there?" he inquired.

I could not say a word. I leaned against the wall and tried to stop trembling.

"Wendy…"

"Sorry, I'm here," I blubbered. "Brian's really, really sick," I continued. "He has a brain tumor. The neurosurgeon just left. He will need to have radiation and chemo."

"Wendy, I am out at the beach with the family for the weekend. Do you want me to come back?"

"No. I'll be fine," I said without any real conviction in my words.

"It's no trouble, I can drive back," Ricardo added. "I'm so terribly sorry for you and Brian. Have you met with the oncologist? What can I do?"

"I don't know Ricardo. They just got the results of the biopsy today. I would appreciate if you could call Dr. W, the neurosurgeon, and go over the results so that I know for sure I understood what he was saying. I think I did, but you would be able to talk Spanish to Spanish and I would feel better having your opinion."

"I will call him first thing Monday and arrange to meet with him. Call me if you need anything over the weekend."

"I will. I am just waiting for Brian to get released."

I walked back into the room. "That was Ricardo on the phone."

"How's he?" Brian asked.

"He's good. He is going to meet with Dr. W to go over everything for us."

"That's nice of him. What are we waiting here for?"

"I will go check at the nursing station and see if we can leave," I said as I walked out of the hospital room. I stood at the counter as the nurses were all busy on the phone or reviewing charts. I wanted to just fall to the floor and sit and wait for the world to quit spinning. I felt like I was on a merry-go-round and just couldn't get it to slow down so I could jump off.

I walked back into Brian's room. "They are working on it."

We sat in silence for what seemed like forever, but in reality was less than five minutes. A nurse came in and asked me to follow her to the front counter where I signed a few more forms, and she said we could leave.

I talked about how sunny it was to divert our attention as we rode down the elevator. Brian looked dejected, and I wanted to talk about anything but the biopsy. When we stepped outside the sliding doors of the hospital the warm air greeted us and Brian smiled.

"God I love this place," he said.

When we got home I settled Brian into one of the white leather chairs in the living room. I went into the next room and mixed both of us a strong rum and Coke. I handed Brian the drink and sat down in the matching chair to his left. I swivelled the chair to look out to the ocean. We both were silent for a few minutes.

"Life sucks," Brian finally said.

"Right now it does, but we are going to fight this Bri and you will be back to your old self in no time. We have too many things left to do. Think of all the countries we want to visit."

We sat for the next two hours, stared out to the ocean and talked. Brian did not have another drink, but I mixed two more rum and Coke for myself. We talked about the blind date that brought us together. I thought back. That was more than 38 years ago. We talked about our life and all that we had done. We talked about how fortunate we had been to take so many vacations to Mexico, Cuba, Ecuador, Costa Rica, and so many more countries. We talked about our life when we owned the ranch in Saskatchewan. As we reminisced we laughed about some weekend visits with family when inevitably something had gone wrong at the ranch.

"Remember how many times we were chasing calves down the ditch after they would crawl through the fence," I said.

"Yeah, and I remember a few times when the cows followed them."

I shook my head, remembering all the work we had running the ranch. There was never a dull moment. I changed the subject and talked about our good fortune to have had the opportunity to work and live in Panama.

Thinking of our current situation we both fell silent.

I spun my chair and took Brian's hand in mind. "We're going to beat this Bri," I said to break the silence.

"I know."

THIRTEEN

*N*othing in life prepares you for what lies ahead. There is no map that you can follow to know what tomorrow holds. Brian lived by the motto *"good things happen to good people."* Most of us try to live a good life, to be good people, to care about others and to set a good example. We pray that being a good person will protect us from anything bad happening to us. I thought about that motto now and hated it. It was a lie. Brian was a good person and yet nothing good was happening to him. What is the sense in being a good person then - I wondered. It would be easier to go through life being an asshole, because in the end none of that matters because it was not up to us. It was up to a higher power that decided who stayed and who went.

Brian got home from the hospital following the biopsy. He had been tired and didn't want to leave the bedroom. He dressed and watched television from atop the bed or while lying down. I hoped that he was just recovering from the anesthetic. I sat and tried to talk to him, but he was distant and silent. I decided to leave him with his thoughts until he was ready to talk more, so I fell silent as well. Within an hour he drifted off to sleep.

While Brian slept I started up the computer and researched what I could. When I searched brain tumors, I was drawn to the Brain Tumor Foundation of Canada and registered to receive ongoing updates and information in the fight against brain tumors. The handbook was 294 pages, so I printed out the index pages so that I could concentrate on only those sections that related to us. I was able to skip sections on surgery, clinical trials, etc. I was able to skip the descriptors of tumors from low grade to high grade, non malignant to malignant ratings. I knew where we stood - in the worst quadrant on the chart. High grade IV.

I read stories from families whose family members had survived years with a brain tumor. I was optimistic until I discovered that the type of tumor did not match Brian's diagnosis. I searched further and found that the stories from families with a glioblastoma multiforme tumor were less positive, and life expectancy was less than 12 months. I closed down the page and did not return to the site for more than a week. I needed to get used to the diagnosis before I could interpret the website information. I wondered if there was anything we could have done sooner. Was there a sign that was overlooked?

How could he be so full of life and within hours be facing such devastating news?

For a few weeks it had been necessary for me to learn the jargon of medical acronyms and then try to interpret them from Spanish to English. I was so lucky to be able to rely on my associate, Victoria, who helped me beyond what I could ever thank her for. Victoria gave me constant encouragement and a shoulder to cry on. Right then I did not have the control to call her. I would have just blubbered on the phone. I had put enough on her shoulders, and so I sat alone in my thoughts.

When Brian woke up we discussed what Dr. W had told us. Brian did not want to tell anyone. We agreed that we would only tell those people that we would need to rely on in the coming weeks.

When I mentioned his mother, Brian said he only wanted to tell her once we were back in Canada and could be together. We talked about her upcoming ninetieth birthday party, which was in four months. Brian wanted her to be able to enjoy her party that had been planned for so long. After a lot of discussion, we decided not to tell other family members either until we could talk face to face. There was no point in alarming everyone when there were so many miles between us.

I knew that there was only one person who knew the whole truth, and that was me. The doctor's words rang out in my mind. *'Brian will not survive'.*

Only my brother Wayne and two of our closest friends knew Brian was undergoing more testing. I had told them about the tumor and would update them on the biopsy results. I steadied myself to call them in Canada. I wanted to be careful not to share the full extent of Brian's condition, because I wanted everyone to remain positive. I wanted them to believe that the chemo and radiation treatments would make Brian well again.

I called my brother first and cried so hard that I had to hang up and call him back to get through the conversation. Wayne cried as well. We are the closest of our siblings, and we have shouldered considerable burdens in the past few years, being the executors of our parents' estates. No matter how close a family is, and ours was, there are always hurt feelings and words exchanged that change the course of the future once you start to deal with the death of a parent. Emotions drive the words, yet once spoken they cannot be withdrawn and the pain of some of those words and accusations aimed at us had weighed heavily on me.

Wayne naturally wanted to return to Panama to see Brian, but I knew that was just not realistic. I would need to rely on Wayne to help me bring Brian home to Canada once we made that decision.

The next call was to Brian's best friend, and I cried once more but steadied myself to get through the conversation. He immediately made up his mind to travel back to Panama and spend time with Brian, so there was no talking him out of it.

I did not have the strength to call our friends, Belinda and Scott. I knew I would break down. It took me a week to advise them by email.

I sat with Brian and watched TV. He was quiet, and I wondered what he was thinking. The previous night he enjoyed a drink and sat with me at our bar, but I knew that desire was gone. I was sad. I looked at the man who I had shared more than 38 years with. He was slowly slipping from my fingers, and there was nothing that I could do to stop it. I lay down beside him and draped my arm over him. He took my hand in his and we lay in silence. Sometime later I got up, undressed, and crawled back into bed and cuddled against him.

The next day Brian wanted to go down to the pool. I was elated that he was acting like himself again. We talked about the biopsy results and he was clear-headed. He knew we were in for a fight, and he said we would beat this thing. We clinked our beer cans together in a sign of solidarity against the tumor.

When we came back up from the pool Brian lay down to rest and I took time to catch up on our personal emails. I read an email from my brother Wayne. He apologized for his grammar. He was trying to type and was having a hard time seeing the keyboard through the tears. I cried. I knew how hard the news of the biopsy result was on Wayne. I walked to the kitchen and got a beer to steady my nerves before I replied. I was grateful that Wayne and Melissa had been here to visit before the biopsy and we'd been able to enjoy ourselves without the diagnosis overshadowing everything.

On Monday, Ricardo met with the neurosurgeon as promised. He came into my office later that day and sat down across from me. He told me what they discussed and confirmed that I had fully understood the neurosurgeon's explanation. Secretly I had hoped that Ricardo would tell me that things were not as dismal as I had thought, that Brian would be cured. But that, of course, was not the conversation.

FOURTEEN

*I*t had been fewer than eight weeks since Brian complained of a headache. I noticed changes almost daily. One day he could walk a short distance in the apartment with the aid of his cane, and the next day he required my assistance to stand. At some point every day I had to help him. He relied on the cane in his right hand, and my hand holding his left arm. Today as we left the bedroom he stopped in the hallway and looked at the framed collages of family photos we had brought from Canada. I knew when we left Canada that the photos would give us comfort when we were feeling lonely, being so far away from home.

Brian stared at the photos but said nothing. I wondered if he knew who was in that specific frame.

"Remember that?" I asked.

"Not really," he said.

"It is of all of us when we went horseback riding in the mountains in Kananaskis. This is Darrell and Jason," I said as I pointed to our nephews. I went through everyone in the photo. Brian said nothing.

"Do you want to sit down?"

"I think so," he said turning his face from the photos.

I led him down the remainder of the hall and got him settled on the couch. I was sure that his memory no longer related to the faces of family in the old photos. I hoped that when we got back to Canada, seeing everyone in person would be easier for him. I looked at him as he sat in silence. I felt so sorry for him.

"Would you like a donut?" I asked to lighten the mood.

"Sure," he replied.

I walked to the kitchen and came back with a box of six assorted donuts from Dunkin Donuts. "Which one would you like?" I asked showing him the box.

He picked one as the phone rang. I put the donut box down on the coffee table and walked into the office to answer the phone. It was my brother, Wayne, in Canada. We talked for a few minutes about the changes in Brian and he updated me on our family in Canada. I relished the news from Canada as I felt so cut off from everything now except Brian's condition.

"I'll let you talk to Bri for a minute," I said, as I walked back into the living room. Brian still had a donut in his hand that he had just bitten into. I looked down at the box and there was only one donut left in the box. That meant that the one in his hand was the fifth donut he had eaten.

"Bri you ate the whole box," I said stunned.

"How come?" he asked.

"Here, talk to Wayne," I said handing him the phone. He started to talk but did not have the telephone handset near his mouth or ear. I sat down beside him and held the phone for him, trying not to burst out in laughter over the donuts. After he had talked for a few minutes his attention went back to the donut in his hand, so I took back the phone and told my brother about the donuts. We both laughed.

FIFTEEN

I drove to the hospital without Brian and steadied myself to meet with the radiation oncologist. He ushered me into a room and closed the door. He moved to sit behind the desk and I sat in an uncomfortable arm chair. I did not lean back in the seat but perched on the edge, anxious to hear his comments.

"I wanted to go over the treatment plan with you so that you can make a decision whether you want to proceed. The type of tumor is very aggressive. We cannot be sure how long it has been growing, but it has most likely not been there for a long time. I think that it is important for Brian to receive treatment, but the decision is not mine. You must decide together."

There was an unusual picture on the wall and I stared at it. I did not want to look the doctor in the eyes. I could feel the tears coming and knew that I must not break down. I needed to stay strong to hear what could be done.

"I have a chart based on statistics," he continued.

I looked at the chart which had been drawn in ink. Time-lines and x's denoted different periods on the chart.

"This is where we are today," he continued, pointing at the start of the line. "We are recommending an aggressive treatment plan over the next six weeks. There would be radiation every day, Monday to Friday, nothing on weekends. This will give him a break between each week. We will also be recommending chemo treatment five days each month." As he spoke he pointed to the chart denoting the treatments.

"We have looked at statistics for this type of tumor and matched the treatment plan to what has been used with other patients."

I said nothing. I just stared at the chart and tried to count the little x's.

"Miss Wendy, do you have questions? Do you understand what I have explained?" he asked.

"What about without any treatment?"

"I have asked another doctor to look at the test results. We agree that Brian would have only four to six weeks without treatment."

I gasped. Fuck. That was like a month from now I thought. A fucking month.

"We can't be certain that the radiation will be beneficial, but our hope is that it will stop the tumor from growing and give Brian maybe nine months," he continued. "We won't know for sure, but the research shows that the treatment will extend his time. There is no cure. I think Dr. W explained that to you."

I burst out in tears. I reached into my purse for something to wipe my face with. Dr. Y reached for a box of tissues and pushed it across the desk at me. I whimpered.

Dr. Y walked around the desk and sat in the chair next to me. He placed his hand on my shoulder. "I am very sorry for you and Brian," he said with true compassion.

Through quivering lips I was able to say, "We definitely want him to get treatment."

I walked out to my car like a zombie. I did not hear the birds chirp or feel the heat of the sun on my face. I was numb. Once inside the car I cried. I was in shock. I could not grasp the thought of losing Brian. How could this be happening? Why so rapidly? God, he was fine on holidays just two months ago and now this. I had expected that radiation would be the cure and chemo was just added protection. The thought had never crossed my mind that Brian would not recover. When Dr. W had said Brian would not survive, I hoped he meant that Brian would not survive without treatment. I never understood that even treatment would not change the path the cancer had chosen. I realized now that I never really asked Dr. W to explain. I was in shock then too. I had formulated in my mind what I wanted to hear, not the truth of what was being said.

The air was being sucked from the vehicle. I was sure of it. I gasped for air like a gold fish that comes to the surface. I had to open the car door and step outside to get air. I stood and breathed in. Tears ran down my face and I knew my mascara was running as well. I didn't care. I couldn't go to work now – not with this news. I needed to go home to our apartment, but first I had to get air into my lungs so that I could carry on.

I wondered how a tumor that planned to kill you could grow inside you, yet you got no signal that it was there. Shouldn't there be a warning so that you got a fighting chance? There was no positive outcome. One day you are alive and enjoying life, and the next day you get a death sentence.

I wanted someone to hold me. Someone to wrap their arms around me and tell me that everything would be okay. I wanted someone to tell me that the doctors were wrong and that Brian would recover after treatment. I needed someone, but there was no one. We were alone in Panama with no family to stand by us. Brian and I would be facing this challenge together. I wasn't sure how I would handle it.

I gathered myself together and drove back to the apartment. Brian had lain down on top of the bed. The television was on, but he wasn't watching it. He looked up at me when I walked in.

"Where were you?" he asked.

I sat on the edge of the bed and explained to him about the meeting at the hospital with Dr. Y and the radiation treatment plan. I spoke for several minutes, but Brian never said anything.

"Do you know why you will be getting radiation?" I asked him.

"Not really." There was such a pained look in his eyes I started to cry.

That evening I woke up when I felt the bed moving. Brian was shaking. I turned on the light and jumped out of bed. I walked around to Brian's side of the bed and put my hand on him. I thought at first that he was having a nightmare but with the light on I could tell he was shaking uncontrollably.

"Bri, you need to wake up. Are you okay? What's happening?" I asked as I shook him.

"I don't know. Can you get me a Tylenol?" he asked matter-of-factly.

"No. I think something is wrong. I don't think you should take anything. I think we should go to the hospital," I replied.

"Let's just wait. I think it will pass," he said.

The doctors had told me to expect that Brian could experience seizures caused by the tumor. He was on a high dose of a drug to minimize the severity of a seizure should it occur.

We were treading on new ground, and neither of us knew what to expect. I had a flashback to the epileptic seizures my cousin had when we were young. My parents had taught me and my two sisters what to do in case our cousin had a seizure and no adults were around. There is an emotional trigger that comes to the surface when an epileptic has a seizure. I wasn't sure if that was what we would experience with my husband.

"It has been more than an hour, so I think I should call an ambulance," I said.

"OK."

This of course was a great idea, but I had no idea how to get a hold of an ambulance in Panama. It wasn't as if I could dial 911. I called down to the security desk in our building hoping that Daniel or someone who spoke English would answer. No such luck. I kept repeating, *"ambulancia es necessario, para Señor Brian."* When I realized I was making no headway I went down the thirty-five floors in the elevator and walked out to the front gate where the security guard sat. Face to face he understood me and kept dialing the phone but was told that there were no ambulances.

What the hell, I thought. In a city of over a million people, there are no ambulances. I sat down on the curb in frustration and tears flooded over me. In hindsight I should have phoned my friend Victoria, even at this hour. She would have been able to fix everything in no time. I went back upstairs and Brian was resting. I stared out the window and low and behold saw red lights flashing on a vehicle and I prayed it was the ambulance. I raced out to the elevator again. I thought I could run down the road and wave it down. When I got to the lobby, security was just unlocking the door and two attendants with a stretcher stood there. I wanted to kiss them I was so happy.

One of the attendants could speak English. Once we were in the apartment they took Brian's vitals and asked him several questions. In less than five minutes the doorbell rang and two more attendants were standing there with red medical bags in their hands. They followed me down to the bedroom. By this time the seizures had stopped. The four attendants chattered to each other and then one of them dialed the phone, indicating they were calling the doctor at the hospital. In the end the doctor decided that there really wasn't anything that could be done differently at the hospital, so the ambulance attendants stayed until Brian was asleep and then they left.

I left the lights and TV on. I stayed awake the rest of the night fearing that Brian would have another seizure, but luckily he did not. He slept through the whole next day. I remembered that my cousin would sleep for a day or even two days after she had bad epileptic seizures, so I was not worried that Brian rested. When he finally woke up, twenty-six hours later, he was more confused than usual.

The following week I noticed that daily activities were becoming more and more difficult for him. I watched from the doorway. He picked up the socks I had laid on the bed beside him. He stared at the sock in his hand but made no attempt to put it on. Eventually he just dropped them to the floor. He sat staring out the window, watching the ships. I walked over to him and he looked up at me and then he glanced down at the socks. I said nothing as I bent down and picked up his foot, put on the sock and then his running shoe. I looked into his eyes and smiled. I worried that the tumor was growing. I stood and reached out my hands. Brian put his hands in mine and I pulled him to a standing position. I walked backwards guiding him down the hallway to the living room where I had left the television on.

I felt like I was watching Brian from the sidelines. He was declining day by day but there was nothing I could do to stop it. I wondered when we would hear back from the oncologist. When almost two weeks had passed I called Dr. Y and asked when Brian would be starting radiation treatments.

"I do not know yet as we are waiting for the insurance company to approve payment, he said.

"How long will that take?" I asked.

"It is out of my control really. The hospital administration handles all insurance claims. I cannot do anything until I am advised that the hospital will be paid."

I am stunned. I can't believe that it is a matter of money. That had not crossed my mind.

"I don't care what it costs. Can I not arrange for payment and worry about the insurance later?"

"I am sorry, but I must follow the hospital's administration. The form has been submitted to the insurance company," he replied.

I could not contain myself and started yelling. "My husband needs treatment now. We can't wait for insurance approval," I exclaimed. "You know that every day makes a difference for him. We can't afford to wait for the insurance company and the hospital to sort out payment," I said between sobs.

"Wendy, I know you are worried. I will see what I can do, but please call the insurance company and get them to respond today if they can."

"Gracias. Thank you Dr. Y," I said. It was an instinctive answer as I really had nothing to thank him for as no progress had been made in getting treatments started.

In addition to obtaining insurance approval, time was required to schedule a simulation to align the actual treatments. I wondered how long that would take. I was really worried as Brian was declining every day.

I was overjoyed later that afternoon when I got confirmation that the treatment had been approved. It was a step in the right direction.

The next morning Dr. Y called me to confirm that the simulation would be scheduled within the next week. I silently thanked God.

Brian was feeling weak and had been throwing up all evening. I hoped that he would feel well enough by morning to make the appointment at the hospital for the radiation simulation. I worried that if we missed the appointment it would mean a longer delay in treatment.

Luckily the next morning Brian felt fine and I drove him to the hospital for the simulation appointment. The radiation oncologist explained that before radiation treatments could be started there was a process to create a mold of Brian's head. The head mask would be worn during each treatment, and it ensured radiation was directed exactly where intended to ensure only the tumor was impacted.

When I returned to pick up Brian I was taken aback by the mold. It was daunting to look at. It was a clear plastic mold that would fit over Brian's head with only his ears protruding. There were lines identified in tape which created an intersecting point. The lines would be utilized to focus the radiation treatments. Brian was not affected by all that was going on to create the mold and just sat and smiled. I wondered whether I would be able to wear such a contraption without being claustrophobic.

SIXTEEN

The plan was approved for Brian to receive thirty radiation treatments, on weekdays with weekends off to give him a chance to recover.

Finally, the day arrived I had been waiting for. It was March 27th and Brian received the first treatment. He got two treatments before the Easter holiday weekend. I thought about the vacation we had discussed for this weekend. Those plans seemed so long ago now.

We were fortunate that the appointments were scheduled for 9:00 am which was generally when Brian was feeling at his best. He got progressively more frustrated and confused as the day progressed.

Neither of us knew what to expect. I was anxious and had Brian up and dressed early. I didn't want to rush him. The treatments were at a different hospital, but still in close proximity to our apartment. The traffic, however, was crazy as we had to intersect a main artery. With no traffic lights you had to just trust that the oncoming three lanes of traffic would yield, which in Panama was not always the case. I gritted my teeth as I drove across the road. I was relieved when I pulled into the parking lot with time to spare.

I parked the car and walked around to the passenger side. Brian was fumbling with the door handle, and I was happy that he could not get it open. With my assistance on his left side, and the cane on the right, he was able to walk across the parking lot. We sat on the bench outside the main doors and enjoyed the aroma of the beautiful flower beds and listened to the melodic chirp of the birds. The gardener was hand watering. As he held the hose on the hedge, the birds flocked to his feet, followed the spray of water and flapped their wings, bathing in the coolness of the spray. Every day of Brian's treatment we followed this same pattern. We arrived early and sat outside for a few minutes on the bench.

So that we were not late, I stood and helped Brian through the doors and down the short hallway to the oncology unit.

Three people sat waiting. I looked at them and wondered if they were patients themselves or family. The doctor was very punctual, and we were only there about five minutes when he stepped through the door.

"Señor Brian. How are you?" Dr. Y asked.

"Fine Doc," Brian replied.

"Good morning," I added.

He walked us down the hallway to the treatment room. This became the pattern for every treatment. Dr. Y told me that he wanted to watch Brian's ability to walk. Once we reached the door of the treatment room I returned to the waiting room. I stared blankly at the TV that had the morning news on. I could keep up with some of what was being said, but the announcers spoke so rapidly in Spanish that it took real concentration to catch all that they said. That day I just didn't have the concentration.

On April 2nd, eleven weeks after Brian's stroke, he was increasingly confused. He questioned me on where we lived, what we were doing, where I was going when I left for work. I tried to explain, but tears flooded my eyes with every question. I tried hard to hide my pain. The doctor had said that Brian's memory should improve about halfway through the radiation treatments. I prayed that we would be that lucky. It broke my heart every day to watch him lose more and more of himself. He had been a voracious reader, but he no longer picked up a book. He always used to keep up to date on current affairs, but now he no longer watched the news. He had always been an extrovert, but most days he was silent.

As I looked at him I thought of the incredible life we had had together. I talked to him about all the trips we had taken to so many countries, but he no longer had memory of most of those trips.

I was fortunate that my office was not far from our apartment and I was able to leave Brian alone when he was sleeping so that I could attend meetings at my office. Emails and telephone calls I did from home. I was feeling the strain though. I felt guilty when I left Brian, but I didn't know an alternative way of doing things. In another week, Larry, Brian's friend, would be arriving from Canada. He would stay for just over a week. It would be nice to have someone to talk with.

When I arrived at work, one of my managers, Alexis, came into my office and was talking quickly about a big deal with a client. I had my back to her as she talked excitedly. She was a high energy person, and I waited for her to take a breath before I turned to face her. I wanted so much to care about what she was telling me, but the weight of everything was crushing me. When I looked at her I started to cry. She closed the door and put her arms around me. We sat down. I felt silly. I was the boss, the mentor, the coach. I was the person that was supposed to be giving guidance to my employees, not the other way around.

"You can't keep doing this. You need help. I am going to call my mom and find you a nurse," Alexis said.

And that was how it happened. The following day I found myself interviewing Anna. Right from the moment she walked into our apartment I liked her. She was confident, caring and I knew Brian would be in good hands when I could not be home.

Anna started on April 4th. She was thoughtful and understood that Brian would no longer eat a big meal, so she would put together snack plates that combined fruit, cheese and of course the candies Brian was always asking for. This way she would give him a smaller meal at lunch and then supplement with the snack plates.

Brian had never been a big eater of fruit, but since the stroke he began to crave fruit. In all the years that we had been together Brian would only eat watermelon, oranges or grapefruit with seasonal fruits like strawberries only occasionally. He rarely ate an apple. Yet following the stroke he ate two or three apples every day. I was amazed. Our family would joke about his new found love of fruit. His mother was pleased that he finally would eat fruit. Brian of course thought that he had always eaten fruit, so that added to the humour of the moment.

His new appetite for fruit was a great way of getting more nutrition in him. He would eat a combination of pineapple, watermelon, grapes and apples every day. Anna made sure Brian drank lots of water by giving him fresh lemonade, which he would drink in an instant.

As the weeks passed I appreciated Anna even more. She would make a list of vegetables for me to purchase so that she could make soup. I walked through the grocery store searching out vegetables that I couldn't pronounce let alone understand what they were. But Anna said the vegetables were good in soup and would heal Brian. I didn't argue as I would take any help we could get.

One day when we were having a discussion about Brian and his care, she told me that her full name was Gladys Anna. I looked at her, not sure if I heard her correctly. I felt a cold chill and a shudder run through me. Brian's grandmother's name was Gladys. I knew then that Anna had been sent to us from heaven. Gladys was not a common name, and I still wonder to this day where the name Gladys came from in a country with Spanish heritage.

I thought of Brian's grandmother and knew that she was still taking care of him, even if it was from heaven.

SEVENTEEN

At the start of the second week of radiation treatments, Brian was cheerful, but I saw the strain and confusion in his eyes. He asked me that morning where we were going when I had got him into the car. I explained it to him as we made the trip to the hospital.

Every day Dr. Y asked Brian how he was doing and Brian's answer was always the same.

"Good, Doc."

Brian never complained. The loss of his short-term memory was a blessing in some ways, as the seriousness of his illness had not caused him concern. When we talked about the tumor and the treatments he would be in the moment, but once we stopped talking he quickly forgot what we talked about. I, however, could never push it out of my mind. Every day I saw pieces of him slipping away.

As we walked down the hall to the treatment room, Dr. Y steadied Brian on his right side even though Brian had a cane in his hand. The cane was now a constant companion as Brian's eyesight continued to deteriorate. I was, as usual, on his left side.

I returned to the waiting room. I looked up as the outer door opened and a woman walked through. Behind her was a man. Draped over the man's shoulder was a girl, about ten years old I guessed. Her body hung limply down his side. Her head rested on his shoulder and one arm clung to his neck. I felt sorry for them, assuming this was their daughter. There was pain in their eyes and deep sorrow was etched on their faces. I started to well up as I looked at them. I couldn't imagine what it would be like to have a child this sick. The girl's head was completely bald, and they no longer covered her head to hide it. There was no life in her eyes.

The receptionist jumped up and held the interior door so that the couple could walk straight through without stopping in the waiting room. I stood and looked through the glass in the door. I watched them enter the chemo room.

Before Brian's treatment was done, an attendant with a stretcher arrived and the girl was wheeled away. I assumed they were admitting the girl to the hospital.

I never saw the family again and always wondered how the girl was. I knew that cancer ravaged many families, but at a time like that you thank God for the years you have had. Brian and I had enjoyed life. This girl would not.

When Brian was home from radiation he slept until Anna made his lunch. I decided to go to work for the afternoon. Only my managers knew the extent of Brian's illness. The rest of my team knew that something was wrong, as I was no longer the first person in to the office. They were respectful and did not ask me what was wrong. I was thankful for that, because if I had shared the extent of Brian's condition with all my employees I would not have held up.

I was in my office when there was a knock on the door. I looked up to see Deidre and Felipe standing there. Felipe was one of my managers and Deidre was part of Felipe's team. Deidre hugged me and told me in Spanish that she had been praying for Brian. She had brought me a gift of a book. I looked at the book and was surprised that it was in English. In addition to being kind enough to buy me the book, Deidre had taken the time to find an English version in Panama where predominantly all books are in Spanish. The book was titled - *Proof of Heaven*. It was a neurosurgeon's journey into the Afterlife. I got a chill. Deidre did not know about Brian's tumor or the terminal diagnosis. I wondered how she selected this book. It was as if God had sent her with it.

When they left my office I flipped through the book and then placed it in my briefcase.

When I arrived home, Brian was resting, and Anna said he did not have much of an appetite. She left for the day and I walked down the hallway. Brian lay on his side in the bed. I walked around the bed and spoke to him, but he did not respond to my words. I bent down and kissed his head. He did not stir, so I let him sleep and went to the kitchen in search of food.

On the kitchen counter was a note written to Señor Brian on a small piece of yellow lined paper. It was from Mercedes, the daughter of our domestic employee. It had small hearts drawn around her words. She was praying for Brian to get better. What a touching note I thought. Since Danya became our employee, whenever Mercedes did not have school she would come to the apartment with Danya. Many days Mercedes watched television with Brian while Danya cleaned. Brian always gave her candy and they would chat in Spanish. I picked up the note and guessed that Mercedes had been at the apartment today while I was gone. I took the note and placed it on the dresser in our bedroom so that I could read it to Brian when he woke up.

I grabbed some cold chicken from the fridge and made two pieces of toast. I looked in the crisper, saw vegetables and thought of a salad, but didn't have the energy to put it together. I sat in our bedroom and ate off a TV tray. It was only 7:30 pm, but I undressed and crawled into bed next to Brian. I propped up the pillows so that I could watch television. He did not stir. I rested my arm over him as I flipped through channels. Two hours later I shut off the television and curled up next to him.

I was in a deep sleep when I heard a crashing sound. I reached for Brian, but the bed was empty. I turned on the bedside light and jumped to my feet. I called out to him as I headed into the bathroom. He did not respond and my heart sank as I saw him lying on the floor next to the toilet. I gasped, assuming the worst that he had hit his head on the toilet.

"My God, Brian what happened?"

"I don't know," he replied as he looked up at me.

"Are you okay? Did you hurt yourself?" I asked, as I looked around him for signs of blood. I was relieved when I couldn't see any cuts on him. "Let's get you back to bed. You aren't supposed to get up without me," I added.

It was a struggle, but I got Brian to his feet. I had him sit on the toilet before attempting to walk. He looked up at me confused.

"Can you walk?"

"I think so. Where are we going?"

"You're going back to bed."

I helped Brian to stand, and he was steadier than I had expected. I got him tucked back into bed and then looked at the clock, 2:35 am. I knew I wouldn't get any more sleep tonight. My mind was racing with thoughts of Brian wandering at night. Then it came to me. I would tie him to me. I walked into the closet and looked at my scarves. I reached out and touched a blue silk scarf that I had rarely worn. Behind it was a heavier cloth scarf which I had worn more often as a belt than a scarf. It had yellow, green and black stripes. I slipped it off the hanger, and had a flashback to the client who had given me the scarf as a gift. I smiled remembering him as I walked back to the bed. I picked up Brian's wrist and tied one end of the scarf to him, making sure it was not tight, but tight enough that he could not slip it off. Then I walked around and got into bed on my side. I picked up the scarf, made a loop and slipped my right hand through it. At least now I would know if he tried to get up.

EIGHTEEN

*T*hen came the day we met with the chemo oncologist. He was a friendly man who made Brian feel good about his progress. Chemo pills had been approved for one week each month after the radiation treatments were completed. Brian would start on the pills the week of June 2nd. One of the side effects of the tumor had been that Brian's eye sight was deteriorating. I was uncertain day to day as to how much he could see. As part of the check-up, the oncologist questioned Brian about what he could see.

After we finished the appointment I helped Brian to his feet and placed the cane in his right hand. Brian was on my left as I extended my right hand to the doctor to thank him. When I stopped, Brian stepped out of my grasp and in a matter of a second walked smack into the door jamb.

"Oops. I guess I misjudged that," Brian said with a chuckle as he stepped back.

I quickly stepped forward, grabbed Brian's hand and placed my right arm the length of his left arm.

The doctor stepped forward and placed his hand on Brian's shoulder. "It's okay. I've done that before too," he said encouragingly.

Brian stepped backward and then leaned forward once again banging into the door jamb. This time we all laughed. I pulled him hard to the right and we got through the doorway.

The oncologist saw how unsteady Brian was and suggested I purchase a more stable cane. Brian had been using one that had just one foot and I had to find one with four feet which was less likely to slip out from under him.

Anna had come with me to help with Brian. She was waiting in the lobby and together we got Brian down the elevator and into the car. All the movement wore Brian out, and he closed his eyes on the drive home. Once we arrived at the apartment, Anna helped get Brian into bed before she left. I sat on the side of the bed and looked down at Brian.

The following week we went to the ophthalmologist and she made every effort to determine Brian's vision level because she expected glasses may be beneficial. Brian had always worn contact lenses, and now of course those were out of the question. The glasses he had were an old pair so I was uncertain as to the prescription. Brian sat in the chair and the eye chart was projected on the wall.

"Can you read this line for me?" the doctor asked as she pointed to a line of letters.

"Five, six and I think nine," Brian replied.

The doctor looked at me and raised her eyes.

"Bri, they are alphabetic not numbers. Can you try again?" I asked.

"Yeah, I know it's the alphabet," Brian said, and then he proceeded to call out numbers once again.

The doctor changed the chart to numbers. "Let's try this page," she continued.

"P, K, M and I think a Z or maybe an S," Brian said proudly.

I chuckled as it truly was funny. Brian had called out numbers when the alphabetical chart was reflected, and once she changed the chart to numerical he called out the alphabet. He had it totally backwards. The doctor at this point also smiled.

"I'm not sure we can pinpoint the problem here today, so I am going to have new glasses made with the same prescription as your contact lenses," she said.

"That will work great, I think," Brian answered.

On the way home I explained to Brian what had happened at the appointment and we both laughed about his answers.

NINETEEN

*I*t was the day of his 15th radiation treatment. As I helped Brian to dress I tried to cheer him up with the news that we were half way, but he was tired and weak. The sparkle had gone from his eyes. The shirt I pulled over his head hung looser than it did before. His chest and arms had shrunk from a lack of exercise. I combed his hair and picked off the loose strands of hair that fell on his shoulders.

I walked him from the apartment in my usual manner, me walking backwards with his hands in mine.

"Where are we going?" he asked as I clipped on his seatbelt.

"You have radiation today. Remember?"

"Why am I doing that?"

"You have a tumor so they are killing it."

"Oh," is all he said and then he leaned his head back and closed his eyes.

"Tomorrow we can go to the beach if you want," I said as I pulled out of the parking garage.

"Ok."

Brian could no longer walk across the parking lot, so I pulled up to the hospital doors. I sat him on the bench and left him while I went to park the car. I prayed that he wouldn't attempt to stand and walk without me at his side. When I joined him on the bench I noticed how pale he looked. He had trouble stepping over the threshold into the hospital and hesitated. He stopped several times as we walked the length of the hallway to the treatment room. When Brian came out of the radiation room Dr. Y was holding his arm and guiding him down the hall. I walked through the doors to take over from the doctor. I pursed my lips but said nothing.

"See you on Monday," Dr. Y said. He then turned and walked back up the hall. He did not wait for a response. Brian said nothing.

We walked out of the hospital and I had to leave Brian on the bench again while I got the car from the parking lot. There was a man standing waiting, so I asked him to please make sure Brian did not move until I got back with the car. The man nodded at me. As I walked to the car I wondered if the man understood English and would still be standing there when I got back.

When we got home Brian wanted to go directly to bed. As soon as he lay down he was sick and threw up repeatedly. He was so apologetic for being sick all over the sheets. I didn't care about the bed. I was just worried as he looked so pale. I went and got him some ginger ale. Both Anna and Danya were working today, so together we were able to roll Brian over to take the sheets off the bed. With military precision they had the bed made up again and Brian resting comfortably within ten minutes.

Brian was feeling no better on Saturday, so we didn't go to the beach. I knew how important it was for him to rest. He ate only a little of what I gave him, so I made up small plates of fruit and snacks like Anna did and offered him something every time he woke. I sat on the couch in our bedroom with my laptop on a TV tray. I attempted to get caught up on my work and personal emails, but I couldn't concentrate. I was up and down checking on Brian and just couldn't focus. I finally shut off the computer. Dr. Y called to see how Brian was today. I was amazed at the compassion of this man to call on a weekend. I updated him on Brian and Dr. Y told me to call him on his cell phone if Brian worsened.

Brian slept most of the weekend. I sat on pins and needles much of the time watching him closely to make sure he did not have any seizures. I knew that seizures would cause him to sleep.

By Monday he was feeling better and we started the day, as usual, with the radiation treatment. Dr. Y was glad to see Brian had not gotten worse over the weekend.

"We have to expect that he will have bad days," Dr. Y said to me.

"I know."

As Brian felt stronger by the time we got home, I left him with Anna and went to work.

I relied on my work colleagues for strength every day. Today Alexis came into my office to tell me she had arranged for a hair stylist to come to the apartment. Brian's hair had been falling out and he had bald patches where he once had hair. I had talked to Alexis about it the day before and already she had solved it for me. I marvelled at the level of service that was possible in Panama. I couldn't image what it would cost for a stylist to come to our home in Canada. Here it was a normal request.

When I got home I took the swivel office chair and put it in the bathroom. A nice young man arrived and I ushered him into the bathroom. I returned to the living room, helped Brian down the hallway into the bathroom, and got him positioned in the chair. By the time we walked down the hall, Miguel, the stylist, had unrolled his scissors, combs, etc... on a towel on the counter. He greeted Brian, picked up the shaver, and within twenty minutes Miguel had given Brian a military-style cut. As he was already at the apartment, I asked Miguel to trim my hair as well.

TWENTY

I looked at Brian every day and wondered if the radiation treatments were making a difference. So far he had completed twenty of the thirty radiation treatments. I had expected to see improvement by now, but sadly Brian continued to slip away from me.

In the beginning after the stroke, Brian was able to dress himself each day. Less than four months after the stroke he could no longer focus to dress himself. I tried to challenge him each day to dress, rather than just stepping in and helping him. Some days he could get his mind focussed and would follow my instructions to put on his socks, his running shoes and his tee shirt. Other days he just stared at me when I spoke, and I knew that he did not have the capacity to understand and get the thoughts from his mind to his limbs. On these days he just sat and waited for me to dress him. I always made a joke out of it to keep him from feeling bad about not being able to help. He had long since quit brushing his teeth and shaving. I stood at the sink with him and moved his hand in a motion to get his teeth brushed.

I had been shaving Brian with a standard razor, but he began moving too much for me to shave him safely with a blade. I purchased an electric shaver instead, but it took longer every day. Sometimes Brian got restless while I shaved him, so one side would get completely done in the morning and sometime later in the day I would finish the other side. I was glad that he did not have a heavy beard or he would have gone out to his radiation treatments each day looking half shaved.

When Brian started radiation I was able to gauge the time we needed to get ready and it always allowed us the luxury to sit outside the hospital for a few minutes enjoying the surroundings. I had to start getting Brian up more than an hour earlier than before as I never knew whether he would be able to get his thoughts working in his favour. Walking was slow and he made numerous stops even over a short distance.

We started the day with the same conversation we'd had several times in the past.

"I think there is something wrong with me," Brian said.

"Yes. Do you remember what the doctor said?"

"No. I think I had a stroke though," he replied.

"Yes, you had a stroke, but you are going to be okay," I said with reassurance.

Brian looked at me but said nothing more. I turned on the TV for noise more than anything. Brian never liked silence and would have the TV on even when he wasn't in the room watching it, so now I turned it on for the same reason.

I thought he was listening but it was hard to tell. I knew that his eyesight had deteriorated to the point that the screen was unclear. He could no longer read. For a man who used to read a novel in two days this was devastating, however Brian took it in stride. He flipped through magazines, but I knew he was only doing it to pass the time. Toes, was resting on his chest. She had flattened herself like a badger against him. She purred as he talked to her. I watched as his hand ran down her back followed by his other hand in a flowing motion.

I looked out the window and saw clouds rolling in. It looked like it was raining already in the distance. An overcast day has always made me feel sluggish. I'm the type of person that needs sunshine to energize me. The greyness encouraged me to enjoy an afternoon nap. I took Brian to our bed then I got undressed and lay down with him. I ran my hands through what was left of his hair. I cuddled up to him and pressed my chest against his back. In happier times he would have rolled over and taken me in his arms, but I got no response. I continued to hold on to Brian, and the comfort of his body helped me to fall sleep. I felt refreshed when I woke and realized how deeply I had slept.

I walked to the kitchen and stood with the fridge door open wondering what we would eat for supper. I looked inside the casserole dish and was thrilled to see that Danya had left us pollo con papas (chicken and potatoes). Brian loved her cooking, so I removed the casserole and put a small amount in a pot to warm up.

I was able to encourage Brian to eat, but he would only sit on the edge of the bed so I placed the meal on a TV tray. I sat beside him to help. I knew I should have eaten as well, but I had no desire to do so.

When Brian went back to sleep I walked to the kitchen. I grabbed a beer from the fridge and sat down in the living room. We had purchased tall white leather chairs, and Brian and I used to sit in them and look out at the ocean. We would watch all the ships that were queuing to enter the Panama Canal. I took a drink of beer and looked over at the vacant chair. I reached out with my foot and spun the chair. Tears filled my eyes. I wished Brian was spinning in the chair but tonight, like so many nights, I sat alone.

I carried the burden of Brian's terminal diagnosis alone. I was feeling the pressure of keeping Brian's condition a secret from our family in Canada. That night it was too much for me. I stared out blankly to the ocean as tears ran off my chin. I didn't care. I was too emotionally drained to even get up for a tissue. I leaned back in the chair and took a big gulp of beer.

I wanted so much to make a bargain with God, to reverse what had happened, to return us to the life we had. I knew that I would give up everything to have Brian back. There was no value in living without him. We had so many plans for vacations, and I wondered whether we would ever go away together again. I wanted to believe that we would. I wanted to believe that Brian would get better. I had to believe it. I had to be strong and get Brian back to Canada. I wanted so much for him to be able to attend his mother's 90th birthday party. I prayed that when we got to Canada some of the pressure would be lifted off my shoulders.

TWENTY ONE

It was a Wednesday and Brian received the 23rd radiation treatment. I felt happy that the end of the treatments was nearing. Then, and only then, would the oncologist be able to determine if the radiation had stopped the growth of the tumor. I worried everyday as I saw no big improvement in Brian.

He looked as tired as I knew his body must be. He did not complain and did not say anything when I asked if he was tired. He just sat in silence, as if the life had been drained from him. Brian had always been boisterous. You always knew when Brian walked in the room. But sadly, the man who had always garnered the centre of attention was no longer able to enjoy life. He was strangely quiet, and I saw no sparkle in his eyes.

We used to talk for hours but our conversations became short. He did not remember the holidays we had enjoyed, and even though I tried to encourage him by discussing upcoming vacation destinations, he'd forgot what we were talking about and so did not respond. It saddened me.

When he lay down to rest I went to work and left him with Anna. Three hours later my assistant interrupted me to advise that Anna had called and needed me to go home. Brian had been resting on the couch in our bedroom, and when Anna went in to check on him he was sitting on the floor. She was unable to get him to his feet.

I arrived home and looked down at Brian who was making no attempt to get up.

"What are you doing?" I asked.

"I don't know. I was waiting for you to come home." He looked up at me and my heart broke. I could tell that he had no idea where he was.

"We need to get you up and maybe have a nice shower," I said as I sat down beside him.

Brian looked at me. "I'm okay. I'm just going to have supper here and watch television."

"But you are on the floor. You need to get back up on the couch," I said, putting my hand under his arm. Anna was on the other side. Brian looked at us but made no attempt to get to his feet.

"Bri, you need to help us. We aren't strong enough to lift you if you don't help."

"Why can't I just stay here?"

"Because you are on the floor! You will get cold," I said.

"I'm not cold," he said, and I realized my comment about getting cold had got him thinking of that rather than about getting up.

I looked over at Anna and told her to leave me alone with Brian. I knew by the look on her face she was disappointed with herself for what had happened. As Anna walked out of the bedroom, I sat down next to Brian. After half an hour I got him to understand that he must get up off the floor. Brian was able to lean one arm on the couch, and with both Anna and I on the other side we were able to maneuver him to a standing position. We quickly walked him over to the bed and got him settled on the edge. I changed his clothes and we got him under the covers.

Brian fell asleep. I was grateful that Anna was at the house. I was fearful of what would have happened had Brian hit his head. I knew the dangerous situation we averted.

The next day I decided to work from home to be with Brian, even though Anna would also be at the apartment. I wanted to be sure that Brian was not experiencing seizures that caused the confusion the day before. As the day went on Anna told me how much more relaxed Brian was when I was there. Normally he asked her over and over where I was, but that day of course he did not. Anna got him to stand and walk around the apartment with her for exercise. Every time they walked through the office he said hello to me as if it was the first time he had seen me that day.

We had friends arriving from Canada. Dudley and Lauretta had planned this trip for months. They were going to come to Panama and stay with us and then go on to Peru to walk the trails of Machu Pichu. I was disappointed that we could no longer enjoy their visit like we would have just five months earlier. We had met Dudley and Lauretta on vacation in Mexico ten years earlier and since then had enjoyed several annual vacations with them. Other friends, Larry and Sally, flew down from Canada as well. We spent a lot of time at the apartment where we could visit and Brian could be comfortable and rest when he needed to. With everyone's help we were able to get Brian into the vehicle and help him walk along the beach. Brian had not complained since he became sick and I knew he would not tell us if the day out was too much for him, so I watched him closely. When we got home we had dinner and then I knew it was time that Brian rest. He could no longer stay up and drink beer with friends and be the life of the party. The party would have to carry on without him.

I went to his left side as he stood. He leaned on his cane and I steadied him as we walked through the living room and down the hall to the bedroom. Dudley and Lauretta were leaving the next day, so they followed us down the hallway so that they could say goodbye to Brian. Brian sat on the edge of the bed and chatted briefly with our friends. I saw the pain in their eyes. We had spent many vacations together and between Brian and Dudley there was never a dull moment. Now Brian's life was being sucked from him and we all knew it. Lauretta leaned in to hug Brian. I snapped a photo. Dudley did the same and I took another photo. I looked at them and tried not to cry. I wondered silently whether they would ever see Brian again.

TWENTY TWO

The day I had been waiting for had finally arrived, May 8th, the last day of radiation treatments.

Brian and I were both excited that morning to have reached the final day. It was the realization that we had done what we could to conquer the tumor. I knew later in the day Brian would have no memory of our discussion, but at least for the time being he knew we would not be coming back to the hospital and we were saying goodbye to Dr. Y.

Brian seemed to walk with a spring in his step at the realization he would never be coming back again. He said hello to everyone we met walking the corridor of the hospital.

"You're in a good mood," I said as we walked.

"Yeah. I feel good today."

I smiled and squeezed his hand. I was carrying a gift for Dr. Y and our camera so that I could capture the radiation team with Brian. After the treatment, Brian was given the plastic molded mask which had been fitted over his head for each radiation treatment. I tucked it under my arm. We each hugged Dr. Y and thanked him. I tried not to cry. I knew that we would not see him again. Brian could not receive any more radiation.

We walked out of the hospital and the warm air was a welcome blast from the coolness of the hospital air conditioning.

"It's nice here, isn't it," Brian said.

"Nice here as in the hospital, or you mean it is nice in Panama?" I asked.

"Both."

Rather than leaving Brian on the bench while I went to get the car from the parking lot, I decided to sit with him on the bench.

"Yes, it is wonderful here," I replied. "I will be sad to leave here."

"Are you going somewhere?"

"We're going back to Canada to see your mom. Remember? She will be turning 90 in July," I said.

"What month is it now?"

"Today is May 8th."

"Good. Then we don't have to leave for a while. I like it here."

"We have had a good time here in Panama. Maybe we could go to the beach on the weekend. For now, we should go back to the apartment and have some coffee."

I stood and walked to the car. I took a longer route home with the windows rolled down so that we could smell the air, even if it heated up the car. I drove along Avenida Balboa and told Brian he could see the ocean if he looked to his right. He turned his head and looked out.

I had planned for us to be alone that day. I had cancelled both Anna and Danya for the day and had arranged to take the day off work. I didn't want to think about anything today except the fact that tomorrow we wouldn't be going to the hospital. It had been our pattern Monday through Friday for six weeks. It would be nice for Brian to be able to sleep in the next day.

The treatments were marked on the calendar, and we had crossed the finish line. In anticipation, I had bought a bottle of champagne to celebrate. After we ate supper, I selected two champagne flutes from the bar. I opened the bottle and poured Brian a small glass. I filled mine to the brim. I talked to him about the treatments being over and why we were celebrating but he is only mildly interested. It breaks my heart. After I settled him in bed, I drank the rest of the bottle. I slept peacefully, partly helped by the champagne.

Now that the treatments were over I turned my attention back to my work responsibilities.

When we had received the confirmation of Brian's tumor and the dismal outlook, I had talked with my employer about retiring once we returned to Canada. I loved my job and always had. I was fortunate to have had many opportunities in my thirty-five years with the company. I was a good employee and they were a good employer. However, it was time for Brian to be my main focus, and I could not accomplish that and carry on any level of work responsibilities. Since we were returning to Canada, it made a good break to leave my job in Panama and retire.

I sat down and made phone calls and sent emails to advise our family back in Canada that I had made the decision to retire so that I could spend all my time with Brian. Retirement would mean that we would return to Canada. Brian's mother was so happy with the news as she desperately wanted to hug him.

My retirement was a surprise to everyone. Most of the family, of course, had no knowledge that Brian had been undergoing the radiation treatments. They only knew about his stroke.

I felt relieved to know Brian was well enough to fly back to Canada. A couple of months before, he would not have survived the flight at such high altitudes. I felt a weight lifting from my shoulders. Once in Canada I could be honest about Brian's condition and the past few months. I prayed that everyone would understand our reservation in telling them sooner.

At work I gathered my management team in my office. I had prepared myself to tell them that I would be returning to Canada. I had practiced what I would say so that I would not get emotional, but the minute I looked into their eyes the tears started to flow. They all knew how sick Brian was. They had been my support for the past few months. They had all shouldered extra work responsibilities in my absence. I owed them so much, but all I felt was sadness and regret.

I was relieved when the weekend arrived. It had been an emotional few days.

"I thought we would go to the beach today and then stop somewhere for lunch. How does that sound?" I asked.

"I don't think I can drive," Brian replied.

"No, I will drive," I answered chuckling. Brian was unaware that he had not driven for more than three months. The loss of his short-term memory caused by the stroke meant that we had the same conversation over and over, and some days I laughed rather than cried. Today I laughed as I got him ready.

I took a familiar highway and described to Brian where we were as I drove. In less than an hour, I turned off the main highway onto the secondary road that would lead us to the ocean.

I was able to park close. I bent down and untied Brian's runners. I did the same to mine and then kicked my feet, freeing them from the runners. Brian did not kick off his runners so I bent down and slipped his feet out. I grabbed both pairs of runners and hid them in the bushes along the ridge above the beach. I took Brian's hand in mine and we walked barefoot in the sand like hundreds of times over our life together. We walked as we talked about vacations, of the life we had, of our good fortune. We talked about Panama. Normally Brian would want to drink a beer as we walked on the beach, but he didn't mention it. I talked continually describing what was around us and all the times we had walked on this exact beach. He looked at me and smiled when I mentioned family who had been here with us.

As Brian no longer had stamina so our trip to the beach was short, but I am thankful to have gotten him out of the city. He'd had a love of the ocean since he joined the Canadian Navy at the age of seventeen. All of our vacations were planned around beach destinations. We never travelled to Europe as Brian always wanted to go to the ocean.

Within an hour I took him back to the car and we drove back to the city. I stopped at a hotel that had a welcoming area around the pool that was easy for Brian to walk to. I ordered Brian sliders, which are small hamburgers and easy for him to hold and eat. He smiled at me and I almost forgot the situation we were in. Brian looked like himself, somewhat thinner and with less hair, but the sparkle was back in his eyes. I wanted to hold on to that day as I knew that tomorrow was no longer promised to us. I had brought the camera and got a hotel employee to snap a photo of us.

TWENTY THREE

I sat down and read an email from my brother Rod. He congratulated me on my decision to retire and commented on how happy Brian and I would be once we were back at our acreage in Canada. He looked forward to visiting us during summer and sitting on the deck to enjoy a beer together. His words brought tears. He of course did not know about Brian's tumor. He had no idea that Brian was no longer drinking beer and wouldn't have the ability to walk in the fields or ride the horses. I felt guilty when I replied as I hid the truth.

The next email was from Maggie. She talked about how relieved she would be once she heard that Brian was back home and cutting the lawn on the riding lawn mower, beer in hand. To her that would be the sign he was well and back to being himself. I wiped away the tears and once more sent a reply that was not fully truthful. Brian could not walk without assistance. He would never cut the lawn again.

Belinda and Scott had been friends for almost forty years. Even though distance separated us, they were the kind of people we could always count on. They would stand by us. They were aware of Brian's condition and knew how important it was for us to be back in Canada. When we moved to Panama they were our first visitors. They offered to help in any way they could. They sent the most heartfelt emails, and I always enjoyed opening a message from them.

As I had considerable work to wrap up my position responsibilities, I left Brian with Anna and went to the office every day.

I opened an email from a friend and colleague in Toronto, and it brought me to tears with the sincerity. He had never worked with Brian. He was my work colleague. He had met Brian on several occasions and they took an instant liking to each other. His words were so truthful and described Brian perfectly;

'I am very fond of Brian and like to picture myself like him in 20 years into my own future. He is calm and capable, balanced and clear sighted. Everybody likes him and everybody wants to know what he thinks about things. I'm really sad.'

His words cut me to the bone. I decided to wait a couple of days before I replied. My thoughts were interrupted by conversation and laughter outside of my office.

We had planned a team-building event, which also became my going-away party. Maria, my assistant, was a great organizer and had motivated the whole team for the upcoming event. The staff had been divided into teams, and they were busy selecting songs to sing at karaoke. The discussion outside my office was about the songs they would perform.

As with other staff events, everyone was increasing the competitive environment by creating costumes to portray the singers they had selected. There would be judging required for their efforts. Practicing on lunch hours and after hours became the norm each day, and the upcoming event had created a real hum around the office.

Secretly, Felipe and I were meeting as we prepared to surprise the staff with our rendition of - *You're The One That I Want.* Me, as Olivia Newton-John and him as John Travolta.

For me it was a pleasant diversion from the pressure of Brian's illness. On the evening of the event, Anna had agreed to stay overnight at our apartment. That way she could give Brian supper and then be there until he went to sleep. It was comforting to me and allowed me to go to the party prepared to enjoy the evening with my staff. Additionally, with Anna staying overnight, I would not have to worry about her travelling home on the bus in the dark.

The evening was a celebration. Teams sang and entertained us and a true sense of camaraderie permeated the air. I cried when Felipe and I finished our duet. They were tears of regret at having to leave these people who had become so much a part of my life. Throughout the evening, between performances, I gathered with staff and photos were taken that I treasure.

A few days later I walked from desk to desk, hugged each employee and tried to hold back my tears. I loved my job. I loved the team I worked with, and I had grown to love Panama. The dream was coming to an end.

TWENTY FOUR

*O*n May 31st we had an appointment with Dr. W, the neurosurgeon. We brought a gift to thank him for everything he had done for both of us. We both hugged him. Dr. W was caring and compassionate and saw me every time I needed to talk. My eyes filled with tears.

As we turned to walk out he said, "Go back to Canada and be with your family. Enjoy the time you have left and do not focus on what you cannot change."

There was no way to prepare myself when tragedy struck. Many people would probably say that I was lucky that my husband had survived a stroke. In reality the diagnosis that he had an aggressive brain tumor which had ultimately caused the stroke was something that I could not look beyond. There was no sugar coating the prognosis – the tumor was inoperable, aggressive and would ultimately take my husband's life. The only unknown was how long Brian had. No one knows how they will react until they are faced with that situation.

I tried to smile as I led Brian from the office. Within thirty minutes we were back at our apartment. Brian sat with the television on. I sat down beside him, but I could not focus. The weight of Dr. W's words was crushing me. I thought back to the conversation we had following the biopsy.

"The brain is very powerful. It can work in Brian's favour, or if he becomes depressed over the diagnosis, his brain could become his enemy and no amount of treatment will help."

On that advice I had sheltered Brian all these weeks. I tried not to talk to him of the devastating tumor which was now changing both our lives.

TWENTY FIVE

We were at the last day of work for Anna. In a week we were going back to Canada. I hugged Anna and was truly sad when I said goodbye to her. I would never have gotten through the previous two months without her. She said goodbye to Brian, but I knew he did not relate to the fact that he would not see her tomorrow. I saw in her eyes that she was sad when she walked out the door.

Over the course of the previous month I had been packing small personal items and clothes into suitcases to take back to Canada with us. The majority of our items were to be handled by the movers and would arrive in Canada by air and sea. I thought I was packing too much, but based on our experience when we arrived in Panama, the air shipment with our clothes had taken more than three weeks to clear customs. I was probably packing the right amount to ensure we would have enough clothes with us to manage those first few weeks once we arrived home.

Brian sat on the couch in our bedroom and watched me put items in the suitcase that I had laid open on our bed.

"We'll be coming back to Panama?" he asked.

"Yes. We'll go home to your mom's birthday party and to check on the farm and then we will come back to Panama," I replied. I walked into the next room and wept. For the first time in thirty-eight years I had lied to my husband. I did not know for certain that he would ever be back to Panama again. I wanted to believe that we both would. I needed to hold on to that dream.

When I stepped back into our bedroom, Brian didn't notice my tears. He focussed on putting on his socks and shoes. I looked down to see his shoes on the wrong feet.

"Good job," I said as I knelt and switched his shoes. I stood, taking his hands in each of mine to steady him as he stood. I walked backwards down the hall as I led him to the living room. He sat down and I switched on the television.

"Wayne will be here tonight," I said, referring to my younger brother. I had asked Wayne to come and help me get Brian home to Canada. He would be here for almost a week before we would all fly back to Canada. I planned it so that there would be time to take Brian to the beach one last time.

"That will be nice," Brian said, not asking why Wayne was coming.

Wayne arrived and the two of us stayed up late enjoying a drink at our bar and talking about the changes in Brian since Wayne's last visit less than four months previous.

The moving company was booked to start packing our items. I had to go to the office to finalize my work commitments, so Wayne was staying at the apartment with Brian. I waited for the packing crew to arrive before I left for work. I reviewed the instructions with the jefe (boss) as the workers started wrapping the furniture. In order to be shipped out of Panama and be allowed back in Canada, all the furniture had to be wrapped in cardboard to ensure no pests travelled along with it. That was a monumental undertaking.

I was at work less than two hours when the phone rang and I saw my home number on the call display.

"You need to come home or talk to these guys," my brother said. "They keep asking me stuff and I don't have a clue what they want. Brian was able to answer a couple of questions, but I don't know if he gave them the right answer."

My brother was referring to the fact that the men packing the apartment only spoke Spanish.

"Where is the boss?" I asked.

"I don't know. I haven't seen him for a couple of hours."

Just then another one of the crew walked up to my brother and chattered to him. "I'll be home in ten minutes," I said.

When I arrived home things looked pretty much under control to me. All the crew was sitting on the floor in the living room eating their lunches. They were enjoying the view out the floor-to-ceiling windows. I expected many of them had never enjoyed such a view.

"How do you guys handle it here? My nerves are fried with all their questions and I've only been here four hours," Wayne said when I arrived.

"Well for the most part I can understand them. You just get used to it," I said. We had left Canada with only basic Spanish language skills, so over the course of our time in Panama we had to adapt and learn Spanish along the way.

It took another full day until everything was wrapped and packed into the trucks. Despite the fact that all the furniture had been moved out of the apartment, Brian still thought we would be back to Panama. He could not process what was going on around him and the fact we would not be taking all the furniture if we were just going back to Canada for a vacation, like we had several times before.

Brian had always wanted to go visit the San Blas Islands off the coast of Panama. It was an archipelago with uninhabited islands and glistening crystal waters. We had travelled to Bocas del Toro in January for the exact same reasons. It was after the Bocas trip that Brian suffered the stroke.

In appreciation of Wayne coming to help us, I had booked the trip. I had arranged for a driver to take us across Panama from the Pacific side, where we live, to San Blas on the Caribbean side. The road across the mountain range was difficult to traverse and a four-wheel drive vehicle was necessary. The trip took us longer than we had anticipated. There were clear skies in Panama City, but the clouds closed in as we travelled closer to San Blas. There were light rain showers when we finally stopped.

Wayne and I looked at the small boats that lined the dock and I wondered how we would get Brian to step down safely. As we had travelled three hours, I did not want to turn back without reaching the larger island where we would have lunch. I was disappointed as I watched the threatening clouds surround us. I had wanted this to be a great memory, and the weather needed to cooperate as we were fully exposed out there with nowhere to take cover. I prayed it did not start lightning.

We walked with Brian down the dock, me on one side and Wayne on the other. Our friend, and the driver, walked behind us. The boats had been converted to bench seats for transporting as many people as possible from the mainland to the outlying islands. There were several people already waiting in the boat.

I stepped down into the boat and held my hand out to Brian. With the help of someone else in the boat who took Brian's other hand, and Wayne steadying him on the dock, we were able to get Brian safely into the boat.

We had a thirty minute boat ride to the island we were visiting. I looked at Wayne as the rain started to sprinkle. I cringed. We had no choice, as there was no turning back. The boat captain soared across the ocean waters and we were pelted with rain. I dreaded each minute that passed. It was not a pleasant rain that refreshed us on a hot day. This was cold as it hit our skin and soaked into our clothes. The rain was intensified by the speed of the boat, so drops felt like pellets hitting us.

I looked at Brian who had his head bent trying to keep the rain from hitting his face. The hat he had on was doing little to keep him dry. Wayne and I were both just as wet. By the time the boat finally pulled up to the shore we were soaked to the bone. Brian was shivering and my plan to give him one more memory had been dashed. I looked at Wayne who looked like he wanted to be anywhere but here.

"We will have to make the most of it," I said.

"That won't be easy," Wayne replied.

I looked around. The conditions were more rustic than described online. The lodge had just four walls and a thatched roof. The palm fronds did little to keep out the rain and the floor of the lodge was damp.

The rain finally stopped, but as we had not planned for rain we had no dry clothes to put on. In the almost three years we had lived in Panama, we had never had a rain experience like that. The sun just wouldn't break through the clouds, so we couldn't even sit and dry on the beach. The boat to return to the mainland wouldn't be back for a couple of hours, so we had no option but to try and smile about our misfortune with the weather. We took photos and tried to look like we were enjoying ourselves, but we looked like drowned rats standing next to a palm tree.

The best I could say about the day was that the fresh fish lunch we were served was phenomenal.

When we got home we all had a hot shower and settled in with a drink. We were able to laugh about the bad luck we had with the weather.

"Why did we go there anyway?" Brian asked. "It was cold."

"It was San Blas. You have wanted to see it for months. Remember trying to plan a trip there?"

"Not really. It wasn't much fun," Brian said, and I had to laugh otherwise I would have cried.

The next day we had plans for lunch with our friends at Gamboa Rainforest. It was to be our opportunity to say goodbye. Brian and I had celebrated the past three Christmases with these friends at this same restaurant. It was a beautiful, warm sunny day and we stood on the balcony of the restaurant, looked down on the pool, and listened to the soothing waters that trickled over the rock flower beds. I breathed in the clean air and the scent of the hedge. I knew that I would miss this country and the smells that made me feel like I was on vacation every day. It was nice that Wayne had met our friends as well.

Julia was the first expat we met. She was a genuine person who organized monthly luncheons for a large circle of friends who had all found themselves in Panama from different countries. Richard was a wonderful man whom Brian always enjoyed talking with as they discussed everything from education to politics. There would no longer be any of those discussions. Our friends were all saddened that Brian had a stroke, and not knowing if we would see each other again, we took photos to capture our time together. Richard told Brian that he was praying for him. I knew that Richard more than anyone would be heartbroken when I finally advised them of Brian's tumor. On this day, I wanted them to enjoy the time we had together. There were lots of hugs when we departed.

For our final days we were booked into the Hard Rock Hotel in downtown Panama. We were in a two-bedroom suite, which allowed Wayne to be available to help me with Brian. The hotel had given us a wheelchair, and Brian was comfortable being pushed around in it. Brian had never complained once, but I knew that his getting in a wheelchair was a sign that he was declining. A couple of months before he would not even consider getting in a wheelchair when we were offered one at the hospital.

Breakfast was served by the pool. It was a clear sunny day when I left Wayne and Brian chatting as I went to finish up paperwork for our return to Canada. At the end of the day we returned to sit by the pool and enjoyed a cold beer. We talked about everything, and while Brian didn't say much, he laughed and smiled and I knew he was grasping sparks of memory from our discussion.

It was our last night in Panama. We were having cocktails with our best friends, Victoria and Jorge, plus Felipe and Leira. Brian was in good spirits and we laughed about the great times we'd had in Panama. I knew that Brian would never see them again and that weighed over me. I was sad for Brian and for our friends, but also for myself as I did not know when I would see them again either.

TWENTY SIX

June 18th, and we were flying home to Canada and leaving this life behind. Brian was still sleeping. I stood and looked out the hotel window at the Bay of Panama. There were small boats leaving the marina with their booms geared for fishing. The sun was just rising, and already I could feel the heat on the window. I bent my arms and leaned on the window sill. I couldn't stop the memories from flooding in. Brian and I both loved Panama and I was saddened to be leaving.

It was only 5:00 am but I had already showered and dressed. Brian stirred, so I turned my attention to getting him dressed. I heard my brother Wayne making coffee. I stepped from our bedroom.

"Good morning. How did you sleep?" I asked.

"Okay. Just thinking about the day ahead and how we will manage everything."

"Yeah, me too," I answered, as I grabbed a cup of coffee and went back into the bedroom.

Brian was sitting on the bed with his running shoe in his hand. He was looking down at his feet. I bent down, took the shoe and placed it on his foot. He lifted his other foot so that I could do the same. I looked up into his eyes from my kneeling position and reached out to touch his hand. He smiled back and squeezed my finger.

I took both his hands in mine and pulled him to a standing position. I walked backwards, and led him into the living area. I positioned him on the couch.

"Hey, Bri, how are you?" Wayne asked.

"Great Bud. How about you?"

I pulled the suitcases to the door and realized that six suitcases were just unmanageable. I had packed enough clothes to last more than the two weeks we would be in a hotel before we moved back into our acreage. I knew that having to leave the hotel to do laundry would be difficult to organize with Brian's condition. Now as I looked at all the suitcases I wished I had packed lighter.

"What time do we have to leave?" Wayne asked.

"Where are we going?" Brian asked.

"We should start heading downstairs in a couple of minutes. Manuel will be here any minute," I said to Wayne. Then I turned to Brian and explained that we were going home to Canada.

With the help of the bellmen we got everything loaded into Manuel's vehicle. Manuel was a private driver who we hired on multiple occasions, and he had taken Brian and me all over Panama in the past two and a half years. He had in turn become a trusted friend. We chatted easily on the trip to the airport. Manuel came with us into the airport, which was not his normal practice. Usually he left us curbside. I knew that he wanted to be able to say goodbye to Brian in a proper fashion.

We had a long, thirteen hour travel day ahead of us, and I was so grateful to have Wayne to lean on. Our first leg was flying from Panama to Houston. Then we had a three-hour layover. Luckily our luggage was tagged all the way to Canada. The second leg of the trip was from Houston to Edmonton, Alberta. Brian was exhausted when we arrived and Wayne and I were only slightly better.

I was thankful for the letter I presented at Customs which explained our situation, returning to Canada from a work assignment in Panama. The Customs Agent looked at Brian in the wheelchair and cleared us quickly.

We proceeded to the luggage area and waited for our bags. Brian was in the wheelchair holding our backpacks and we had two luggage carts with the six suitcases. Wayne was frustrated with me for packing so much, as one of us had to push Brian and it was impossible for the other person to push two luggage carts. It became a game of leap frog, moving one luggage cart, and then returning for the other one. A young girl saw our plight and offered to push one cart to the final Customs clearance area for us. Before we were allowed to leave the Customs area, I had to turn in the paperwork which indicated we had baggage that was not accompanying us and would arrive by air at a later date. It only took a few minutes before the documents were copied and stamped and we were allowed to leave.

We had arrived back in Canada at last.

TWENTY SEVEN

On our first few days' home we visited Brian's mother, arranged to rent a vehicle, and moved into a hotel. It was a comfort to be home, but confusing for Brian as we were not in a familiar place. We did not have a wheelchair, so Brian was relying on his cane once again.

I had to face the truth now that we were in Canada. We met first with his mom. It was a difficult conversation to tell her that Brian had been diagnosed with a brain tumor. We both talked and explained why we had withheld this information. We told her about all the treatments and I assured her that Brian would get well. I knew it was important to stay positive and I needed to hang on to a glimmer of possibility that the treatment would work. We all cried.

I telephoned my siblings and one by one told them about Brian's tumor. I tried not to break down but with each conversation it became increasingly difficult. They were exhausting discussions. I let everyone talk with Brian as I knew hearing his voice would be comforting.

We were fortunate to get an appointment with a top neurosurgeon at the University Hospital. The appointment had been arranged by the parents of our friends, and I am eternally grateful to them. Dr. Z was friendly and I knew he was accommodating us into his busy schedule. Before we left Panama the medical team had given me the CT and MRI test results as well as a detailed outline of the radiation and chemo regimen in digital format. Dr. Z was impressed with the detail that was contained in the reports. The information was required so that Brian could continue with the chemo treatment in Canada. We saw Dr. Z on June 21st and the second week of chemo pills was to commence July 1st. I was pleased when we got referred to the oncologist who would arrange for the blood testing necessary before each chemo regimen.

We were going to spend two weeks in the hotel, so I chose a hotel where we had a living room and a small kitchen, which we needed as breakfast was the only meal offered in the hotel. With the fridge I was able to have food in the room to snack on. It was not the best situation, but I knew it was only temporary. Because I was afraid to leave Brian alone, I had to take him with me every couple of days to get food. Places were unfamiliar to Brian, so the daily trips in the vehicle were confusing for him. Also it was difficult for him to walk the long hallways from our room to the elevator and out to the vehicle.

On one of our trips to the grocery store I made a second stop and purchased a wheelchair.

I woke up to the sun shining through the small hotel window. I looked over at Brian, who was still asleep. I stood up and looked out the window and saw clear blue skies. I decided that today I would take Brian for a drive to Elk Island National Park where we used to go golfing and to view the bison. The park was a wildlife conservation park for a variety of animals including elk, moose and bison.

I made coffee as I didn't dare get in the shower until I had Brian resting in the living area, otherwise he might try to get out of bed without me.

Brian was happy and smiled when he woke up. He was unsteady on his feet, but I managed to get him into the wheelchair. I left him in the hotel lobby until I brought the vehicle up to the door. A man was just coming in to register at the hotel as I was exiting with Brian. He put down his suitcase to help me. As I held the car door open he got Brian to his feet and in to the passenger's side.

"He's a big guy. How do you handle him yourself?" he asked.

I clamp my lips in a half smile. "Thanks," I said, not wanting to explain how worried I am every time I load Brian alone. As I folded up the wheelchair and put it in the trunk, the man gave me his name.

"I'm here for the next week if you need help," he said before he walked back into the hotel.

"That was nice of that guy to help us, wasn't it," I said to Brian as I got in the car and started the engine.

"What guy? Brian asked.

"A guy helped you get into the car."

"Yeah, that was nice," he answered. "Where are we going to?"

"I thought we would go to Elk Island."

Brian did not reply while I pulled out of the parking lot into the traffic. Within a few minutes we were on the highway. I talked to Brian as I drove describing where we were and all the things that should be familiar to him. We had driven this highway for seven years before moving to Panama.

When we got to the National Park I was thrilled that a herd of bison and their calves were in clear view from our vehicle. I drove slowly through what was termed *buffalo loop*, pointing out bison for Brian. When we finished the loop I drove further into the park to the picnic area. I was able to get Brian out of the car and we sat at a picnic table, looking out to the lake. I talked to him about all the times we had been in the park viewing wildlife and also the golf games we had played here. I wanted to take him to the clubhouse, but it was on a steep incline from the parking lot and I knew he couldn't maneuver it. After an hour we got back in the car and drove back to the hotel.

Finally, the day had come and we had checked out of the hotel. We were excited as we were moving back home to the forty-acre property we owned. When we moved to Panama, our goddaughter, Lauren, and her boyfriend, Trent, had moved in to the house and taken care of our many pets.

When I stepped out of the vehicle it felt like it was just yesterday that we had lived here, but then again it felt like it had been years. I had mixed feelings but was glad to be HOME. I helped Brian out of the vehicle, and he was able to walk with me steadying him on the left side and him holding the cane in his right hand. Our dogs, Danny and Hayley, who had stayed at the acreage in our absence, were glad to see us again. They sniffed us and wiggled with excitement. I was careful that they did not trip Brian as I led him up the step onto the deck. We both just stood there and looked around. The smell was distinctive, a mixture of horses and hay fields. I could also smell the flowers in pots on the deck. The silence was broken by chickadees and siskins that were buzzing through the trees.

I got Brian into the house and let him rest on the couch while I went to unload the vehicle. I moved from room to room in the house, like a walk down memory lane. I stopped and looked out windows, taking in the familiarity of the surroundings. I was happy to be back here at the acreage, and at this time it was the right place for both of us.

I got another load from the vehicle, and when I came back in the house, I let Danny and Hayley in so Brian could visit with them. He was thrilled to see them and they sat at his side as he patted their heads. Danny rolled on her back and Brian reached down and rubbed her stomach. This reminded me of when Danny entered our lives, thirteen years earlier. I recounted the story to Brian.

It was the summer of 2000. In the night we were awakened by one of our dogs, Keilly barking incessantly. Brian knew that Keilly was warning coyotes to stay away from the barns. In the morning I left for work and Brian called me a couple of hours later to say that there was a small black puppy under our deck. We found out later that the puppy was only six weeks old and had walked away from the litter at the next farm. She had walked across eighty acres and must have walked towards the barn lights at our farm. We believe that the barking we heard in the night kept the coyotes from getting the puppy. Keilly had in fact saved her. Even though we already had two dogs, Brian did not have the heart to give the puppy away, so she stayed and joined our growing pet collection.

Being back at our acreage was wonderful, but the yard required a lot of work and I was short on time. The riding lawn mower we had was no longer working so I had to go out and purchase a new one. I went to Home Depot where I stood and stared at all the riding lawn mowers that were lined up. I looked at the spec sheets but had no idea what questions to ask the salesman when he approached. I left the store and returned home. I asked Brian about the size of lawn mower we'd had and what I should be looking for. He gave me an answer which was totally unrelated to the size of the mower. I called a friend and asked him. The next day I went back to Home Depot and at least came home with information about the cutting radius of the mower, options and price. On day three I finally made the decision and arranged to purchase the mower. The salesman gave me a ten minute overview of the mower operation.

The following day I waited until Brian was resting and then went out to the garage where the lawn mower was parked. I got out the manual and turned to the page for start up. I followed the steps, but to no avail. I couldn't get it started. After more than an hour I broke down in tears of frustration. This was just one more thing that I had to deal with because Brian could not. I asked God to please help me get the mower functioning. I felt physically drained as I didn't need this frustration. Despite my prayer I couldn't get the mower to start, so I eventually went back in the house with the manual in my hand.

When Brian woke up I asked him to help me understand what I was doing wrong. Surprisingly, he gave me a tip that worked when I went back out to the mower. I was so happy that I got it started. I thanked Brian and God. It took a few minutes to understand how to engage the mower, but eventually I was able to cut the lawn without too many problems. I felt proud of myself for accomplishing this small feat.

My next task was to find a vehicle. When we left Canada for Panama we sold our vehicles, so I had been driving a rental car. I was eager to get our own vehicle again. I started searching car dealerships online to find a suitable vehicle which would be easy for Brian to get in and out of. As I didn't want to leave Brian alone at the acreage, every few days I helped him into the rental vehicle and went to car dealerships to test drive vehicles. I had to make a quick assessment of each test drive as it was difficult for Brian to get in and out of the vehicle. Sometimes I just left Brian in our rental car as I took the dealership car for a test drive. This was not the best option, but it was quicker and less stressful for Brian. After a couple of weeks, and several trips to dealerships, I settled on a Ford Escape. I was happy when we turned in the rental car and finally had our own vehicle again. It was one less thing that I needed to worry about.

The next day Brian was feeling weak and tired. He did not want to do anything but sleep, so I sat on the bed at his side and watched television. He was not interested in eating, just took a bite and then drifted off to sleep again. I asked several times if he was in pain, but his answer was always no. I watched him closely as he slept for signs he was having a seizure. It had been a long day and other than a few minutes taken to feed our dogs and cat, I remained in the bedroom with Brian. Eventually I too drifted off to sleep.

The next day brought a smile to my face. Brian was happy when he woke and he had a coffee with me. By the afternoon he wanted to go out on the deck where he could see the horses. He stood, and with my help he was able to maneuver himself into the wheelchair. I pushed him out onto the deck and we both looked out towards the pasture and the horses.

"Can you see Jesse and Dustin?" I asked Brian, referring to the two horses that remained at the acreage when we moved to Panama. We chatted about all the horses we had owned. We lost one to West Nile virus, one to a heart attack and one to old age. We had Wacey Cathey for more than twenty-five years, and she had been the mother of three of our horses. She lived a good life, was a loyal companion and passed away at the age of thirty-four the year before.

As we chatted on the deck about the acreage and our horses, Brian attempted to stand, slid from his seat to the deck and became wedged between the feet of the wheelchair. The supports for the foot pieces were rubbing against his back.

"Damn it," he swore.

"Let me help you," I said, as I placed my hand under his arm pit and tried to lift him back into the chair. I couldn't move him at all. He was dead weight, and without his help I knew that I wouldn't get him back up by myself.

"I think I will have to call for help," I said. My first call was to Brian's best friend and I was relieved when he picked up on the second ring.

"How are you?" I asked. "Bri is out on the deck. He slipped from his wheelchair and is stuck between the feet of the wheelchair. I can't move him at all and really need your help to get him back into the house."

"I'll be there in ten," he said without hesitation.

When Larry stepped from his truck he joked with Brian about being stuck, and we all laughed. It took the two of us to get Brian lifted and back into the wheelchair. We went in the house afterwards and had a beer and a visit.

A couple of days later when I came back from walking our dogs, the light on the answering machine was blinking. I asked Brian if the phone rang while I was gone.

"I don't think so," he said. I looked from him to the phone knowing that any message would have been recorded aloud, so he most certainly would have heard it. He was preoccupied with the television, so I walked over to the answering machine and hit the message button. When I heard her voice I immediately hit the save button. I knew that I would have to listen to the message over and over until I could finally listen all the way through, as hearing her voice made me emotional. The caller was the doctor Brian had in Canada before we left the country. Dr. U had been Brian's general practitioner for more than seven years, and over that time the relationship had turned to a friendship. The pain in her voice was audible.

If you could love your doctor, Brian did. He would dress in his jeans, cowboy boots, western shirt and always a cowboy hat for his appointments. He looked forward to seeing Dr. U and talking about the events in his life.

When we had moved to Panama it was important to Brian to bring gifts for her on his return trips to Canada. He planned to surprise her and quizzed the nursing staff to get the sizes of the doctor's two sons so that he could bring them both back shirts from Panama along with his gift for the doctor herself.

I listened as Dr. U expressed her concern and shock over hearing of Brian's diagnosis with the brain tumor. I could sense the tears that I knew she was holding back.

"Bri, Dr. U called and she wanted you to know she was thinking of you."

"That's nice," Brian said.

The day passed with us spending most of the day in the living room watching television. Brian was having a really good day, and we were able to have several lengthy conversations. He asked for mac and cheese for supper. I watched as he lifted his right hand and dipped the spoon into the bowl and ate as if there was nothing wrong. Most days I had to help him eat. I stared at him tonight as he seemed to have better coordination than on many days. I called his mother and gave her the good news.

"Brian is feeding himself mac and cheese," I said when she answered the phone.

"Excellent," she replied.

After I chatted I held the phone so that Brian could talk.

I went to bed feeling positive and cuddled up next to Brian. Toes jumped on the bed and wedged between us.

A package arrived from my colleague in Panama. Inside was a prayer book from one of the Missionary Sisters of Charity that Brian and I had met at Hogar San Jose. I was in complete awe. I thought about what a tremendous sacrifice it was for her to send her personal prayer book here to Canada so that it would provide God's comforting hand over Brian. The prayer book was composed entirely from Mother Teresa's own words.

I read from the daily devotional to Brian. He would close his eyes and listen. When I finished he would always say, 'That was nice'. I reminded him each night where the prayer book came from. I hoped that the prayers would help, that we would get a message to God, that Brian would get well, that life would return to normal.

Brian's sister Katie, and her husband Reggie, brought Brian and Karen's mother to visit. It was a beautiful sunny day and we enjoyed sitting on the deck. The horses were drawn to our voices and whinnied from the corral. I walked over with Katie and fed them horse treats. They nuzzled our out-stretched hands and we rubbed their noses. By afternoon it was too warm, so we moved our chairs to the shade under the large pine trees and enjoyed cold drinks. Over the afternoon we took several group photos. My plan was that the photos would be our gift to mom on her 90th birthday which was in less than a week.

TWENTY EIGHT

"I'm going to start packing so we can leave tomorrow morning early to go to Calgary for your mom's birthday party," I said to Brian. I knew she would be happy once we arrived. I was thinking of my mother in law, who had spent months thinking about and planning her 90th birthday celebration, and now the day had almost come. There had been much emotion leading up to the party. For many relatives and family friends, this would have been the first time they had seen Brian in almost three years. We discussed Brian's diagnosis and decided not to tell anyone about the tumor until after the party to ensure the celebration stayed focussed on Brian's mother. Everyone was aware that Brian had experienced a stroke, so the fact he was in a wheelchair was explainable.

I drove the three hours from our acreage to Calgary the day before the party so that Brian would have overnight to rest at a hotel. The day of the party I encouraged him to have a sleep after lunch so that he would have full energy when we arrived at the party. He woke up and was feeling great. His smile and unwavering attitude was what had always attracted people to him like a magnet. We dressed and waited for our friends who were also staying at the hotel.

We pulled up in the vehicles and I opened the door for Brian. With the help of our friends we got him into the wheelchair. We wheeled him up the ramp and before we reached the doorway his best friend Larry said, "You ready to do this?"

"You bet, Buddy," Brian replied. What we were talking about was having Brian walk into the party. It was important for both Brian and I to show his mother that he could still walk. He wanted to be viewed as the strong man, her only son, her cowboy as he entered. Brian smiled at me as I placed my hand under his left shoulder. With Larry on the other side Brian stood and we walked through the doors. There was instant excitement as people announced his arrival. His mother's eyes were brimming with admiration as she walked over and wrapped her arms around him. I knew that inside she had been worried that Brian may not be well enough to attend her party, and that would have broken her heart. He was her first child and still her baby boy.

The party was a great venue for allowing so many friends and relatives to visit with Brian. Eventually the hum of all the festivities settled down and everyone was absorbed in a conversation. Brian and his mother sat side by side on a small flowered couch. As they talked she placed her hand on his cheek and looked into his eyes. Brian raised his hand to cover hers. It was a conversation between just the two of them as if there was no one else in the room. As I looked at them I thought about how many times when he was a boy that his mother would have placed her hand on his cheek as she spoke. He was her first child and her only son. They had always had a special bond. Brian had always been close to his mother, and she had always been supportive when his father was not.

When he was young, Brian had taken music lessons and learned to play the accordion, because it made his mom happy. He said she loved to listen to him play. I remember him telling me about practicing for a music festival and how his mom was always encouraging him. When he was a teenager and came home late at night he would always wake his mom and would sit on the side of her bed and they talked no matter what the hour. When Brian enlisted in the Canadian Navy at the age of seventeen, it was his mother that he missed most. We have a picture of Brian hanging in our kitchen that was a gift from his mom. He was maybe three or four years old. He was dressed in his western clothes with play six shooter guns hanging from his belt. His mother called him her little cowboy. As a child Brian had been mischievious, but no matter what he did, his mother melted under his smile.

I knew there were countless times when he was small that she had protected him, but now there was nothing she could do to protect him from the demon that was consuming him.

As I looked at them lost in their own world, I reflected on how just the previous year Brian's mother had come to visit us in Panama and we celebrated Brian's birthday. She was 89 at the time. Brian had flown to Canada to travel with her, and he was so excited that she had agreed to visit. We had planned as many activities as we could to show her all the tourist sites. Brian and I were both proud of what we had accomplished in our lives that had resulted in our living in Panama. It was the chance of a lifetime to experience another country and we could not stop talking about how great it was. On Mom's last night in Panama we sat in the wine bar at Trump Tower and looked out over the pool at the sun setting. We talked about the preceding several days and agreed we could not have squeezed in anything more. Little did we know that less than twelve months later Brian would be in a fight for his life.

Our nephew Ken and his wife, Shelley, were at the party. Brian beamed when he saw them. We took some amazing photos of them together. Ken held a special place in Brian's heart. When Ken was young he had travelled alone from Calgary to spend a week with us at our ranch in Saskatchewan. Brian had taught Ken how to fix barbed wire fences and how to look for problems as they would walk through the cattle herd. Most importantly Ken got the chance to hang out with his Uncle Brian. It had been a typically hot

110

Saskatchewan summer, so to cool off Brian would take Ken for a swim in the South Saskatchewan River. Brian had taught Ken how to swim safely, how to react to the current and how to respect the river. It had been a week full of adventures and new experiences that we all enjoyed.

As the party came to a close we returned to our hotel room. I had invited close family and friends to join us. We had just a standard hotel room, but we were able to cram ten people besides ourselves, plus a dog, into the room. Everyone scrambled for a place to perch on the two beds. Brian sat in his wheelchair between the beds. Brian enjoyed all the activity and had not gotten tired, so everyone stayed later than expected. It was good for all of us to joke around over a few beers. As we visited I snapped photos. The next day our nephew Matthew came to visit us at the hotel. Matthew had flown home from University to see Brian. I took what would be the last photo of the two of them.

The next morning we went for coffee at Brian's mom's. It was a beautiful morning so the two of them sat on the garden swing. We talked about the party and all the people who had attended. Brian's cousin, Ricky, also came by for coffee. We laughed and I took photos. Mom had on a dress she bought in Panama and Brian joked about the day we bought it.

Eventually it was time to leave and start the three-hour trip back home. The first hour Brian was occupied with conversation about the party and everyone he had talked with. After that he started to get restless and undid his seatbelt.

"I want to get out," he said.

"You can't get out! I've driving at one-hundred-twenty kilometres an hour. You can't open the door," I shouted.

"Okay."

That lasted only a few minutes, and he once again unhooked the seatbelt. I was sweating with anxiety. I couldn't just stop on the highway as it was very busy. It was the main corridor between Calgary and Edmonton, the two largest cities in the province.

"Bri, you have to do your seatbelt up," I said with emotion and tension evident in my tone. He made no movement to do up the belt and it kept beeping, which meant I had to find a place to stop. I searched the signs on the highway for somewhere to exit. When I finally was able to stop, I turned to Brian. "You can get out now if you want." He looked at me bewildered. "We're stopped now. Do you want to get out for a minute?" I continued, as I undid my seatbelt. Looking confused all he said was *no.*

I started the vehicle and turned back onto the highway. This scenario played out four more times on the drive home and was frying my nerves. I was worried that he would just open the door and fall out. It was a terrifying trip home. By the time we arrived safely at our farm my stomach was in knots and my nerves jangled.

"Bri, you scared me," I said as I helped him from the car.

"How come?" he asked.

"Because you kept undoing your seatbelt and I was worried you were going to open the door."

"I wouldn't do that," he said.

I realized it was a pointless conversation, so I dropped it. I got him settled in the house with the television on and went to walk Danny and Hayley who were happy to have us back home.

TWENTY NINE

*I*t was July 25th, and we had been home for three days after our trip to Calgary. I woke as the bed was shaking. I reached over and grappled to find the light on the night stand. When I turned the light on I realized Brian was shuddering so bad it was more like convulsions. God, please don't let this be happening I thought. I knew the shaking was most probably a result of seizures. I got up and walked around to Brian's side of the bed. He was covered in perspiration. I sat with him and held his hand all the while measuring the time between each convulsion. He would shake and then things would be calm for fifteen to twenty minutes and I'd think it was over, but each time the convulsion was followed by another and another.

"Bri, I think I should call an ambulance," I said trying to remain calm.

"They aren't going to do anything," he replied. "I think the seizures are getting shorter and probably almost done. I'll be fine in a few minutes," he continued.

The seizures were shortening in length but coming more frequently, so there was now only about five minutes between each convulsion. I knew that Brian did not want to go to the hospital, so I sat beside him and talked to distract both of us, all the while watching the minutes on my watch. We had been through this twice before while in Panama. As time passed I became increasingly worried that maybe this time it was something more.

"Bri, I think I will call the Health Link nurse and get their idea of what we should do. Then we will know if we have to go to the hospital or not," I said as I dialed the phone. Health Link was a free service of the government health care system and you could ask questions of a Registered Nurse. When I explained the situation and the time that had elapsed, the nurse advised me to call an ambulance. I knew Brian was scared. God, we were both scared, but I knew it was time to call 911. Within twenty minutes the ambulance had arrived. Unlike earlier, Brian was now unresponsive to questions. He just stared at them as they spoke. I rubbed my arms as the room all of a sudden felt cold. The attendants decided to transport him to the hospital. I sat up front in the ambulance and Brian was in the back on a stretcher. He only spoke once and that was to ask where I was.

"She's sitting up front," said the medical technician who was monitoring Brian in the ambulance.

I looked over at the ambulance driver and smiled. I turned as much as I could with the seatbelt fastened and talked to Brain. I thought maybe hearing my voice would help to keep him grounded.

The trip seemed to take forever, and by the time we arrived at the hospital Brian was asleep. He did not wake up when he was wheeled into the emergency department. I met with the attending doctor and updated her on Brian's current status plus what had transpired as far as his treatments in Panama. She was able to see Brian's CT and MRI scans that had been uploaded to the Alberta Health Services site by the neurosurgeon we met with after arriving back in Canada. The medical team in Panama had provided us with all the tests, diagnosis and treatment on CD's that were easily transferable to the computer and allowed us to carry on with the chemo regimen. The doctor looked at all the information that now popped up on the computer screen. She looked over at me and then at Brian who continued to sleep.

"He is very sick," she said.

"Yes I know."

"When was the last time he had chemo?"

I took a few minutes to think back and wished I would have brought my notebook where I had recorded the scheduled dates for chemo.

"It was the first week in July, I think."

We continue to talk and I told her the amount of Brian's other medications. I knew them all in my head. I had to, as Brian could not be in charge of his own medication. I had to keep all pills out of his reach. I had even hidden all Tylenol and Advil in the house for fear he would eat some without my knowledge.

The doctor left the room and I walked to Brian's bedside. He looked so peaceful, like there was nothing wrong. I leaned down and kissed his forehead, trying to stem the tears that were building. The doctor returned and we continued to talk as Brian was admitted to the hospital. The seizure medicine was tripled from the level Brian was currently taking. I knew from past discussions with the medical team in Panama that high dosage and long term use of the drug was dangerous. It was constantly being monitored. I also knew that given the seizures there was no alternative.

The doctor told me that they would sedate Brian for the next twelve to twenty-four hours to give his body a rest after the stress of the seizures. They would also schedule a CT scan.

Brian slept for the remainder of the day after being admitted. I sat by his bed. I thought back to just four days earlier when he sat on the garden swing on his mother's patio and chatted. Now he was silent. I would never have guessed that I would be sitting here now looking at him. I prayed to God to help Brian. Then I prayed that God would help me.

The following day Brian slept on and off. He never spoke or acknowledged the nursing staff when they came into the room. He just stared at them as they bustled around. He would smile at me when I spoke, but he did not reply. I sat by his side and counted the hours.

The doctor came in while I was there. She advised that the CT scan showed considerable bleeding. She gave me no comfort with her words.

"I must be honest. I am not optimistic about Brian's future," she said.

I looked at her and then back at Brian. I could not process what she was saying. I wanted to tell her he was fine. That he had just gone to his mother's party and was walking and talking. He had things to do yet. We had things to do.

"Let's see how he is in the next few days."

With that she left. I stood at the end of Brian's bed and looked at him. He was perfectly still. It was difficult to see him like this. I wondered if he would wake up again. I got increasingly concerned that maybe I had waited too long to call the ambulance.

I walked down the hallway outside Brian's room to the quiet area. People were sitting and visiting. I knew it was time to call our family.

The following day Brian's mother and sister, Katie, drove up from Calgary. On our way to the hospital I updated them and cautioned them that Brian may not be awake. I was relieved when we walked into his room and he was in a sitting position. I couldn't believe the improvement over the past two days. He smiled when he saw us. He was still confused and did not say much, but at least he was awake.

The rest of the family in Calgary was shocked by the sudden change in Brian from the previous weekend when we had all been together at the party. By the weekend Brian had improved enough that my brothers and their families drove up from Calgary to visit.

Brian was happy to see the group of them. They had brought candy, and that always put a smile on his face. There were too many to visit in the room without disturbing other patients, so everyone took turns with the rest waiting at the end of the hall. Brian tired quickly and wanted to go back to sleep, so the visits were short. It was difficult for everyone to see him in the hospital and there were lots of emotions over the weekend.

I couldn't help but reflect on the fact my grandmother had died of cancer as had my aunt. I remember being at my aunt's bedside with Brian. Also on my mind was my mother whom we had lost to cancer less than four years before. I had stood at mom's bedside with my siblings. Now we were facing the grips of cancer once more as we stood at Brian's bed side. I silently hoped against hope that we would not lose him as well.

Brian underwent more CT scans and MRI's. He had good days and bad. Some days he would be able to carry on a conversation and the following day he would struggle to find words. On days when he was alert I was optimistic that the worst was behind us, and then a day later he would be withdrawn and unresponsive. It was like a roller coaster ride where your stomach tosses and turns in the curves and then in the straight stretches you feel fine. Whenever the medication was reduced he would experience a seizure, but it was a balancing act as there were consequences to extended use of the medication. I had learned all this while in Panama as I needed to closely monitor his daily condition and watch for any signs that would result in an increase in the daily dosage.

Brian was blissfully unaware of all this. He had been in the hospital for ten days and yet he had no idea how much time had passed. The loss of his short-term memory had been a blessing for him. It kept him from stressing over his condition which would have increased the seizure activity.

Brian's mother stayed at our home and went with me daily to the hospital. Other visitors came and went each day with the majority coming on the weekends.

It was Saturday and family was coming from Calgary. When we arrived at the hospital Brian was sitting in a wheelchair. We were able to push him outside to the healing garden for fresh air. Brian chatted and ate candies as if nothing was wrong. It brought everyone comfort to see him in such good spirits. I, of course, was internalizing everything as I tend to do, and my stomach was in knots most days.

The following day he was quiet and slept without much interaction with us. His mother and I stayed until after he had eaten supper. As he closed his eyes once more, we said goodbye. We were both silent as I drove the forty-five minutes back to our acreage. The dogs were glad when we arrived and I took them for a short walk in the field before I fed them. It was a nice evening and my thoughts drifted to visions of Brian lying in the hospital bed. When I got back to the house I opened a beer, which I needed before I prepared for Cindy, Lauren, Trent and their friends who were coming for a visit.

It was an enjoyable evening as we sat on the deck and enjoyed a beer. I was distracted for a few hours. They planned to build a ramp on the deck so that it would be easier for Brian to move off the deck in his wheelchair. The boys searched through the wood shed and came up with scrap wood to build the ramp. Then they took turns riding down the ramp in Brian's wheelchair to determine the angle required before they permanently affixed the ramp to the deck. We had some great laughs as they spun around in the wheelchair. By the end of the evening the ramp was done. I was proud of these young men who could be doing many things on this evening, but they choose to come to our acreage and do something for Brian.

When we arrived at the hospital the next day, I was excited to tell Brian about the ramp.

"Remember I said that Cindy and Lauren were coming to visit at the farm last night."

"I think so. How are they?" he asked.

"Trent, Carl and some friends built a ramp onto the deck so that you will be able to get into the yard in your wheelchair. It was a wonderful night. We had beers and lots of laughs. The boys were trying out your wheelchair."

"That's nice."

While we were talking an attendant showed up to take Brian for more tests.

"I will be back later Bri. I'm going home to cut the lawn."

He smiled at me but said nothing as they spun the stretcher and wheeled him away. I wondered what was going on in his head.

When I got home I changed my clothes, but before I went outside I noticed that the answering machine was beeping. I hit the blinking button. Two messages.

"We're just calling to advise that your sea shipment has arrived and will be ready for delivery later this week once the customs papers are finalized. Please call....."

Damn, I thought. How the hell was I going to deal with that now? With everything that had happened I had totally forgotten about the furniture and personal items we had shipped home from Panama. I sat down. I bent my head into my hands, and rested my elbows on the table. I rubbed my forehead. Tears flooded in. I was too tired to even get a tissue to wipe away my tears. Instead I let the tears drip off my chin and make tiny little puddles on the table. What the hell was I going to do?

My thoughts were interrupted when the phone rang. I stood up and looked at the call display first. Recognizing the number from Saskatchewan, I reached out and picked up the handset.

"Hi. How are you? I wasn't sure we would catch you at home. I thought I would just leave you a message," Belinda said.

"I'm okay," I lied. "Actually I came home to cut the lawn. I left his mom there so that they could have some personal time and then I will go back and get there around supper."

"How is Brian?"

"He is up and down."

"That's why I'm calling. We are going to drive up tomorrow and stay overnight with our friends and then we thought we would go and see Brian on Thursday. We weren't sure if he would be sleeping if we went tomorrow night when we arrive."

"Either way is fine. I am there every day with his mom and we stay most of the day. I might take a day off when you are here as I got home today and I have a message about all the stuff we shipped from Panama. I need to call and organize a day for that to be delivered."

I proceeded to explain to Belinda all that was shipped and I was sure that I must have sounded overwhelmed, which of course I was.

"Maybe I can help you while we are there. Scott and I can help you with whatever. We just have to be home by next Wednesday," she said.

"Thanks, that's great," I said before we hung up. At least that would be some help, I thought.

When I got back to the hospital Brian was chatting with his mom and eating supper.

"Looks good," I said looking at the tray of hospital food. Everyone knows that hospital food is never good, but what else could I say.

"Belinda and Scott will be here Thursday. Won't that be great," I said knowing that Brian would be happy to see our lifelong friends.

"Are they here now?" he asked.

"I think they are driving tomorrow and will come and see you the next day. It will take them all day to get here," I said referring to the eight-hundred kilometre trip from their home in Saskatchewan.

"Where are they living now?" he asked.

"They are still in White City, outside Regina."

Brian did not say anything, and I think he was trying to relate White City to where we had all last lived in Calgary. On some days I could tell that Brian's reduced memory made it difficult for him to interpret and understand everything, but on other days he would surprise me and be able to quickly relate to information.

Over the course of the next few days I was able to organize the delivery of our furniture shipment to coincide with Belinda and Scott's visit. Delivery day had arrived. In the morning Scott drove to the hospital and took Brian's mother. Belinda and I sat in the kitchen waiting as we poured our second cup of coffee. Another friend had offered to help and I saw her vehicle pull into the drive minutes after Scott left. I was grateful for all the help.

When the movers arrived they handed me the packing slips. I had almost forgotten how many items would be arriving. I flipped the pages and saw it contained one-hundred-fifty-four items. What a full day we have ahead of us, I thought.

The movers opened the truck. I looked in and wondered where all the items would fit in our home which was already furnished. Some of the items were pieces of furniture and of course some were boxes. Everything was wrapped in cardboard. In order to leave Panama, and enter Canada, all items have to be insect free, so even the chairs from the dining room suite were wrapped in cardboard. So it looked like a chair but was enclosed in a cardboard sweater.

Each item that was delivered had to be checked off from the packing slips. As each item was unloaded the men would call out the packing label number and I had to check off each item and try to direct traffic for placement. It was quite a daunting task as the men continued to call out packing numbers when I was still trying to locate the previous number called out. There was no order to the numbers so it was a bit of a hunt and peck routine.

Belinda took over and checked off the items so I could just focus on what would be unloaded into the house and what would be going into storage. My other friend worked in the kitchen unpacking boxes and finding somewhere to put everything in the cupboards.

By lunch we were ready for a break. I was glad for a few minutes to slow down. All morning I had worried how Brian was without me at the hospital, even though I knew his mother was there with Scott.

Belinda was out on the deck enjoying a much deserved cigarette. It was just my closest friend and me making sandwiches. We stood alone in the kitchen.

"We don't think you should bring Brian home. He would get more care at a rehab centre," she said.

I looked at her not believing my ears. Move him from the hospital to another facility. For what, I wondered. A rage welled in me.

"No, I am bringing him home," I exclaimed.

"How are you going to care for him?" she asked.

"Well, to be honest, I thought with the help of all of you," I said making reference to her family. "I'm not leaving him there," I barked. I was so mad that I exploded on her before I walked away. I was hurt that she would even suggest that I consider not bringing Brian home. How could Brian be better served by sitting in a facility, deteriorating day by day, waiting for visitors. Never, never, never, would I allow that to happen.

Brian and I had a strong bond and we knew that we would care for each other until the end. I just never expected to be faced with this decision so soon. I always thought we would grow into our eighty's together. We used to see white-haired couples walking hand in hand or enjoying a cocktail and we would say in unison, *"that will be us. Still drinking beer into our 80's."*

At home Brian would never be alone. He would never lie in bed at night waiting for the next day's visiting hours, like he was enduring currently at the hospital. We stayed as long as we could each day, but eventually we were ushered from his room when the visiting hours were over. I did not want that to become his life for whatever time he had left.

My rage turned to frustration and hurt. I knew I would not be able to count on her for support.

The afternoon was difficult as her comments kept coming alive in my mind. By late afternoon everything was unloaded and the moving van pulled out of the drive. We sat down for a beer and to relax. There was still tension between us, but I tried to push it from my mind.

The next morning, I looked at all the boxes that still needed to be unpacked. I rubbed my head. It was overwhelming. I guessed there were probably one hundred items to deal with which were either in the garage or throughout the main floor of the house. I walked around and looked at the boxes wondering how I would tackle it. Since everything was packed by the movers I would need to open all the boxes just to determine what was inside and whether it would stay or go back into storage. Boxes had no words to identify contents. Large furniture pieces were marked in Spanish as to what was hidden under the cardboard. The glass coffee table, for instance, had been broken down into six pieces. When I looked at it I wondered if I would be able to put it back together. Would the screws be inside one of the packages?

"There's a lot of stuff here," Brian's mother said as she walked into the sun room where I stood befuddled.

"Yeah, there is. But we got a lot accomplished yesterday. At least we got the kitchen unpacked. I will go through the rest of this as I find time," I turned and smiled at my mother-in-law.

"Are you sure you want to stay home?" I asked referring to her decision not to go to the hospital this morning. I knew she was getting tired of the daily trips.

"I will go back with you later," she said.

I hugged her and walked out the door.

THIRTY

I was standing outside Brian's room waiting for the doctor to arrive. I had to meet him there as Brian was in a ward with four beds and there was only the canvas curtain to give any sense of privacy. I leaned against the wall and stared up and down the hall watching the constant movement of people. The walls were painted a blah color which matched my mood. I wondered why hospital walls weren't painted cheerful colours. Children's wards are painted to make patients feel more at home with bright pictures and graphics. Where I stood there was nothing in the décor that would make you feel uplifted. It actually was making me feel worse. I saw the doctor approaching me and I tried to smile. There was no expression on his face.

"Let's go down the hall and sit," he said, pointing to a lounge area. I was anxious and felt weak as I walked down the hall. I sat in a chair in the corner and the doctor took a seat across from me. He talked for a few minutes about Brian's condition when he had been admitted to the hospital, the tests that had been performed and Brian's current condition. Of course I already knew all this and wondered what he was leading up to. And then it came.

"There really isn't anything else we can do for your husband in the hospital," he said pausing momentarily. "There are options to consider." I knew the option the doctor was going to suggest was to move Brian to a long-term care facility and there was no way I would agree with that.

"I want to take him home," I interjected.

"Are you sure about that? It is a lot of work to care for him."

"Yes, I'm sure," I said, knowing that I could never agree to anything less.

"We can see what help you can get through Home Care," he added.

"Is there anything medically that he will require that I could not give him at home?" I asked.

"No."

He paused and just looked at me. We sat in silence for a couple of minutes, then he continued. "I will arrange for someone from the palliative unit to meet with you later today." With that he stood to leave. I did not attempt to stand as I was unsure if my legs would hold me up or betray me and let me collapse into a puddle on the floor.

I looked into his eyes. I uttered a weak thank you before I started to cry.

"Good luck to you both," he said. Then he turned and walked away.

I turned my attention to the tile floor. I continued to look at the floor as I did not want to make eye contact with the people who were walking down the corridor towards me. The sound of their shoes on the tile floor grew louder, so I knew they were almost to where I sat. I did not want them to see my pain and ask if I was okay. Once they passed I leaned back in the chair and pushed at my hair that had fallen in my eyes. I reached for the tissue I had put in my jean pocket before I left Brian's room. I wiped tenderly at my eyes. My eyelids were sore from days of sorrow.

That was it then. Nothing else they could do in the hospital, so we would go back home and try to continue with the chemo regimen. I wondered if I would have the strength to get through it. I shook off the negative thoughts that were starting to overtake me. I straightened myself and breathed out. It was time to get back.

I walked back into Brian's hospital room where his mother stood at his side telling him stories of when he was a boy. Brian had a smile from ear to ear and was laughing. She was talking about one particular time when he and his cousin Ricky had gotten into trouble. There were so many stories about the two of them when they were little. Ricky and Brian were like brothers and inseparable when they were growing up. They spent many weekends and family vacations together. I thought now of Ricky and the pain that was expressed in his silence when I had told him the truth about Brian's condition.

"Well, that story has you laughing," I said as I stopped at the bottom of his bed.

His mother continued. "We were just talking about Brian and Ricky. They were such a handful as youngsters. You couldn't take your eye off them for a minute or turn your back as surely they would get into something!"

"Two peas in a pod," I added. "I always laugh about the time they painted the basement floor."

"Not sure whose idea that was. We were sitting upstairs having a coffee and Brian and Ricky were in the basement. As we were visiting, it was probably quite a few minutes before we noticed that they weren't making a lot of noise, which was unusual. I went downstairs to see what they were doing. I had hoped to find them reading. Instead I saw them each with a paint brush in hand, and they had opened all the cans of paint in the basement and were painting the floor. It was every color you could think of and the paint was on the floor and on them," she continued.

Once they were caught all Brian had said was, *'doesn't it look nice.'*

His mother chuckled, remembering the incident. "I really had to keep a straight face. I wanted to burst out in laughter, but I knew his father would not find the paint job very funny. Remember, back in those days, paint was oil based. It didn't just wash off like it does now."

We carried on talking about Brian growing up. It gave us all something to focus on and was so important for Brian and his mom.

When there was a break in the conversation I changed the subject.

"I think it is time we blow this pop stand Bri," I said, taking both him and his mother by surprise. "They aren't really doing much for you in here, so we might as well be at home. What do you think?"

"I'm ready when you are," he answered. "I've been waiting to go home for days."

"Are they going to release him?" his mother asked with concern.

"I think so. The doctor is just checking into it. I need to have a meeting today with them, so it probably won't be until tomorrow. We need to arrange for the hospital bed and stuff first," I added.

The hospital had a wonderful healing garden outside with beautifully arranged flower beds boasting an array of colours. The flowers were complemented by bubbling ponds. It was a welcome break from sitting in the hospital room. We had taken Brian out there when the visitors were too many to fit in his room. The Palliative Coordinator suggested we meet out there where we could speak openly. She started by talking about being a caregiver and the emotional stress of caring for a loved one. She went on to explain options such as a long-term care facility and hospice. I sat there wishing I could be anywhere but here. Brian didn't deserve this. Here we were discussing where he would spend his remaining time. Here or there; blah, blah blah.

"Have you thought about what you would like to do?" she asked.

I looked at her but said nothing. I just stared at her and wondered how many times she had repeated this same conversation with families. Did they all feel like I did? Did they all wish they could be somewhere else, anywhere else?

"Have you thought about what you would like to do?" she repeated.

"Yes. I am taking him home." My lips quivered and I burst into tears. She placed her hand on my shoulder.

"I need him and he needs me. It has been difficult to see him here in the hospital and I just can't imagine going to visit him in a facility for months. I can't leave him. All we have is each other. We don't have any children. It has always been just the two of us," I continued.

I was shaking and stood up so that I could regain control of my emotions. I felt light-headed and wanted to curl up in a fetal position. I wondered if I could just lie down amongst the flowers in the garden and hide. My heart was pounding and I felt weak. I bit my lip trying to stop the tears. I turned around and looked at her. She motioned for me to sit down.

"Are you all right?" she asked.

"No, but I don't think there is anything you can do to help me." I never knew what it would entail to care for Brian every day, but I knew I had to face it as best I could. I owed it to him, and I knew he would do the same for me if the tables were turned.

The Palliative Coordinator continued talking. I looked away at the flowers and the calm ripple of the water. I thought of my father. He had always been terrified of going to the hospital as he thought it would be the end for him. He was convinced that the doctors would never send him home again. My dad was terrified of being separated from our mother. She was his anchor. She had always been there for him and for us six kids. Mom was what grounded us. No matter what we faced we could always go to our mother. I wanted to call my mom, but that was no longer possible. My mother had lost her battle with cancer less than ninety days after diagnosis. My father died fourteen months after Mom.

God, had I not been through enough, I thought. I had lost both my parents in the past four years and now was having to go through it all again with Brian's illness. I felt numb.

"I will need you to sign these forms," she said breaking my concentration.

I turned my attention back to her, and listened as she explained about the palliative drug program. The word palliative said it all. I signed the forms where she pointed to.

"I'm available if you have any questions. The nurses can page me as I am usually here somewhere in the hospital," she said as she stood and extended her hand.

"Thanks," I said and took the envelope of information from her. I watched her walk back into the hospital. I emptied the contents of the envelope on the bench. In addition to the documents she had talked about there was a book. I stared at it. It was titled: *A Caregiver's Guide to End of Life Care.* End of Life. There it was in print.

I stood and followed the path that led around the gardens. I looked at the bed of red geraniums in various stages of bloom. To the left were pansies in such vivid colours they looked artificial. One plant had a dark purple core with the edges of the petals pale pink. Behind, in the next row, were yellow plants. I could not think of the name of the flower. I knew I had planted some in my garden last year, but the name escaped me. They were bright yellow and stood tall reaching their little heads up to the sun. I don't know why, but I bent down and picked a few weeds from the edge of the flower bed and discarded them in the garbage receptacle. I walked past four people who were seated on one of the benches. I smiled and they smiled back, but we did not exchange words. I imagined they too were facing tough decisions. Once I had walked around the garden I stopped at the sliding glass doors that led back into the hospital.

I took a deep breath and walked through. I walked slowly down the hallway until I reached Brian's room, wondering what the days ahead would bring.

"Where were you?" Brian asked when I stepped around the curtain.

"I just had a meeting with the hospital so that you can go home. We need to organize the hospital bed and stuff," I said.

"Is he going home today?" his mother asked.

"No, it will be in the morning."

I kissed Brian good night and told him we would be back in the morning. Brian had been in the hospital for fifteen days and his mother and I had spent every day and many nights there at his side. It was going to be nice to have him at home.

In true bureaucratic fashion, the hospital bed that was to be delivered that day in order that Brian could come home, was nowhere to be seen. I finally tracked it down and delivery was scheduled within the next two to five days.

The next day, through a series of mix ups, the ambulance to transfer Brian back home was cancelled, so he never got home until 7:15 pm. Of course because the release forms were signed just after breakfast the hospital had cancelled his lunch and supper. Luckily we were there at lunch and had gotten him something to eat. He was confused when he arrived home, but he had a big smile on his face when he saw all the pets.

The following morning Brian's mother returned to her home, three hours away. She was satisfied Brian would be okay now that he was at home. I knew she was missing her cats and the familiarity of her own home. It was time to get back to a routine.

Brian was weak and tired, and I knew it was because he had been in the hospital bed for so long. His muscles had not had to work. He did not want to get out of bed. I looked at the calendar. It was August 9th. Less than three weeks prior he was at his mother's birthday party, chatting with everyone and so full of life. All that enthusiasm seemed to have seeped away. Because we didn't have the hospital bed yet, Brian had to sleep in our bed. Without bed rails I worried about him rolling out of bed or getting up in the night, so I barely slept for those first few nights. Once again, like in Panama, I tied his wrist to mine with the scarf so I could feel his movements.

The next few days were a blur as I had telephone calls and meetings with Home Care as well as a private home care provider. There were lots of questions and discussions on what services would be covered through the Provincial Health Care Palliative Services program. I tried to listen intently. While there would be help scheduled each day it was clear that I would be responsible for a substantial amount of his care, alone.

I was a career Banker. We had never had children, so I had missed all the mothering instinct that comes from that role. I wondered how well I would be able to fill the role of caregiver and nurse. I loved Brian with all my heart and would do anything for him, so I needed to adapt to my changing role.

Brian had been home for four days and this was the first day that a Home Care Aide had shown up. I greeted her at the door. I expected that she would stay for the one hour scheduled and was surprised when fifteen minutes later she told me she was leaving as she had a busy day. Not knowing any better, I allowed her to leave. This was the pattern for the balance of the week where an Aide arrived twice a day and stayed less than thirty minutes. The weekend support was even worse, with only one visit on Saturday and no one showing up at all on Sunday. On Monday morning an Aide came, late, and was in my view, uncompassionate. She rolled Brian on his side so quickly that he had a seizure and she did not even notice. I was mortified and tried to explain his condition to her. She chattered on about how overworked she was, and she only had so much time for each visit, plus she needed to travel from home to home which required her to hurry with each patient and how it wasn't her fault, and on and on. I couldn't care less. All I cared about was her care with Brian. I called the company and asked that she never be sent to our house again. Their response was that as this woman was scheduled for the next couple of days the company may not be able to reschedule someone else, so I may not get any support for a few days. They were true to their word as no one showed up for the following four days.

Brian had only been out of his bed twice in the fifteen days he was in the hospital. He no longer had the strength to get himself to a sitting position and into the wheelchair. He had no idea how long he had been in bed, so he had no desire to get up and moving. To care for someone who was bed-ridden was exhausting. I had only been responsible for Brian's care for several days, yet I was already feeling the strain. I wondered how families with chronically ill children managed to care for them at home year after year.

I looked at the saline bag and watched the drip down into the line leading to Brian's arm. I wondered whether I was changing the saline IV bags correctly. The nurse had explained it all in a few minutes. To her it was second nature, but to me it was something totally foreign. I looked at the bags constantly and wondered whether the last bag dripped quicker or was it just my imagination. I started to write down the time I changed the bag so that I could calculate time frames.

I had a meeting today with the Home Care Nurse. She was a wonderfully caring person and someone I knew I could talk with.

"How did you manage last week?" she asked.

"It was hard. I don't think the same person (referring to the Home Care Aides) came more than a couple of times. It seemed like every day there was someone new and I needed to explain Brian's condition to them. I thought they would know about him and why they were here. I was three days without anyone showing up. I did it all myself." With that I broke down. I just couldn't hold it in any longer.

"I am so sorry. Anyone sent to the house should know fully about Brian. The Company is provided with each patient's medical situation so that they can ensure the employee that is scheduled has the skills to manage the tasks required. I will call and find out what happened last week and make sure that they are here when they are authorized to be. I don't know why someone would not have come on Sunday. And then this week you had problems again. That is just unacceptable." With that she picked up her cell phone and called back to her office.

I was pleased to see that she was taking me seriously and was going to resolve it. I gathered control over my emotions and while she talked on the phone I poured us both a coffee. We sat down and over the coffee we talked. She listened to me. I told her how healthy Brian had been and how much we loved Panama. Before I could carry on I started to cry again. She reached out and placed her hand on my shoulder.

"It's okay to cry."

I rubbed at my eyes with the tissue. I couldn't remember if I had put eye shadow on this morning, but if I did it was going to be a mess now. I sighed and went on to tell her about Brian's diagnosis, the treatments in Panama, our return to Canada, attending his mom's 90th birthday party and the most recent hospital stay. I shared with her how lonely I felt as we didn't have any family close that I could rely on. During our conversation Brian slept.

"I am here for you as well as Brian. I am going to see if I can get the same Home Care Aide to come throughout the week and that should help. On weekends it is more difficult to get the same staff."

"Thanks. Even if the same person came a few times it would help. I felt like I needed to train each person that arrived," I said.

"Also make sure that they stay for the allotted time. They are being paid for a one-hour visit, so they should be staying for that time frame. They can help you give Brian a meal or whatever else you need help with," she added. "I'll call you at least once a week and I will also come for a visit once a week but you can call me at any time that you want to talk."

By then Brian was awake so she spoke with him for a few minutes and then left.

I felt better after her visit. At least I knew that I could insist on the Aide's staying for the allotted time and that would give me a chance to at least run to the basement with the never ending laundry basket, or take a quick walk or weed my flowers. My flower beds were overgrown, and while that should be unimportant, it was something I enjoyed doing and it gave me something else to focus on. If an Aide was in the house with Brian, I would not have to keep running in the house to check on him.

Talking with the nurse had given me a new strength.

THIRTY ONE

rian's cousin Ricky had been anxious to talk with him since he went into the hospital. I had emailed Ricky to organize a call between them. The phone rang and after I said hello, I held the phone to Brian's ear and listened as Ricky started to talk. To say they were cousins does not truly reflect their relationship. They were more like brothers at heart. They talked briefly and Brian laughed. I knew that Ricky was kidding him about being sick to get attention. It had only been six weeks since they had been together at the birthday party, but much had happened in that time.

After the meeting with the Home Care Nurse the support improved. They arranged for the same Aide to come to the house from Monday to Friday. They would not make any guarantees for the weekend support, but at least I would receive some consistent care for Brian during the week.

Heather, the Home Care Aide, became the stabilizing factor each week. She was scheduled as the Aide from Monday through Friday. Heather had a friendly disposition, a wonderful smile and a caring manner. From the first time we met I thought how well suited Heather was to the position. Brian would smile when he heard her voice as she walked in the front door. Heather would talk with him and joke as she went about her duties.

Heather became a friend and someone I could talk to, someone I could cry with. We had many long conversations and Heather gave me a hug on the days when the strain was breaking me down. On Friday afternoons Heather was scheduled for a three-hour period which was my approved respite time. Of the approved three hours, I had to deduct forty minutes which was the travel time back and forth from our acreage to the city. That left me with two hours and twenty minutes to get everything accomplished. With the list I had prepared I would strategically drive from store to store. I needed to purchase groceries, then go to the pet food store, stop for medical supplies and lastly stop at the pharmacy. In addition to refilling prescriptions which continually changed, I needed to pick up saline solution weekly. I constantly had to look at my watch to ensure I stayed within the allotted time frame. On the days that Heather didn't have another client after Brian she would let me know, which gave me some flexibility if I ran late.

I felt pressured every week as I ran from store to store and worried I would forget something. I was constantly making lists and always watching the clock. To resolve this I hired a companion for Brian four hours per week through a private home care company. That allowed me sufficient time to travel to the city and catch up on errands and it gave me time to breathe without having something to do. The girl they sent to our home was a university student and we scheduled her weekly visit around her class schedule. She visited with Brian and read to him or talked about her classes. They shared the candies and snack I left out. After her fourth week visit we both realized that Brian needed more care than she could provide, so it was the last time that she came to the house. Wherever she is, I'd like to thank her for how caring she was and want her to know that Brian loved those visits.

When the strain got to me I tried to break down each day's tasks into which ones were necessary to be accomplished, and that kept me from getting overwhelmed. It was natural for me to feel under pressure. Of the one hundred and sixty-eight hours in every week, I was absent from Brian's side just seven hours. I relied on lists and a notebook in which I wrote down everything that the Doctor, Home Care Nurses, and Aides told me so that I could refer to it. When I worked I never had to write down such trivial details, but I felt like my brain was on vacation. The simplest task seemed to drain me. I couldn't keep thoughts together and I was so worried about doing something wrong.

With Heather's help, we got Brian into his wheelchair and were able to push the chair on to the deck where he could enjoy the beautiful day. It was sunny and warm, and I knew it was good for him to get the fresh air.

"Can you see Jesse?" I asked, pointing to the corral where one of our horses stood.

"Not really."

"He's standing right at the fence. Probably wants a treat," I said.

"How old is he?" Brian asked.

"We have had him a long time. Remember when he was born?" I asked thinking back and trying to remember the year.

Brian changed the subject entirely and asked to go back in the house to lie down. I realized that he had no interest in the horse as he could not see that far. I could only imagine that everything outside was a blur and the glare of the sun was probably not helping. Heather and I got him back in bed, and while she sat with him I quickly cut the lawn.

When I came back in Brian was asleep and Heather had done the dishes for me.

"Thanks. You didn't need to do that," I said.

"No problem. Brian was sleeping so I quickly washed them up."

Just as Heather was saying goodbye the phone rang and I quickly picked up the handset without looking at the caller ID.

"Hey, how are you?"

I recognized Dudley's voice and was shaken. I tried to brace myself before I spoke. "We're okay," I said, but there was no strength in my voice. I felt the tears building and as Dudley started to talk I broke down and had to say goodbye through quivering lips.

The voice of male friends brought me to tears when I was not prepared. The previous week the same thing happened when Scott had called. I didn't know whether it was my subconscious that a male voice reminded me of Brian or what, but I just could not stop myself from breaking down. An hour later I emailed Dudley, apologized and suggested another time to talk.

My thoughts got diverted when Cindy called offering to help me unpack some of the boxes from the shipment from Panama. I thanked her. I had slowly been unpacking a box at a time when I could, but it was still a mess and some days I just couldn't face having to organize the items that got unpacked. With Cindy's help we unpacked two large boxes and got everything put away. All the while she was able to visit with Brian.

When Cindy left I sat down with Brian and we talked about the vacations we had taken while living in Panama. Brian had always dreamed of visiting the Galapagos Islands. Living in Panama gave us the opportunity to travel to Ecuador and visit the Darwin Research facility. I went and found the photo album of that trip. I sat at Brian's bedside and described the photos as we talked. Brian closed his eyes, but every few minutes he would respond to what I was describing. Eventually he drifted off to sleep. I placed the album on the table thinking I would show him more pictures once he woke up.

Later that night I stood and watched the sun set. The orange glow melted into shades of pink and purple. The colours danced behind a thin line of clouds. I wanted to go grab my camera but was frozen in place knowing that the colour would have faded by the time I returned, and I didn't want to miss this sight. I have hundreds of photos of sunrises and sunsets. They are soothing to me. Both my mother and Brian's grandmother loved sunrises and sunsets as well, and we often talked of the wonderful colours we had seen. I turned from the window and looked at Brian as he slept. I wondered if images of the sun rising and setting would change for me when Brian was no longer at my side.

THIRTY TWO

*B*rian and I both laughed as he brushed his teeth with the coordination of a first grader. I squeezed out the toothpaste and passed him the toothbrush. Some days he just dropped it, and other days he was able to put it into his mouth but did not remember what to do from there. On this day I had to help him brush his teeth and to wash and shave. I remembered my dad using a straight razor, and Brian had showed me many times how to give him a close shave, so this was now our ritual. I laughed as I spread the shaving foam on him and he moved his head getting shaving foam in his mouth. He just talked through it and I almost doubled over with laughter as his lips moved and the shaving foam moved as well.

Once we were through the morning routine I got him some dry cereal to munch on. It was Saturday, so I never knew if a Home Care Aide would be arriving or not. I waited to bathe him in the off chance this was a lucky day and someone would arrive.

I poured myself coffee and sat at Brian's bedside and we talked. I knew Brian could not remember all that we had done in our life together, but I thought it was important to keep talking about it. I spoke to Brian often about where we would vacation next and told him he needed to get well so that we could get away before the winter came. *"We need to blow this pop stand Bri,"* I said almost daily, as encouragement for him to want to get up and out of bed.

To pass the time I started to play a game of remembering what we were doing in a particular year. "Let's see what we were doing in 1992," I said and then I went and got the photo album. I lay the album on the corner of his bed and flipped through it until something jumped out at me. I had always been the camera buff and printed pictures immediately after events and organized them into albums. Our life together was neatly captured in more than twenty-eight albums. Looking through the albums had always given me comfort.

"Do you remember this?" I asked holding up a photo of us at Christmas when friends were visiting.

"Not really. Where were we?"

I knew Brian's eyesight did not allow him to see the photo clearly. We spent many Christmases together with our friends, and there was always lots of laughter and activity in our home. The picture took me back to that happy time and I recounted the event to Brian.

Remember on Christmas Eve how the smell of ham permeated the kitchen? We would be waiting with your mom for everyone to arrive. Mom would always want to eat when they arrived, and you would want to sit down for a beer first.

"Mom was always hungry, I know that. And Larry did always want a beer first," Brian said with laughter.

I remembered standing and looking out our kitchen window and announcing their arrival when I saw their truck turn into our drive. This was a bi-annual event when they would travel five hours through snow and ice to spend Xmas with us at the farm. We all watched as they drove up the long driveway and within minutes chaos erupted as the four of them and the dog squeezed through the front door. While Sally and Larry unloaded the truck, Cindy and Lauren came in to find Uncle Beanie. I was always the second to be hugged. Brian, a.k.a. Uncle Beanie would always be first. Misty, their Lab, had no job but to sniff, so she went past us all and greeted our three dogs. Our dogs lived outside and stayed in the old dairy barn, which was bedded with deep straw and we even had a radio playing for them. The barn provided protection, warmth and allowed them to run around and play without having to be out in a Saskatchewan winter, which can be brutal. We brought the dogs in daily for a few hours, and because it was Christmas they were enjoying a stretch by the fire. Our house, which was usually quiet with just Brian and me, had five adults, two children and four dogs plus the cats who had scattered when Misty arrived. It felt like the Tasmanian Devil was swirling around and it took a few minutes to get the pets under control. Larry and Sally unloaded everything they had brought, which made it look like they were moving permanently into our house, but was in fact just the Christmas presents, winter clothes and half their kitchen I'm sure.

A tradition was to decorate gingerbread cookies on Xmas Eve, so that was always an event in itself. They would bring the cookies with them so after supper we would make a big batch of icing and then spoon it into little dishes. We would all gather around the table and mix food colouring into the icing to make an array of interesting colors. Then the real fun began. We would each decorate our cookies. Brian of course always made strange patterns on his cookies and the icing would be a quarter-inch thick. We had gingerbread people in an assortment of clothes and colours. After a couple of hours, we each ate a couple of our creations before it was time for our goddaughters to go to bed.

"Do you remember decorating gingerbread cookies and all the icing we went through?"

"I do remember that. It was fun fighting over the colours. I think I used a lot of blue," Brian said laughing. Blue was his favourite colour, so he always used that colour the most, and we would have to make more than one dish of blue icing so that everyone else could get some blue into their decorating.

Christmas day always brought another series of events. Brian and I always had champagne Christmas morning, so he got out the glasses and organized that while I made the coffee. The kids would always be excited, and of course the dogs were back in the house and running around trying to be a part of the excitement. There were Christmas stockings stuffed to the brim, one for each including the dogs and cats.

As I talked to Brian I kept pulling out the photos taken at Christmas that year. We were sitting on the floor in front of the fire opening presents. Several showed us laughing when Brian and Larry exchanged gag gifts. There were photos of us all sitting down at Christmas dinner. We were always sad to say goodbye when it was time for our friends to return home, but we knew that in a few months we would see each other again.

Brian drifted off to sleep as I talked. I closed the photo album and returned it to the shelves with the others. I poured a cup of coffee and turned on the laptop.

I read an email from my sister Penny. She asked when her daughter Sophie could come and visit Brian. Sophie, or Chip Dip as Brian had named her, was away in British Columbia working.

I replied to Penny that I did not see any reason why Sophie needed to come quickly to visit as she would be home in a few months for Christmas. Brian was home from the hospital and we were all optimistic. In the end, Brian's little Chip Dip never got home to see him again. I regretted this.

I read another email written in Spanish. It was from Anna, Brian's nurse in Panama. She had found out that Brian had been in the hospital. Her email, translated read:

I wish I had wings to be there in this moment. I miss him.

My thoughts got interrupted when I saw someone approach the front door. When I opened the door I greeted another new Aide. It was the first man that we'd had assigned to us. He was friendly and gentle with Brian. When he left, I silently hoped that we would see him again. I also thought it was time to put curtains on the window. We had never had curtains on the kitchen and dining room windows as the view was out to our corral and pastures. Brian and I had always enjoyed the unobstructed view, but now with health care people coming at all hours I thought it best to have curtains to protect our privacy. I added a note to the week's shopping list to look for something appropriate.

The next morning, I called our friends Belinda and Scott in Saskatchewan so that Brian could talk with them. I held the phone to his ear. He talked and laughed. When Brian was done, I updated them on what had transpired that week. Next I called Brian's mom and went through the same routine. Lastly I called my brother Wayne. After he had spoken to Brian, I made a plan for his family to visit the following weekend, along with my brother Rod and his family. They would also bring Brian's mother. I knew that it would be a welcome relief to have the company. Everyone would be happy to see Brian at home and not in his hospital room. I was happy that Brian could recount part of the conversations to me afterwards.

Brian had a mixed week. He felt good one day and then the next day he was quiet and uncommunicative. I never knew what to expect. I kept reminding him that we would have company on the next weekend to keep his spirits up. As we were chatting I noticed how unruly Brian's hair was. Unlike in Panama I couldn't just call a hair salon and have them send someone to the house. I added a hair cutting kit to my shopping list. I had cut my father's hair numerous times, so I knew how the clippers worked and I thought this was the best option for now. I could at least get Brian's hair more even.

On Friday while Heather sat with Brian I went shopping and picked up the hair clippers. After Heather had gone home, I trimmed Brian's hair to a short buzz. I stood back and looked at it, feeling pleased with myself. It was not the quality of a barber cut, but at least it looked better than it did that morning, I thought. I looked at my watch and I knew it was time to get Brian dressed. From his closet I selected a golf shirt which was too small for him six months previously. Now as I slid it over his head it draped off his shoulders. His biceps no longer bulged. I looked at the tattoo on his arm that he had gotten while in the navy. It was a devil. When I ran my fingers over the devil, Brian always flexed his arm, in essence making the devil larger. Now as I rubbed the tattoo there was no movement from Brian. I joked with him, "You need to start lifting weights again. The devil is shrinking."

"I think I did this morning," he replied.

"No, not today, but maybe you can tomorrow," I laughed with him as I was not sure if he was joking or really thought he had lifted weights today.

Brian was sleeping when the family arrived. His mother sat beside him, wanting to be there when he woke up. Everyone else wanted to go for a walk to stretch after the three-hour trip. We walked across the fields with our dogs, Hayley and Danny. Our conversation did not center on Brian. I knew it was because talking about him would bring us all to tears, so we talked about mundane things instead. When we returned to the house my brothers asked what they could repair. I immediately thought of the eaves trough at the front door as it had overflowed just the week before. The pipe ran along the front of the porch and then under the deck where it flowed out onto the lawn. I knew it was plugged. Through the process of elimination, our youngest nephew, Cameron, quickly got voted to crawl under the deck and unplug the downspout, partly because he was the youngest but also because he was the only one that could fit in the space under the deck.

We laid down a tarp for Cameron to lie on and passed him screwdrivers so he could detach the pipe at the last juncture point. When the pipe came apart a rush of water and leaves gushed out and almost soaked him. We all laughed and gave him suggestions and advice, and yet all Cameron wanted was for the job to be finished.

While Cameron was under the deck, his dad Rod got out the ladder and climbed up it with the hose in hand and ran more water down the downspout to ensure nothing else was stuck. It was a comedy of errors as Wayne turned on the water before Rod told Cameron, so water rushed at Cameron for the second time. The rest of us, including Cameron's two cousins burst out laughing. What else could we do?

When we finished that job we gathered around the fire pit and my brother Rod built a fire. There was lots of conversation and laughter. Brian was having a good day and was alert. Everyone took turns visiting at his bedside and having some private time with him. It was a chance for Blair, Cameron and Crystal to talk, laugh and share sour candies with their much loved Uncle.

Outside we were joking and someone decided that we should climb the white rail corral fence for a photo. There was lots of pushing attempting to knock each other off the fence. We even got Brian's mother on the fence for a photo. As always, my brother Rod's antics with Melissa brought us to tears of laughter.

Brian had a short rest but woke with the noise when we all came in the house for supper. Brian talked to our nieces and nephews about their lives. He had always been a driving force, encouraging them to strive to be the best they can be, so Crystal and Cameron talked about their classes and Blair talked about his job and all that he was learning. No matter what the topic was, Brian could add something to the conversation. Blair got out his phone and showed Brian the application that allowed him to see the constellations. Earlier he had searched how many types of mosquitos there are so Blair shared that information with Brian.

"Yeah, and when we lived in Saskatchewan every one of those mosquitoes bit me," Brian said.

I was happy that Brian spent time with the kids. He thrived on the close relationship he had with them. I knew they were proud to tell him about their plans and accomplishments.

After supper we sat around and spent the evening telling stories and sharing memories. Brian had a small glass of beer resting on the TV tray next to his bed. It had been there for hours since I placed it there. Brian took a sip when I first handed it to him and then the glass had been idle. Brian had always been the life of the party and could out-drink all of us, and he had on numerous occasions. We joked with him that he was falling behind. It was all in good fun as none of us expected him to drink the beer. In his mind he wanted a beer when he saw everyone else with one, but the thought passed quickly and he no longer had an appetite for beer. I wanted him to feel like he was a part of the party though, and that was why I still poured him a glass.

It was a good evening and I slept well. In the morning everyone returned to Calgary and it was quiet in the house once again.

THIRTY THREE

On August 30th I stood at the window wringing my hands as I waited for the ambulance that would transport Brian to the hospital for an appointment with the oncologist and blood testing again. He was too weak now, from being in bed, to stand and get into a wheelchair. The blood tests were necessary to determine the strength of chemo pills Brian would require. He was scheduled to commence chemo again later in the week.

With Heather's help, we changed Brian into a nice shirt for the hospital appointment. I went to the closet and stared at all the brightly coloured shirts Brian used to wear on beach vacations. I selected a blue shirt as blue was Brian's favourite colour. It was the richest royal blue with white imprints of hibiscus flowers. It was soft to the touch from the hundreds of washings.

The appointment with the oncologist was short, as she knew Brian tired easily. I was thankful when she approved Brian to continue with the chemo pills. Before we left the hospital, I picked up the pills at the hospital pharmacy.

We were back home four hours after we had left. Brian slept most of the trip home and only opened his eyes briefly when the ambulance attendants moved him from the stretcher back onto his bed. He slept on and off for the balance of the day.

I sat by his side and reflected. I wanted to be able to talk to Brian about our life and the paths we had chosen. I wanted to discuss the decisions that had impacted us. I wondered silently where our lives would have been had we taken a different path. What if we had never taken that first career opportunity and moved to Saskatchewan? What if we would have stayed and lived our entire lives in Calgary? So many times we had sat together and weighed the opportunities that came our way and together made the decision to take a new path. Those decisions had led to a wonderful, fulfilling, life together.

I wondered whether Brian would have another birthday. That was five and a half months away. I folded my arms and bent over onto the side of his bed. I laid my head gently on my arms. The image of one of his birthdays, celebrated in Mexico, popped into my head. I smiled, remembering.

We are with Larry and Sally, Dudley and Lauretta. We have caught a bus into Puerto Vallarta for lunch and beers. We do some shopping at the market and then stop at a restaurant. There is a man there making animals from balloons. All the kids are excited. Because we have had a few beers and are celebrating we pay the man to make balloon hats for all of us. He makes one of bull horns for Brian, which is so fitting. I think of how happy we are and the great day spent with friends.

Brian stirred and that brought me back to reality. I made him a plate of snacks, but he had no interest in eating. Despite my efforts I couldn't convince him to eat anything. I didn't eat either. I just didn't have an appetite. Instead I mixed a drink and watched television to pass the rest of the evening.

The next morning Brian was alert and acting more like himself, so I knew he was feeling better. It was hard to tell some days as he never complained. He had a good day. He was excited as he waited for Lauren and Cindy, our goddaughters, who were coming to visit that evening. He greeted them with a hug. They had brought his favourite sour candies. They told him of their jobs, their social life and then the stories turned to memories of when they would visit us at our ranch in Saskatchewan when they were growing up. There was laughter and happiness. Cindy and Lauren either stood or sat by his bed. I looked at them both and saw the beautiful girls they had grown into. We talked about a particular visit.

They were flying from Edmonton to visit us on their first solo trip without their parents. They remember how excited they were. For them the visits were always about Uncle Beanie as they called him. I was there of course, but Uncle Beanie was always the centre of their affection. Brian had told them that he was going to meet them at the airport with underwear on his head. Cindy was of course mortified as she was of the age that simple things embarrassed her. True to his word Brian arrived at the airport with a pair of white underwear on his head like a hat. He walked into the airport like that and then back out again and all the way back home.

I laughed with them. I remembered the photos of the three of them at our house, eating a bucket of ice cream, Brian still with the underwear on his head.

Two hours had passed since they'd arrived, and Brian began to nod off. I didn't want to cut short their visit as I knew that today was a good day and next time Brian may not be able to converse as well.

Cindy saw him close his eyes and said "We should go Uncle Beanie so you can get some rest."

"Okay, Sweetie," he replied.

They both kissed him and told him that they loved him. He gave them a big hug. I stepped out onto the deck with them and we chatted briefly. They hugged me and jumped into their vehicles. I waved as they drove away. I breathed in the warm night air and looked up at the glittering stars. The sky was clear and the wonder of all the constellations was inspiring. So many times Brian and I had taken the telescope out on to the deck on nights like this. The thought crossed my mind, but when I walked back inside Brian was already asleep. There wasn't much point in looking up at the stars when I had no one to share it with. I walked over and stood at his bed.

While he slept I sat and watched the television. A commercial came on advertising Christmas and an image of Boxing Day shopping popped into my head.

Many men don't like to go shopping on a normal day let alone on Boxing Day. The malls are packed with everyone looking for a bargain. For many years Brian and I would take Cindy and Lauren shopping on Boxing Day. Brian would hold all the packages and wait outside the stores as the girls scurried in and out of the long lines and crazy crowds. Afterwards we would always have lunch before returning home. The girls would add up the savings from the store receipts and be thrilled at what they were able to buy.

Brian went shopping on Boxing Day every year he could, not to buy anything for himself, but because it made his goddaughters happy.

I jumped when the phone rang, and quickly picked up the handset so it would not wake Brian. It was Debbie, Brian's cousin on Vancouver Island. We chatted on the phone for more than an hour and she told me stories that made my sides ache with laughter. It felt good to take my mind off the day to day stresses.

Most days I functioned like a robot. I felt like I was in a trance. I got out of bed, brushed my teeth, washed my face and brushed my hair. I long ago gave up on makeup. I looked in the mirror and wondered where my smile had gone. There were circles under my eyes and my complexion was blotchy. I was tired, not just physically but emotionally. I felt drained of all life.

I gathered my inner strength and stepped across the threshold from the bedroom. Brian's bed was positioned just outside the doorway. I spoke to Brian and tried to hide my sorrow. There was no rest. I could not take the day off. I could not turn back the clock. I had to forge on and so I did. Before I got Brian's breakfast I made a pot of coffee. Next I prepared warm water so that I could wash Brian's face and I poured a glass of water so we could brush his teeth. As part of the daily routine I gave him his pills and checked that the saline solution was dripping at the right level and nothing had happened overnight to pinch the line. In the past Brian had rolled in his sleep and pinched the line between the mattress and the bed rail. He no longer moved in bed, so I just needed to make sure I had not pinched the line while I was changing Brian's clothes.

Saturdays and Sundays were long days. Home care assistance was sporadic, and I had to work the best I could to tend to Brian's needs. It was lonely and quiet as he slept. The phone had not rung. There had been no telephone calls to ask how Brian was or how I was coping. I wondered what everyone was doing.

I spent most of the weekend going over photos with Brian or in silent reflection while he slept. I wondered when I last went to a shopping mall. It was in Panama, I thought, such a distant memory. My life was devoted to Brian's care. I had no time for relaxation. I was on edge every day, trying to be alert for changes in Brian's condition.

THIRTY FOUR

I looked at the calendar. The next day would be September 14th, my brother Wayne's birthday. He and Melissa planned to travel from Calgary to visit Brian and bring Brian's mother. I cooked a turkey in preparation. I knew that his mom would have been busy baking and would bring Brian's favourite cookies.

Brian was resting, so I reviewed the Caregiver handbook while I waited for everyone to arrive. I turned to the page titled *Caring for yourself – the Caregiver.* I read about keeping healthy and knew I was not caring for myself. I read about coping skills and emotions. I stopped at the paragraph titled *Caregiver Burnout.* I was already at this point. It said to ask for help. I knew that I should do this, but it was foreign to me. I had always been a boss in my career, so asking for help was not something I was comfortable with. To me it was a sign of weakness. I knew myself well enough. I would collapse under the pressure before I would admit defeat.

I could not stop myself as I was drawn to the section titled *As Life Ends.* Tears ran down my cheeks while I read:

'Take comfort in knowing that by giving care in the final stages of life, you shared in the most loving act of support and comfort.'

I knew deep down that I was doing the right thing, for Brian and for myself, in caring for him at home. I gave everything I had to care for him.

I closed the book when I saw Wayne's truck through the living room window. I knew they would be up the drive and unloading the truck in minutes. I shook Brian to wake him, so he knew that everyone had arrived. It was Friday night.

On Saturday morning Wayne, Melissa and I went to play golf at a nearby course as a birthday celebration for Wayne. The second reason of course was to give Brian's mother time to be alone with him.

When we got home from golf we decided that by using the manual lift we could get Brian up in his wheelchair so that he could go out on the deck for some fresh air. It was a beautiful day. We thought that between Wayne, Melissa and me we had the strength to handle Brian. We sat him on the edge of the bed so that we could swing the lift over him. We draped the canvas over the bed and then got Brian to lie back down so that we could position him on the canvas. We snapped together all the buckles and slowly moved the lift to the left with the plan to hold Brian over the wheelchair and then lower him into the chair and unhook the lift. As an extra precaution, Melissa held the wheelchair so that it couldn't move. It seemed easy enough, unfortunately Brian started to slip in the contraption and we were worried he would slide right out. He was hanging in the lift and we couldn't swing him into the wheelchair. All we could do was let him down onto the floor. We all laughed because any other emotion would have had us in tears.

"Now what are we going to do?" I asked Wayne.

"I still think we can get him up and into the chair. It would be nice for him to get some fresh air."

"I don't think we can do it."

"Well, let's try," Wayne said.

With that we tried again to lift Brian from the floor, and I realized how difficult it would be to move his body back to a sitting position. Brian had no strength to help us, so he was dead weight to move. We tried moving him into a variety of positions to have him aligned correctly on the canvas. All this movement tired Brian out and I started to worry that it was just too much for him.

"I think we need to just get him back into bed," I said, looking directly at my brother with concern.

"Okay, Bri. We are just going to swing you back into bed. Are you okay?" Wayne asked.

"I think I'm fine, but why am I on the floor?" Brian asked and we all laughed.

It took us a few more minutes before we were able to raise Brian high enough to guide the lift back over the bed. We were all relieved once he was comfortably in the safety of the bed.

On Sunday afternoon Wayne, Melissa and Brian's mother left and returned to Calgary. I sighed deeply as they pulled out of the drive. I wanted so much to share my pain, but I didn't. I shouldered my worries alone.

Monday morning the Home Care nurse arrived to check up on both of us. She drank a cup of coffee and chatted with Brian as she checked the saline bag. She was a comfort to me every time she visited as she was never in a hurry and provided me with someone to talk with. There were days when I felt like the walls were closing in on me and that the air was being sucked from the room. I was able to talk freely to her as she understood the pressure of the caregiver role. She encouraged me to ask for help from family and friends.

As she checked and changed the saline bag I thought about what she had said. I knew she was right about asking for help, but who could I lean on? Family came on the weekend when they could make the three-hour trip. It was just not possible for them to be with us during the week with their careers and other obligations. Friends that have offered to help do not live in the same province, so again it was not a plausible solution. I thought of our friends that lived only minutes away, but they had offered no help and I wouldn't beg to get assistance.

"Dr. T would like us to put in the injection sites, so that when Brian can no longer swallow you will be able to give him the meds by injection," she said looking at me. Then she explained to Brian what she would be doing. She kept talking as she set up the five injection sites. "Just one more and we are done for today."

Brian was the best patient. He just smiled and listened to the conversation without asking a question.

I watched her, and then facing Brian, I spoke. "We don't need to use these now Bri. You will keep taking your pills, but the doctor wants to make sure the sites are set up in case you get a sore throat and find it hard to swallow."

Brian's eyes flashed from me to the nurse. I didn't want to think about the day that he couldn't swallow. I wanted to block it from my thoughts. I grabbed my cup of coffee and took a big gulp. I felt my stomach tightening and my pulse quickening. I grabbed the sheet on Brian's bed, made an effort to straighten it and in the process wiped my palms that were feeling clammy. I looked down at Brian and smiled. I was a career Banker and never expected to become a nurse in this life. I wondered if I was going to be able to give Brian injections. I didn't know, and I was too nervous to say anything as I intently listened to the instructions and took notes.

"Don't worry. You'll be fine," the nurse said as she finished up. I knew she could read the concern on my face. She said goodbye to us both and walked out the door closing it quietly behind her.

I looked at the five injection sites as I pulled down Brian's shirt. I called our friend who had spent her career as a pediatric nurse.

"How's he doing?" Belinda asked.

"He's resting. It was a busy morning as the Home Care nurse set up all the injection sites. I never expected to have to be a nurse as well," I finished.

"You'll be able to do it. With the sites it is easier, and you don't need to worry as you can't hurt him. Don't worry. You'll be fine. You're a strong woman."

If only I had a nickel for every time I had heard someone say 'you're a strong woman.' Being a strong, determined career woman, was different than what I was facing. I felt like that woman had left the building and what was left was a scared, lonely shell of a person, who wished she did not have to face another day. Hearing Belinda's words brought me to tears. "I don't feel very strong," I replied.

"I know. But you are. Do you want us to drive up?" she asked suggesting they make an eight-hour trip.

"No I'll be fine. Really! It is just overwhelming sometimes and today is one of those days. Looking at the nurse put in the needle sites just brings home the fact that someday I will have to give Bri his medication by injection, and on that day it will mean he has turned another page in his journey."

When I got off the phone I sat down beside Brian's hospital bed and just stared at him. At times like this he looked so content and like himself. It was hard to believe how sick he truly was. He had fallen asleep after the nurse's visit, but just opened his eyes.

"Hey, Bri. How are you feeling?"

"Great. Just a little hungry."

I got up and went to the kitchen to heat up some leftovers for lunch. "I was just talking to Belinda," I said.

"Oh great. How are they?" he asked.

"About the same. They send hugs. It really got me to thinking how long we have known them. It is more than thirty-five years, you know."

"Really! Wow."

"Do you remember when we all lived in Calgary? I remember when they called us and said they had good news and bad news. The good news was that they found a house they really liked, and the bad news was that it was only three doors from us. Remember?" I said with a chuckle.

"Yup. We had lots of good times."

"We were all so young. Remember how many beers we could drink?"

"Still can" he replied.

Belinda and Scott had moved into that house and were our neighbours. They also became a part of our family. Most memorable were Christmas dinners at my parents place.

At that time both my sisters were also married so dinners included their spouses, nieces, nephews, our aunt, uncle and cousin from across the street, plus my other three siblings and perhaps the odd boyfriend or girlfriend. Dinner itself was the normal seasonal fare, but the excitement came from my mother's attempt at creating flaming plum pudding. My father would just look the other way as my mother would holler for us to shut off all the lights and she would walk into the rumpus room with the pudding in full blue flame. Instead of just using a small amount of liqueur for taste, my mother would drown the pudding in liqueur as she loved the flame. I never ate the pudding and neither did my sisters. It was left up to the MEN. Mom would give them each a generous portion. Scott was included along with the sons-in-law and they would all laugh at each other as they quite literally, choked down the pudding. The liqueur took their breath away. It was always followed by lots of laughter.

"I can see Mom now dishing up the plum pudding. Remember how she would give Scott an extra helping?"

"It was strong stuff, but she sure loved the flame," Brian added.

As Brian ate I thought about our friendship with Belinda & Scott. As happens in many friendships, our worlds had taken us in different directions. We all moved away from those homes next to each other in Calgary. Even though miles separated us, we always maintained contact through letters and annual telephone calls at Christmas. We had a connection with them built up over many years, and they had always remained close to my siblings as well. Brian and I were thrilled when Belinda and Scott called us in Panama and asked about coming to visit us. They were our first visitors, and we loved taking them to all the tourist attractions and sharing our love of Panama.

THIRTY FIVE

I woke up sad. It was the anniversary of my mom passing away. It had been four long years. I wished that I could hear the comfort of her voice, as she would tell me that everything would be okay. I sat down and talked to Brian about Mom. I don't look anything like my mom. She was less than five feet tall and for the majority of her life never weighted more than one hundred pounds. I, on the other hand, was five foot four inches and weighted over one hundred pounds in junior high. For as long as I could remember I had looked down into my mother's eyes. I went to the spare room and brought back several photo albums so that I could see my mom once again. I traced my finger over a photo of her as I reminisced with Brian.

The photo was from 2003, ten years before. It was when we moved back to Alberta from Saskatchewan. My mother was so excited about us being closer that she talked my brothers and families into visiting us even before our furniture had arrived. There were several photos from that weekend and it was as clear as if it was yesterday. In one photo, my mom, who was seventy-eight at the time, was tucked into a sleeping bag and beside her was her grandson, my nephew, Cameron. And beside Cameron was his dad, my brother Rod. In the other photos are my other brother Wayne, and his children Blair and Brandi, who are also resting in their sleeping bags in front of the fireplace. Rod's wife, Linda had found an unused corner to place her sleeping bag. It was an unusual situation with everyone bunked on the living room floor, but I remember how happy we all were that weekend to be together.

We had many more similar weekends together with everyone sleeping overnight, but we had furniture and beds. I picked up a photo album from an earlier year. I saw more photos of my mom and brothers on visits to our ranch in Saskatchewan. I was so grateful now for all those photos that brought memories to life.

It was September 24th, my birthday. My birthday had never been the same since my mom passed away. My birthday fell only five days after mom's death, so I knew I would never again be in a celebratory mood in September. I made myself a cake anyways and put sprinkles on the icing as Brian liked them. There was no fanfare. Brian did not know the day, and even though I told him, he soon forgot and asked why we were having cake. I cried as I cut him another piece. I talked to him about the weather while we ate. There was no wind and the sun shone down through the pine trees that lined our yard. It was a perfect day for an outdoor party but there was no one to enjoy the day with.

I thought of all the birthday cards Brian had bought me over the years, and I wished that I had another card today, but there would be no card from him, no card from my parents. I wanted to go shopping at the mall, but those were distant memories now. I had not been in a mall for nine months.

When Brian went to sleep I sat down at the table, which was only a few feet from his bed. I checked emails, and along with inquiries about Brian I received birthday greetings from family. There were several emails with the subject line "feliz cumpleanos". These were birthday greetings from my colleagues in Panama. I started to cry all over again as I read and felt their emotion and compassion. I had been gone only three months, but I longed to be back in Panama and to reverse the situation we were facing. I thought back to the previous year when Brian and I flew to Costa Rica to celebrate my birthday. We went on a tour of the Arenal Volcano and basked in the hot spring waters of the resort. We didn't have a care in the world. That seemed like a lifetime ago.

The phone interrupted my thoughts. It was Brian's mother wishing me a happy birthday. I walked into the family room to talk so that I didn't wake Brian. I updated her and she shared news from other family members.

Early in the afternoon Dr. T arrived for his weekly visit. He pulled up Brian's shirt to look at the injection sites that the nurse had set up.

"Is he still able to swallow?" he asked.

"Yes. No problem so far. He is eating less though."

"That's natural. There is good nutrition in baby food, so you may want to buy some next time you go for groceries. Anything purified is probably easiest for him as time goes on," Dr. T added.

I was surprised as I never thought I would be giving Brian baby food.

Dr. T looked at me. "Just see how it goes. Is he in pain?"

"It's hard to tell as he never complains about anything," I answered.

"That's good. I will write you a prescription for morphine."

I know that my eyes must have shown my concern. Morphine. Doesn't anyone realize I'm not a nurse, I thought. Before I could speak, Dr. T did.

"You can pick up the morphine the next time you go to fill his prescriptions. If you don't need to use it that's okay, but it is good to have ready in case Brian needs it. I'll stop by next week."

Dr. T left and I stood and looked down at Brian. He never woke up at all even though we talked at his bedside and Dr. T lifted his shirt to check the injection sites. I marvelled at how deeply Brian slept. He used to hear every noise and would wake up. He would hear the dogs bark at night or a coyote call out, or even cars driving fast down the highway. Now he slept through all of these noises.

As Brian was content I went for a walk in the fields with the dogs, giving us all a much needed break. I fed Jesse and Dustin horse treats. I knew as I looked at them that I should also take the time to brush them. Their manes and tails were tangled, and they had been neglected since we arrived back to Canada.

"Sorry guys, not today," I said, as I walked back into the house to check on Brian. Brian was still sleeping, so I sat on the deck and waited for the evening Home Care Aide to arrive.

The next morning, I finished updating emails and then turned my attention to the Palliative Caregiver guide that sat on my night table. Brian had been home from the hospital for six weeks. I flipped through the headings and stopped at the section on seizures. I learned nothing new.

In my notebook I had been recording the number of seizures that Brian experienced, and that day there were nine. Nothing in the guide told me about the number of seizures, so I turn my attention to the brain tumor handbook. After reading the section on seizures I felt more relaxed knowing that what I was doing was appropriate. The Home Care nurse recommended putting face cloths in Brian's hands so that he did not squeeze his hands too tight when he had a seizure. Instead he held a small stuffed monkey in one hand and a soft rubbery toy caterpillar in the other.

I looked at Brian and wondered what the days ahead would bring. The day before he'd eaten the birthday cake, but today he had no interest in cake or candy. He had always eaten a lot of candy; in fact we had always had a shelf dedicated to candy in our pantry. Instead of eating a dish of candy, he only ate a few and then he turned away. The thing that he'd loved – junk candy, no longer held his interest.

I thought of the previous day's visit with Dr. T and wondered when Brian would need morphine. I was scared to death at the thought of having to inject him, that I might do it wrong, or give him too much.

I was feeling the pressure. I called Maggie to talk with her. I knew she would understand the feelings that overwhelmed me. Maggie had been married to Brian's Uncle Bruce, and we always had a close friendship with them. Maggie understood what I was going through. She had nursed Bruce at home until the end.

After I got off the phone I lay down on the couch near Brian. While I slept I dreamt.

It was 1996, the year we survived a tornado at our farm. We had just enjoyed the July long weekend visit from family. We had no idea that we were about to experience a tornado. All day long the weather had been ominous with thunder storms in the area. We had just finished supper and had not watched the evening news, so we were unaware of the tornado warning which had been issued. Brian was watching the sky as we expected a severe thunderstorm, and we needed the rain, so Brian hoped the storm would materialize. As we stood looking out the patio doors I became nervous, which was not unusual. I had been scared of thunderstorms since I was a child. My mother was terrified of wind, and whenever there was a bad storm and my father was not yet home from work, Mom would take me and my two older sisters, plus our Border Collie dog, Lucky, and we would hide under my parents bed. I can remember being under that bed snacking on crackers and shaking with each clap of thunder. That impression on me had lasted my whole life, and the sound of thunder still makes me shake like a scared animal.

As Brian and I watched the sky we commented about the unusual colour and formations. The sky had hints of green and purple. As we were discussing it, a wall of water rushed at the house. We had only a second to get the patio door closed. The storm was so fierce we knew that this was no ordinary thunderstorm. We raced to the rear door and called our dogs into the house.

We retreated to the basement and sat in a room which had been a concrete cistern seventy years earlier. This room was our refuge for the next few hours until we were certain the storm was over.

The next morning the small community of farmers gathered to assess the damage. There was considerable property damage and loss of livestock, but all the people were accounted for. In the end we were grateful that no lives were lost in our community.

We spent the next few months working to rebuild our corrals, fences and buildings before winter set in. We lost numerous trees in our yard, and I was tearful because we had to cut those trees down and see the gaps in the windbreak. The storm cost us emotionally and financially. I was already scared about wind and storms and now my fear was at a whole new level.

I woke up to a knock at the door. It was Heather, and I realized I had locked the door. Normally she would just walk in, and call out to me if I wasn't sitting right there. She never rang the doorbell, just in case it woke Brian. We chatted as she went about her duties and I told her about the dream I had. I must have been in a deep sleep, because even as I spoke to her I felt drowsy.

THIRTY SIX

$\mathcal{M}$y sister Penny and her husband, Mark, were visiting. I knew it was difficult for them to talk with Brian, and much of the time we sat in silence. The only thing that broke the silence was their dog, Chip, who walked around whining and stopping at the foot of Brian's bed. We assumed he just wanted the food that sat on a table at Brian's bedside. When we made sandwiches for lunch, Chip continued to whine, and even being coaxed by Mark with a piece of sandwich, didn't keep his attention for more than a couple of minutes. Eventually we lifted Chip up on the bed and realized that was all that he had wanted for more than an hour. Chip lay down tucked against Brian's legs and slept. Chip was content. Brian reached down with his hand and stroked Chip. It was amazing that Chip, who has not spent much time around Brian, had sensed Brian's illness and wanted to provide comfort by lying next to him.

Mark helped me with some household chores that I couldn't do alone. It was Saturday, so Heather was not there, but another Home Care Aide arrived. While she was there we took a five-minute drive up to the community centre that was having a bazaar sale. We returned with gourds and pumpkins to decorate the kitchen table for Thanksgiving. We were gone less than 30 minutes.

Penny and Mark only stayed one day and then drove back to Calgary. Once again I was alone. When I had company I could feel the pressure of caring for Brian lift, if only for a short time. I was able to have a conversation and to laugh.

I talked to Brian about when our niece Sophie and nephew Matthew, (Penny and Mark's children), were young and came to stay for a week with us at the farm.

As with all the nieces and nephews, Brian would take them on the tractor and let them steer as he handled the gears. It always brought a smile to their faces and a sense of being older than their age. On this particular trip I remember us eating supper, and of course having laughs as Brian was telling them stories. I remember my sister Penny calling to check on Sophie and Matthew, and I was laughing so hard when I picked up the receiver that I could barely talk. When Brian, Sophie and Matthew realized it was Penny they took cucumber slices and laid them over their eyes. They made faces at me as I was trying to carry on an intelligent conversation with my sister so that she would not question why she had released her kids to a house full of

*crazies. Eventually I had to hang up, and once the silliness calmed down, I called
my sister back.*

This was typical of what happened when our nieces and nephews came
to stay. Brian always entertained them and they would go home full of food,
candy and memories for a lifetime.

After we chatted I started the computer and checked emails. I read Brian
emails that arrived daily, skipping any concerning comments and just focusing
on the positive words of comfort from family and friends. I shared as much
as I could with Brian as I wanted him to know how much he was loved.
Afterwards I walked down our drive to get the mail. There was a letter and
a music CD from my oldest sister. The CD was the newest release of Corb
Lund, an Alberta band. I played it for Brian and we talked about the other
CD's we had from the same band and how we had taken them on vacation
to Cuba with us one year. We laughed about one song in particular. 'Time
To Switch To Whisky.' The lyrics go; *'It's time to switch to whisky, we been
drinking beer all day'.* That song was a real hit around the swim-up bar. All
the Canadian tourists would be singing along and some would even dance the
jive around the pool area. Every day at 4:00 pm the bartenders would play
the CD and the same scenario would play out. The Cubans clearly did not
know the words, but they knew that people loved the music and they loved
watching everyone dance.

The next morning our friends Dale and Bonnie called. We had met each
other when Dale and I worked together in Saskatchewan. They now lived in
the Maritimes. Brian and Bonnie quickly became friends and the four of us
enjoyed time together. That was more than twenty years ago. They moved
away from Saskatchewan, but we remained friends. Our paths crossed again
in 2003 when both families were living in Alberta. I held the phone to Brian's
ear. He did not speak but smiled when he heard their voices. I bent down and
placed my ear to the phone as well. I heard them recounting stories of fun
times from the past. I knew that for Brian, those times were lost and no longer
in his memories. For the time being though he was happy to listen, and he
enjoyed what they were saying even if he couldn't speak.

I looked forward to Fridays as Heather was at the house for four hours with
Brian, which gave me time to go to the city for shopping. I always had a list
and organized my driving in the most efficient circuit of the stores. Walmart
had become my store of choice as I could get dog food, some groceries and
medical supplies in one stop. Plus it had McDonald's, and that was my weekly
treat. Afterwards I drove to the pharmacy to pick up more saline solution and
drop off the prescription for the morphine. Within minutes they asked me to

sign a form for accepting a narcotic. This was when it hit me. On top of all the regular medicines I had to control daily, I had the added component of handling morphine. My hand was shaking as I signed the form.

That evening Brian's cousin, Debbie, called again. I had forgotten that we had planned to talk tonight, and hers was a welcome voice. We were able to talk. Her husband had a stroke five years before. It had been a long recovery. Debbie and I talked about the strain and some of the funny things that happened in each of our lives. We were able to support each other by just listening and caring. I felt uplifted every time after we talked.

The next day I sat with Brian and continued to reflect on our life. It gave us something to pass the time talking about. I pulled out another photo album and flipped through the pages. I stopped at a photo of Christmas. Brian and his cousin Ricky sat in front of the Christmas tree. It was taken when we lived on the ranch in Saskatchewan. Both Brian and Ricky were holding a beer and toasting the season.

"Do you remember the year Ricky came to the farm for Christmas?" I asked.

"No."

"I remember because he came on the bus and left home with his clothes wet in a black garbage bag, direct from the laundry. He was short of time so could not dry everything he wanted to bring. On the bus trip, the bag was placed in the luggage compartment and the clothes froze together. When he arrived the bag was a bag of ice."

Brian laughed. "I do remember that."

THIRTY SEVEN

*I*t was Sept 30th. I stood waiting for the ambulance to transport Brian to the cancer clinic to get another MRI. I watched out the window to ensure they did not miss our driveway, as the address was obscured by the large poplar trees. Finally, I saw the ambulance turn off the highway. I walked out on the deck to greet the attendants and ensured they came to the front door where it was easier to load Brian.

As they backed up to the deck I stood and waited, holding the dogs to keep them from running up to greet the ambulance attendants.

"Sorry we are late," the paramedic said as he jumped from the driver's door.

"It's fine," I replied.

A woman paramedic jumped from the passenger side and walked to join her partner at the rear of the ambulance. They opened the rear doors and pulled out the stretcher, extended the legs and rolled it up the ramp on the deck. Once they got Brian comfortable in the ambulance we made the thirty-minute trip to the hospital. Following the MRI, a different paramedic team transported us back home.

Trips to the hospital took a lot out of Brian. It was all the movement. He had no appetite, and I couldn't get him to eat anything before he fell asleep. When he woke, he looked at me when I asked him if he was hungry, but there was no response. I had a plate of cheese and fruit ready, but he wouldn't eat and then he fell back asleep. I sat beside his bed, and snacked on the handful of Ritz crackers that made up my supper. The desire to cook anything was gone.

It was hard to know when Brian would want to eat and when he wouldn't. Some days I struggled to get him to chew, so I opted for meals like macaroni and cheese or soups. He almost choked on a grape one day so even that scared me now. One day he had a desire and ability to eat and the next day I knew that he was having difficulty processing the need to chew what went in his mouth.

The next day, Dr. T knocked on the front door and then walked in. I stood. I had been sitting with Brian's hand in mine and I was stroking the back of his hand with my finger. I continued to hold his hand.

"How has he been this week?" he asked.

Tears streamed down my face and I choked back my sobs. "He's been sleeping most of the days. Yesterday we went back to the Cancer Clinic for another MRI. Those trips take a lot out of him."

"How are you?"

I smiled at him and pursed my lips trying to not fully fall apart. "I'm fine."

"No, you're not."

I couldn't look directly at Dr. T, so I held my glance on Brian.

"There's no embarrassment in saying you can't do it anymore." He hesitated before continuing. "It's hard work, and maybe we need to look into…"

I cut him off. "No I'm fine really. I need him here with me."

"Are you sure?"

I looked down at Brian and back at the doctor. Tears were streaming down my cheeks and I wiped at them before they dripped off my chin. We stood in silence for a few minutes.

"Call me if anything changes. I'll drop back next week."

"Thanks for coming," I replied.

"Of course. Take care of yourself," he said as he stood and left the house.

I continued to sit beside Brian's bed while he slept. I yearned to lie beside him and feel the warmth of his body next to mine. Those days I knew were gone. I substituted by moving the couch beside his bed. I was able to lie on the couch and reach through the bed rails and hold Brian's hand and rub his arm. I was so lonely and yearned for someone that I could unload all my feelings on. Brian had always been my sounding board. I wanted to cry out loud.

I felt some days like I had lost myself. I didn't even feel like showering, let alone putting on makeup. I must have been a fright for some of the Home Care Aides. I decided that starting the next day I would put on a new face and perhaps that would cheer my inner self. If I looked good on the outside I would feel good on the inside – right?

A few days later the phone rang and I quickly picked it up recognizing the caller ID.

"We have the results of the MRI. It is encouraging as there is no new cell growth," the oncologist said.

I was thrilled that we had finally stopped the tumor from growing. I thought about our upcoming wedding anniversary and Christmas, and for the first time, in a long time, I felt Brian would be there to celebrate both.

"I'm so happy I can't tell you," I said. Then the hammer came down.

"While the tumor has not grown, the swelling has not responded to medication as well as we had expected. I'm afraid that Brian's seizure activity may increase," she finished.

"But no new cell growth is good, isn't it?" I asked confused.

"It's encouraging, but I must be honest that the swelling is still a major concern. I will consider whether we should increase the medication. I will call you in a couple of days." She paused and then added "Call the office if anything changes."

I was deflated. All the treatments had stopped the growth of the tumor and that was what I had always thought was our goal. Now with the doctor's words I realized that was not enough. For some reason the words of the neurosurgeon in Panama popped into my mind – '*go home and enjoy the time you have together.*'

As Brian slept I emailed Maggie to ask if she could come to visit. I needed her to lean on. She was the one person that knew what I was going through. She had been widowed twice.

THIRTY EIGHT

*A*s Brian slept I kept looking through the photo albums. I turned the page and Brian's mother and her friend Mary were sitting on the swing in our yard at the ranch. There were plastic buckets at their feet overflowing with berries. I thought back....

At the end of our ranch fence was a road allowance which led down to the river. Along the pathway there were bushes full of chokecherries, and sometimes when we were lucky, we would find saskatoons. Mary and Brian's mother would drive out from Saskatoon to our farm in their quest to find berries to make preserves. The photo is of such a day. We were out picking chokecherries and together we had filled several one-gallon plastic ice cream pails. The photo was taken after we were back at the farm and they were enjoying a lemonade on the swing and laughing about how much work they had ahead of them to use all the berries.

Brian was awake and I described the photos to him as he lay on the bed and smiled.

The next album had photos of him and his Uncle Bruce walking in our fields. I flipped pages and got new albums and we talked about the many family and friends we have captured in photos. I always had a camera ready.

I showed him the photos of a trip to Huatulco, Mexico. We had just moved to Panama and were meeting up with family and friends in Huatulco.

"Remember when we took this group photo?" I asked. It was a photo of the group taken on a rooftop terrace. Behind us was the resort and ocean. The sky was a bright blue. I named off everyone in the photo - my brothers Wayne and Rod, sisters-in- laws Melissa and Linda, niece Crystal, nephew Cameron and friends Larry and Sally.

After that trip I had taken the photos and made online books as gifts for each family. I flipped to other photos of us on the beach as I talked but Brian didn't say anything. I knew he didn't remember the vacation.

I closed the album and turned the television on while I fixed Brian something to eat. I had to be quick, because if I took more than a few minutes he would be asleep.

"Would you like a grilled cheese sandwich?" I asked knowing it is one of his favourites.

"Yeah. That would be nice."

I handed Brian a dish that had some Fruit Loops in it as well as some fish crackers. I did this so that he concentrated on snacking while I got the sandwich cooked. Luckily he stayed awake until I had the sandwich ready. He ate only half, but that made me happy. Afterwards he ate a chocolate pudding. I was grateful for everything that I could get him to eat.

Just when I was doing the dishes Heather showed up. She chatted with Brian and me at the same time. When she was done work for the day we sat at the table and talked while Brian drifted back to sleep.

As we sat and talked I felt a nudge on my hand. I looked down at our German Shepherd, Hayley. She started whining, her signal for 'it's supper time.' I stood and looked at Brian who was still sound asleep. I walked to the side of his bed and placed my hand on his cheek. Heather looked at her watch and then stood to leave. It was time for her to get home to make supper for her family.

I prepared Hayley and Danny's doggy supper and walked outside to put their dishes on the deck. I went back in the house and got some carrots out of the fridge. I walked over to the barn and filled my pocket with horse treats before heading to the corral. I folded my arms and leaned on the top rail of the corral fence. Jesse meandered over as he was conditioned to know that the chance of my having horse treats was fairly good. Dustin was more reserved and held his stance at the end of the corral. He kept his eyes on me and Jesse just in case something was happening.

Jesse knocked my arm with his muzzle. He could smell the horse treats, but his eyes were on the carrots in my hand. His lips slid down my arm, leaving a wet smudge of the grass he had been eating. I pulled my hand back and broke the carrot into pieces and fed him. Then I walked over and gave Dustin his share of the carrots, also broken in pieces, plus I put some of the alfalfa treats into his feed bucket. Once my pocket was empty of both the horse treats and the carrots, Jesse went back to grazing, slowly moving across the corral and out into the pasture. I stood at the fence and watched him. I laid my head on my arms across the fence rail and closed my eyes. In time I gained my composure and walked back into the house. I sat by Brian's bed and listened to the television for company. Brian slept through the night.

On the weekend my brothers came to visit once again and brought Brian's mom. We sat down, and even though the television was on, none of us was paying attention to it. We were all lost in our own inner thoughts.

My mother-in-law broke the silence by telling us stories about when she was growing up in the 1920's in drought stricken Saskatchewan. She captivated us all as she talked about what day to day life was like. So many people have no idea what hardships the previous generation endured. I had heard the stories many times before, but I enjoyed hearing her talk. So many times I had asked her to write about her life. I had always wanted to write a book about it. Those thoughts were at the back of my mind. For my brothers and families this was the first time they had heard her speak about her life. Everyone had questions and that kept the story telling alive for the evening.

I stood back and listened to them talk. Brian's mother was close to all of my siblings and had been a part of family celebrations for all the years Brian and I had been together. She also was a good friend to our mother. I looked at her now and realized that in a way she was filling a mother role for all of us today.

In the morning we started the day with coffee and a few of us got into the baking that my mother-in-law had brought. It was wonderful to have homemade cookies for breakfast!

Wayne stood at the island and had started to mix pancakes. Melissa was in charge of the bacon. I just stood by and savoured not doing anything. Within minutes the strong aroma of the maple bacon had us all salivating.

Wayne mixed the pancake batter, but it was my brother Rod who was in charge of cooking. Rod could make a joke from anything, and this morning he was making us laugh as he flipped pancakes. He was singing and dancing and it was hard not to burst out in laughter as he was swinging the spatula like he was conducting a band! He bumped hips with Melissa as they both stood at the stove, and the rest of us just shook our heads and laughed. Rod was helping all of us to redirect our attention. Even when we were at our lowest, we could find laughter if we tried.

Brian was having difficulty eating his Fruit Loops which he ate dry like a snack. My brother Wayne sat beside him and picked up the cereal Brian dropped and put them back in the bowl. Wayne tried to joke about it, and Brian laughed.

I looked at Wayne and Brian and so many thoughts ran through my head. I thought of vacations and enjoying beers on a beach and of course the laughter that followed. I thought of our most recent time in Panama. Brian was like the older brother Wayne never had. Their roles now had changed. Wayne looked over at me and I shrugged. I knew how hard it was to sit and pick up the Fruit Loops that dropped. I had done it on many days.

After breakfast was finished everyone jumped into their vehicles and made the trip back to Calgary. For me, I was alone once more.

While I talked to Brian I thought about the upcoming Thanksgiving weekend. I hoped that Brian would see another Christmas, which was only two months away, but I knew that another Thanksgiving, another year from now, was probably not in the cards. I realized this may be our last Thanksgiving together.

I decided to cook Thanksgiving dinner and invite our friends. This way we could all celebrate with Brian like we had done so many times in the past.

I cooked the turkey and our goddaughters, Cindy and Lauren, brought the vegetables and dessert. Brian had a good appetite and enjoyed the turkey, but he truly savoured the apple crisp dessert, which was one of his favourites. Brian fell asleep as we all continued to talk at the dining room table, which was a mere few feet from his hospital bed. We shared a great meal, drinks, good conversation, some laughs and of course lots of hugs with Brian. I captured the happiness of the day in photos.

I went to bed that night content. I got up a couple of times during the night to check on Brian, but overall I had a good night's sleep. In the morning, as always, I went to check on Brian before I got washed up and started coffee. He was still sleeping and looked so peaceful. I spoke to him but got no response, so I decided to start coffee and then shower before the Home Care Aide arrived. As I dressed I talked aloud to Brian, which had become routine.

An hour later Brian still had not woken up. The Home Care Aide came and went and when another couple of hours passed without Brian waking up I was really concerned. I called for support and a nurse came to the house. She was just as shocked as I was. Brian had been sleeping for seventeen hours. The nurse called the doctor. As Brian was not in any distress it appeared that perhaps he may have had a seizure that I had not been witness to, and hence he was just sleeping as part of the aftermath. I sat by Brian's side throughout the day and into the evening and talked to him as if he were awake. I could not eat. My stomach was in knots. I didn't know what to think when I finally fell into bed. I found comfort in knowing that the doctor would be here the next day for his regularly scheduled weekly visit.

I woke up to Brian calling my name. At first I thought I was dreaming. I looked at the clock. It was 3:10 am. I jumped out of bed and was at the side of Brian's bed in seconds.

"I'm hungry," Brian said.

"Bri, I am so happy you're awake. You scared me," I said as I leaned down and hugged him.

"How come?" he asked.

"Because you have been sleeping since Sunday night and it is Tuesday morning!" I answered.

"Really! How come?"

"I don't know. Do you remember Thanksgiving dinner?"

"No."

"Well, we had dinner on Sunday, and Sally, Larry and the girls were here. You had turkey and even apple crisp for dessert. After dinner you went to sleep and then yesterday you just didn't wake up," I said.

"Maybe that's why I'm hungry," Brian added.

He said it so matter of fact that I had to laugh. He had been asleep for thirty-two hours. He had no question as to the length of time that had passed, he just said that he was hungry. Inside the tears were just below the surface, but I did not want to upset Brian by crying. For the next hour I sat and talked with him as he ate a bowl of Fruit Loops, some chocolate pudding and an apple. After that he closed his eyes and went back to sleep as if nothing had happened. I kissed him on the forehead and crawled back into bed, relieved.

Dr. T showed up for his weekly visit and I told him about Brian sleeping from Sunday until that morning. He of course already knew this from the telephone call from the Home Care Nurse.

"It could be the result of more seizure activity. How long was he awake before he went back to sleep?" he asked.

"He was himself, as if nothing happened. He was awake all morning and just went back to sleep after lunch. I'm worried about the ring on his finger though. It is too tight, and I think I should get it cut off when we go to the hospital for his next blood work," I said as I held up Brian's hand. I had taken off his wedding ring a few weeks before and had only left this blue sapphire ring on as it was already tight at that time.

"Have you got some pliers?" he asked.

"Like needle nose pliers?"

"Yes, those will work fine."

I walked into the garage and opened the tool box. I pushed aside some screwdrivers until I found some pliers and walked back into the house. Within a few seconds Dr. T had cut the ring off. I was relieved. Brian slept through it all.

THIRTY NINE

he following week Brian had good days and bad. With each week that passed he slept more and more. His arms looked so thin and his shirts no longer clung to his chest. His skin was pale now with no hint of a tan. He no longer wore the contact lenses that gave him beautiful blue eyes. I talked to him for hours every day, even when he slept. I told him about the weather, how much the hay field had grown, about the sun rise every morning and the colours as it set at night. I told him about the horses, the dogs and even about the barn cat. I told him about everyone that called. I told him every day how much I loved him. I told him about vacation plans that I knew we would never take.

It was October 18th. Brian had slept most of the day. By late afternoon he woke and was alert enough to talk. I got him to eat a chocolate pudding, but I knew that anything more than that would be a struggle as he started to doze off. This was the third day of his chemo regimen, so while he was awake I ran and grabbed the pills from our bathroom.

In those couple of moments, he had closed his eyes once again. "Bri, you need to take your chemo pills before you go to sleep."

He opened his eyes and looked at me. I placed two pills in his mouth and brought the straw to his lips.

"The straw is in your mouth, Bri. Just suck on the straw." There was no reaction. "Bri, you need to suck the straw so that you can swallow your chemo pills. It's really important you get them down. I can't give you an injection for these. We only have the pills." I could hear the panic in my voice.

His eyes rolled and he turned his face away from me. I walked to the other side of his bed. He looked up at me and opened his mouth. One of the pills fell out. I picked it up and placed it back between his lips. I removed the straw from the cup and placed the glass rim to his lips.

"I'm just going to tip the glass Bri, and give you a bit of water to swallow your pills," I said trying to fight back tears. He continued to look at me as the water ran from the corner of his mouth and soaked into his shirt. Following the water, came the two pills.

I picked up the pills and laid the towel over his shirt to soak up the water. I looked directly into his eyes and could not hide my sadness.

"It's okay, Bri. You don't need to take the pills if you don't want to. You just rest now."

Brian closed his eyes. I could not hold back my sorrow. As tears fell down my cheeks I kissed him and told him I loved him. There was no reply. I covered him with the woolly blanket and placed several stuffed toys around him. There were two hedgehogs, a Disney character and a teddy bear. The toys were gifts from his most recent hospital stay. In addition, he had a small sock monkey and a rubbery caterpillar toy which I placed in his hands to keep him from pinching his hands tight if he had a seizure.

I was frustrated. Brian's last MRI had shown that there was no new cell growth of the tumor. The recent blood tests were positive and another five-day regimen of chemo had been approved. Today was day three of the chemo. The pills were in vain if he could no longer swallow.

For the next hour I talked to Brian, knowing that he could hear me even though he did not respond. I wanted something I said to trigger a memory or a feeling and cause him to open his eyes.

I told him about when we met and that crazy first date, about when we moved to the property in Saskatchewan that he always called 'the ranch', while I referred to it as 'the farm.' I told him about feeding the cows on a cold winter day and how we would come in the house afterwards and curl up by the fireplace with a rum and Coke. I told him about how lucky we had been to vacation in Cuba, Dominican Republic, Mexico, Costa Rica, Bahamas, and other destinations. As I talked of vacations I envisioned us walking on the beach. Tears ran down my cheeks and I reached for a tissue. I wiped away the tears and clutched the tissue in my fist, knowing that since I had started to cry I would not be able to stop my tears. It was my emotional release. There was nothing else I could do to relieve the pain.

I talked about living in Panama and all that we loved about the country and the people. I told him about how cheap the beer was in Panama and how he would joke with everyone back in Canada about it. '*I can buy three beers here for the price of one in Canada.*'

Brian was known to everyone as a beer man. No matter the hour he had enjoyed a beer when friends or family were visiting. When we lived on the farm, before going to Panama, having company was our time to relax away from our careers and the chores to keep the farm operating. We would take a much needed break and enjoy beers instead.

I looked at Brian and thought of all the beers we had shared, just the two of us. I pictured us on our deck with our dogs lying in the shade. In the summer Brian kept a cooler on the deck that always had a supply of cold beer. He used to tell friends that if they came to visit and we weren't home, to just pull up a chair, grab a cold beer, and wait for us to come home.

I thought of the last beer we had shared before his stroke. I thought of how we would talk for hours, and now he lay silent. I wanted to hear his voice, to hear him laugh, to hear him telling stories and making us all laugh. I wanted Brian back.

There was no expression on his face. I looked for motion in his eye-lids but there was none. I rubbed his arm as I kept talking. I was scared. I laid my head on the edge of his bed and stretched my arm across his body.

I did not know it then but that was the last time that Brian was lucid.

My strong, confident Navy man, the man I had relied on for more than thirty-nine years was slipping away and there was nothing I could do to stop it but cry. Most days I cried until I could cry no more. I cried for the future that was lost, for the past he had forgotten, but more importantly I cried for Brian as he could not cry for himself. I cried for the life he would not fulfill. I cried for our family and friends who would miss having Brian in their lives.

I knew in time family and friends would survive, I just was not certain that I ever would. I couldn't even remember a time when Brian was not a part of my life. It was as if my life started the day I met him.

I did not sleep that night. I tried to lie on the couch next to Brian and I tried to sleep in our bed but sleep evaded me. I was so focussed on listening for any sign from Brian that I was so on edge I could not relax. I prayed to just get through the night as I knew I would have company the next day as his mother and Maggie would be arriving. I was also nervous as I would need to give Brian all his medication by injection starting in the morning. Nursing was not in my blood.

I got out of bed early as I wasn't sleeping anyway. I made coffee and went out on the deck. Brian still slept peacefully. When my coffee cup was empty I came back in the house and talked to Brian, telling him what a beautiful morning it was. Then I went into our bedroom and prepared all the injections for his medication. Each of the injection sites was named so that I didn't confuse where to put the injections. I lifted Brian's shirt and within ten minutes I was finished. I let out a heavy sigh.

The phone rang midmorning and it was more disappointment. Maggie's plane from Vancouver Island had been delayed due to fog. She would not arrive in Calgary until perhaps later in the day, so they would not be driving up to our acreage until the next day. I could not hide my disappointment. I so wanted Maggie here to have a drink with, to cry with, and just to talk with someone who knew what it was like to be a care giver. Secretly I hoped that Brian would not be worse by the time they arrived. I stood by Brian's bed and talked to him, but he did not stir. After I filled my coffee cup I sat at his bedside and stroked his hand. It was a long day. I wanted so much for Brian to open his eyes and speak to me again, but the day passed without any change in him. I gave him injections that evening and again the next morning without any response from him. It was now Sunday and he had been asleep since Friday evening. I sat at his side and waited for his sister and her husband to arrive with his mom and Maggie.

There was no change in Brian all day. We took turns sitting by his side talking and telling stories as we all believed that he could hear us. At the end of the day Katie and Reggie returned to Calgary.

On Monday morning the Home Care Nurse called to check in. I updated her on Brian and told her that there was no need to visit. She advised that she would update Dr. T. I gave Brian his medicine by injections again and was feeling comfortable that I was doing everything correctly.

Tuesday afternoon Dr. T arrived for his weekly visit. I stood at Brian's side with tears streaming down my face.

"He hasn't really been awake since Friday night," I said. "He couldn't swallow his chemo pills. I have been giving him everything else by injection."

Dr. T looked at me and I could see the compassion in his eyes.

"You can stop all the medication except the morphine. Brian is not going to wake up again."

My eyes darted from Dr. T to Brian.

He hesitated and then added. "Have you made the calls we talked about?"

I knew he was referring to the funeral home, but I could not answer him.

"I am sorry. Brian has less than a week left."

I was shocked by his words. I had always thought that we had weeks left and wanted Brian to see another Christmas. It was only October 22nd. I looked down at Brian. My lips quivered, but I could not say a word. I stood frozen at Brian's bedside and rubbed his arm. Dr. T leaned over and placed his hand on my shoulder. I looked at him with tears streaming down my face.

"Call me if you need anything," he said as he picked up his bag and walked out the door.

I hesitated after Dr. T left, trying to process the information. I wanted to run out the door after him and tell him he was wrong, that Brian would wake up again like he had on all the previous occasions when seizures had caused him to sleep for up to forty-eight hours. He has to wake up. He just has too. I stared down at Brian and wished so much for things to be different. I wished that the doctor had not come. Before he arrived I'd had hope. Now that was all stripped away.

I leaned down and whispered in Brian's ear. *'I love you. Please wake up. I need you'*. Then I walked into the bathroom and looked in the mirror. I blew my nose, and washed my face, lingering with the warm cloth against my face. I breathed in deeply and straightened my stance and tried to repeat in my head what I would say to break the news to his mom and Maggie. I did not want to repeat what the doctor had said. I wanted to be able to walk into the sunroom where they were sipping tea and tell them that Brian was awake. But I could not. I had to be truthful to his mom. She deserved to know.

Despite my best effort, emotion got the best of me and all I could do was cry when I walked into the room. Maggie was a stabilizing factor for me and once we hugged I was able to sit down and repeat what the doctor had said. The look on Brian's mother's face was one that I wished I'd never had to see. We held on to each other and cried. Then we walked back in to be at Brian's side.

There was no change in Brian that day, and we took turns sitting at his bedside and sharing our thoughts.

The next evening, we sat eating supper and chatting just feet from Brian's bed. All of a sudden he opened his eyes and raised his right arm. In his hand he held a small stuffed monkey. His arm stayed upright for several minutes. He did not speak. I looked into his eyes and bent to kiss him. Less than a week before, Brian would have said '*I love you*', when I whispered in his ear. Now there was no verbal reply. I knew however that he heard me. His mother stood on the other side of his bed. She placed her hand on his cheek. I knew her heart was breaking. While he held his right arm in the air he lifted his left arm as well. In that hand he held on to the antenna of a rubber toy caterpillar. We marvelled at how long he held his arms upright. I secretly hoped that this would be the first of more positive movements. I wanted so much for him to be responsive if only for a fleeting moment. It was not to be. Within thirty minutes Brian closed his eyes again and his arms went still by his sides.

There was no change in Brian on Thursday and Friday. I knew it was time to update my siblings. I knew these would be difficult discussions and braced myself, trying desperately to keep my emotions in check.

On Saturday morning Maggie caught her flight home because she had business commitments that could not be changed. My heart broke for her as I knew she wanted to stay to be there for Brian's mother, who was her sister-in-law. I also needed her.

My brother Wayne arrived and we spent most of the day in silence, each of us reflecting on why we were all together. As the day progressed Wayne called my brother Rod. He and my sisters-in-laws drove up from Calgary. By 7:30 that night we were all seated on the couch watching a movie on television as Brian slept quietly. I don't remember what the movie was, and truly none of us was paying attention, but it was a diversion. We each took turns, without saying anything, to stand up and check on Brian. Whispers were all that could be heard, silent words to a friend. I called Brian's best friend and invited him to come and say goodbye.

I chose to not allow our nieces and nephews to come and say goodbye. I did this out of love for Brian and our nieces and nephews. I wanted them to remember him as the loud and fun Uncle, who told them he loved them and gave out big bear hugs. The Uncle who encouraged them to be all they could be. The Uncle that made them feel special. Now he lay motionless, unable to communicate. This was not the image I wanted imprinted on our nieces and nephews. I knew in my heart I had made the right decision, even though at the time not everyone agreed with me.

One by one we all said goodnight to Brian. I had not been in bed more than a few minutes when I heard Brian's breathing intensify. I jumped from my bed and my movement woke Brian's mother who was in the next bedroom. I don't think she was truly asleep. I spent most evenings getting by on cat naps and getting up and checking on Brian several times through the evening. His mother was subconsciously on alert as well.

I bolted to Brian's bedside, with his mom right behind me. We stood and looked down at Brian. I rubbed his arm and talked to him. I didn't know what else to do. My heart was pounding so hard, and I could not detect a pulse in Brian. *Oh God, please don't let this be happening. I am not ready to let go of him yet. Please God.*

Then I ran to the stairs leading to the second floor. I tripped trying to climb the staircase and almost fell on my face. I lay on the stairs and called out to Wayne. My yell woke Rod and Linda who were asleep on the sofa bed in the room next to the stairs. Within minutes we were all at Brian's bedside.

My prayer was in vain. Brian was gone. He had silently left us. I wept. There were no goodbyes. No exchange of words. I had lost everything that meant anything to me in a code of silence. Brian was not in pain and I was grateful that he passed away peacefully. I was selfish though, because he had not fulfilled his life. He, we, had plans. There were things to do. Brian had no regrets, I knew that. We had lived life, but he would want to keep living. What destiny awaited him?

We all cried and hugged. What else could we do? Then we silently parted, each of us moved to a corner of the living room and stood alone in our grief. One by one we returned to Brian's side and said our goodbyes. It had all happened so quickly and so silently. I had never expected that it would be this way.

As part of the medical instructions that had been given to me, I was told that we could take personal time before we called about Brian's passing, which is what we did.

In time I called 911, for the paramedics as I didn't know who else to call. Within minutes of the ambulance arriving, two police officers knocked on the door. Within a couple more minutes we saw the reflection of headlights on the deck and two more officers came through the door. And lastly a more senior officer arrived. We all stood next to Brian. There was myself, Brian's mother, Wayne, Melissa, Rod, Linda, two paramedics, and five police officers.

I should have expected that the police would be dispatched based on what I had seen on all the crime television programs I watched, but it just wasn't something I had thought about. The police, I was told, were here to investigate.

I am glad we took the time to say our goodbyes before they all arrived. It now felt official. Our home had been taken over and I was no longer in charge. Linda and Melissa made coffee and tea. I needed something stronger, but I accepted the cup of hot liquid that got placed in my hand. Four police officers sat at the kitchen table next to where Brian lay. They asked questions and wrote notes in tiny flip open notebooks. The more senior officer advised the ambulance attendants that they were not required, so they quietly walked out, closing the door behind them. Then she went and sat in the living room, where she started to conduct interviews and took our statements. I was still surprised by it all but politely answered her questions, describing what had transpired.

My sister-in-law Linda made sure that everyone had something to drink and kept offering something until they accepted. I knew that was her way of getting through what was happening. It wasn't until months later that I realized that Linda was not only coping with the current situation but also it was the anniversary of her mother's passing. I wonder now what was going through her mind. She must have been struggling to just get through those hours.

When I was done talking with the officer I went back and stood at Brian's side. As I looked at him, I wanted to crawl on the bed with him and hug him one more time. Bending over him just was not sufficient for me. I rubbed his arm while I listened to everyone talking around me.

I remember the attendants from the funeral home arriving. I had not called them so I guess the police have. I stood silently as they covered Brian and slowly left the house.

Within a few hours everything was concluded and we were back to just the family in the house. We stood quietly and looked at each other. The strain was evident on everyone's face. None of us knew what to say.

Within a day everyone had returned to their homes, more than three hours away. They all had obligations. The house was silent and I was totally alone.

PART III

Life without Brian

FORTY

wonder what I have done wrong to be punished by losing Brian. I think of family and friends who had all faced incredible cancer diagnoses and they had all pulled through. Why couldn't Brian have been lucky and been a cancer survivor? Why was he chosen to be a statistic? He had faced all obstacles with optimism and believed that together we could overcome anything. But this monster tackled Brian's brain and removed his ability to formulate a defense.

I look out the window and feel the heavy weight of being left. There is no one to talk with. There is no one to listen to me. I am totally alone. I want to yell at the top of my lungs.

I go to the cupboard and pull out a large black garbage bag. I pull the sheet from Brian's bed, and not wanting to ever see it again, roll it into a ball and place it in the garbage bag. I do the same with the spare sheet and pillow cases. Then I pull out the sanitizing wipes and wash the mattress thoroughly, twice. The antiseptic smell reminds me of all the times the bed has been washed, one half at a time, while Brian lay on his side. The bed would be sanitized from top to bottom and a clean sheet slipped over the corners, and then Brian would be rolled back and the same process would play out on the other side. In less than ten minutes the bed was sanitized and tidy with clean sheets.

I turn and walk to the back door. I pull on warm clothes and go outside to walk in the fields. I take our dogs, Hayley and Danny. The walk and fresh air do nothing to take away the pain in my gut. Every part of my body seems to be aching. I want to crawl into a ball and hope that things will be normal when I wake up.

Many people will tell you that God only gives you what you can handle, but I wonder what my limit is. Brian and I had so many plans. We had lived for today, not putting off travelling for when we retired. We had, however, foregone going out for expensive dinners and we only rarely went to a movie or concert. We saved our money for the annual vacation that was for many years to a beach destination. We had saved for retirement, and in the past two years had started to make more detailed plans. We were looking forward to travelling for long periods and getting away from the rush of day to day living and two careers. We even have a retirement home that we expected to live in for a few months to get away from the cold grips of winter in Alberta. Now all those plans are meaningless.

My thoughts turn to my mother. I could hear her telling me to sit down with a beer, relax, reflect and things will be better. Professionals will tell you not to drink alcohol when you are depressed, but for me, I much prefer a beer to a pill. I decide to have a rum and Coke instead, a preferred drink for Brian in the cold winter months. Dark rum and Coke always reminds me of our years on the farm in Saskatchewan.

We were in our mid 30's when we bought a one-hundred-sixty acre farm just outside Saskatoon. We were young, in love with life and wanting to make the old dairy farm our piece of heaven. It was a dream come true for Brian. As a young boy Brian had spent many summer vacations at his Uncle Johnny's ranch in southern Alberta. Those days had a tremendous impression on Brian. Wide open spaces, stars at night, total peace and quiet. For a kid you would think it would have been lonely, but not for Brian. There was always something going on, and when there wasn't work to be done, Brian would sit with a book and read while perched on Chapel Rock overlooking the farmstead. I was lucky to have met Johnny several times, and he was a one of a kind true pioneer.

I take a long sip of rum and savour the taste in my mouth before swallowing. Dark rum has a distinctive taste. Dejavu waves over me.

We are on our property in Saskatchewan, which I always referred to as our farm. Brian always called it 'the ranch'. It is bitterly cold outside, but we must go out and feed the cattle. Brian ventures out to start the tractor as I struggle to pull my padded overalls on over my jeans and sweater. For those of you reading this that are familiar with the Michelin man commercials, you will know how I feel. In the depths of a minus forty degree temperature, you dress in layers, and a pair of quilted overalls will keep your skin from freezing, but they also make you feel swelled all over and make you walk like a penguin. I am finally done and open the door. The cold air slams me. My God, why do we live here, I think to myself.

As I step from the door I see Brian on the tractor with a bale of hay on the picks. I walk ahead and open the gate to the corral. The cows have heard the tractor running and know that means food, so they are all standing ready to greet me as I swing the gate open. I must push them back. I do not need to worry about them escaping into the yard as they will follow the tractor once Brian drives through the gate. Once Brian drops the bale in the feeder he returns to the stack and picks up another. I stand with my back to the wind waiting for him to return. This is repeated three times with feed and then Brian makes two other trips to bring in straw for the shelters.

Spreading straw has always brought me joy. When he drops the bale in the shelter my job is to cut the bale strings that hold it together. I pull with all my might on the strings trying to free them. When Brian drops the second bale he jumps down from the tractor and together we roll the bale across the shelter. This is not an easy task and takes all the energy I have to help him. The calves are always excited when we put out straw and they are not afraid of us. They romp and play butting each other and us while waiting to get in the warmth of the straw. Brian always leaves a part of the bale unrolled and the cows and calves play with it and spread it farther. When we are done I close and lock the gate as Brian puts the tractor back in the shed. We go into the house and I make us a rum and Coke and we sit by the fireplace.

I open my eyes. God, we were so happy in those days. It was just the two of us, working together. I stand and walk into our bedroom. I crawl under the covers with my clothes still on and try to garner some comfort.

I wonder why I am all alone. Was there not someone who could be with me? I drifted off to sleep.

I think of calling my brother Wayne. He has always been my closest sibling. When Wayne was still in his teens Brian had hired him and that was the beginning of a friendship and unique bond between them. Wayne was fifty-three and Brian had been a part of his life for thirty-nine years.

I think the first born son in all families takes on a responsibility reserved for their position in the family chain. My brother Wayne was no exception. He is a carbon copy of our father and is more and more like him with each year that passes. Our father was an honest and loyal friend; steadfast; unflinching in tough times and someone you could count on in a pinch. These words also describe Wayne.

In recent years Wayne and I had relied more and more on each other with the death of our mother and father. Wayne is also the one I called to come to Panama and help me get Brian back to Canada. I know that calling Wayne will probably only make me cry when I hear his voice so I decide against it.

Everyone will tell you that when faced with adversity you will get through it. You work on instinct because you have to. Now was not the time to fall apart. I had a difficult job ahead of me. I had to make arrangements for cremation.

I was fortunate that Brian and I had taken the time and effort to have wills drawn up and I knew what his wishes were for all of our married life. We had written our first will shortly after getting married. Before we left Canada to live in Panama in 2010 we had updated our wills and added personal directives and power of attorney documents. At the time of course we never expected that one of us would need to rely on these documents so soon. I was grateful now that our affairs were in order.

I stand for a minute staring at the dresser. Then I open the drawer and look at Brian's things. I take out a pair of white socks and blue underwear. Then I pick a pair of his jeans from the shelf. I look in the closet at all his shirts. I pull a sleeve to my nose and smell it, hoping to capture his scent. The only smell was of laundry detergent. Everything is laundered. I need to feel Brian close, so I walk into the bathroom and spray his cologne on the back of my hand. I lift my hand to my nose and close my eyes, visualizing Brian as I breathe in.

I return to the closet and stare at all his western shirts. I select a striped multi-colored shirt that he had worn often. I pictured him in the shirt at the rodeo.

I fold everything neatly, tucking the socks and underwear between the jeans and shirt and place it in a bag to take with me. I sip my coffee and pace as I wait for Larry to arrive. I climb into his truck and settle the bag on my lap. I stare out the window at the fields along the highway. Neither of us speaks as Larry drives to the local funeral home.

I dread the job ahead of me. We walk through the large wooden door into the lobby. We look at each other and both continue to stand, even though there were comfortable armchairs. I step over to an end table and take a couple of tissues from the box and hold them in my hand. There is peaceful music playing that makes me feel even worse. It would be nice to hear something upbeat, but of course that is not the music of a funeral home. We make small talk until we are ushered into a meeting room. It is a brief conversation as I explain that we only require the cremation service and that Brian's Celebration of Life will take place in another city. The Funeral Director completes the paper work explaining everything and then hands me the papers to sign. I gulp and close my eyes, not wanting to be making arrangements to have my husband cremated. Next it came to selecting the casket. I know already what Brian wants, and as Larry and I walk through the room listening to the Funeral Director describe each type of wood and the expensive linings, we both point to a plain pine box and in unison say *'This will do.'*

The Funeral Director probably thinks we are cheap, but in actual fact Brian would prefer to spend money on lunch or beer for family and friends than a box that is going to be burned. Brian and I have joked about it numerous times in the past, never assuming that either one of us would need to be making the decision any time soon. *Just put me in a pine box'* Brian would say.

I do not sleep that night replaying the meeting in my mind. Today I will be saying my last goodbye. I make coffee which I drink as I shower and dress. I sit on the edge of the bed and bend my head. I feel weak and am uncertain if I can stand. The pounding of my heart is ringing in my ears. I know I must pull myself together, so I reach deep inside and find the inner strength to face the day. I wipe away the tears and stand. I take in a deep breath and walk past the hospital bed which still rests in our dining room. I think how nice it will be when this is removed.

I wish there was someone I could call. I feel so all alone. Even more I wish I had someone who would comfort me through the day ahead.

Like a robot I remove a metal travel mug from the cupboard and fill it with coffee. I walk into the garage and climb into my vehicle. I double check my purse for tissues and place some on the passenger seat for easy access when I am driving. As the garage door rolls up I breathe in deeply and turn the key in the ignition. Even as the engine comes to life I am unable to put the vehicle into gear. After a few minutes I back out of the garage and sit in the driveway watching the garage door slowly roll back down. I want so much to run back in the house and hide under the comforter. My lips are quivering and I know that it will only be seconds until the tears flood in. I lean my head on the steering wheel. I am alone, all alone and I can't help but wonder why I have no friend at my side. I must drive alone to the funeral home to see Brian for the last time. The tears run steadily down my face as the full weight of Brian's loss is upon me. My hands are trembling as I turn the steering wheel to pull out onto the highway. A car swerves and goes around me. I look down at the speedometer and realize I am way below the eighty-kilometre speed limit. I step on the gas and merge onto the main highway. I stay in the right lane of the divided highway allowing vehicles to pass me. I am in no hurry to get to the city.

I am trembling when I arrive, but I am not cold. I folded my arms across my chest and rub my upper arms as if it would bring me comfort.

"Are you ready?" the Funeral Director asked.

I shook my head.

"Follow me, please."

I walk behind him to the end of the hall where he stops and opens a door. He does not step into the room and keeps his hand on the door handle. I step past him into the room.

"Take all the time you want," he says as he pulls the door closed behind him.

I stand frozen in place. I look across the room and see Brian resting in the pine box. I want to walk over to him but my legs feel like rubber and I don't think I can move. I breathe in and close my eyes. My heart is racing. Finally I gather strength and cross the room. I look down at Brian.

His hands are folded neatly on his stomach and I place my hands over his. Cold, so cold. I rub his hands trying to bring warmth to him. He does not look like himself. His face is gaunt and pale. He is always so tanned I thought. There is no life left. Tears run down my cheeks and I wipe away the tears with the tissue that is squeezed in my hand. With my finger I trace the lines on his shirt up his arm. I cup his face in my hand. I touch what is left of his hair. I wish I could wrap my arms around him and take him back home with me. I want to turn back the hands of time. I stand and stare at him. I start talking to him not wanting to leave for fear of being lost in my grief.

Finally I bend down, kiss him for the last time, and whisper in his ear. *Goodbye my love.* Through eyes that are flooded with tears I turn and leave the room, not looking back.

I do not stop to talk to the Funeral Director who stands outside the door when I exit. I walk past him, and leave the building and walk to my vehicle. I climb inside and weep. I do not know how long I sat there before I put the key in the ignition and drove the vehicle out of the parking lot. I do not remember driving the twenty minutes it took to get home. I was on instinct, following the road I had driven hundreds of times, back to our acreage. I walk into the comfort of our home and collapse on our bed. I pull my knees up to my chest and rock. I weep out loud. I wish there was someone at the house with me. I wish there was someone to talk to. My mind and body are just worn out. I pull up the comforter over my head to block out the light. As I doze off I am grateful that there is time before I must deal with another Funeral Director. It will be almost another two weeks until the Celebration of Brian's life will take place.

I wake up and realize less than an hour has passed. I get up and walk down the driveway to get the mail. Three more cards arrive today. I walk back and sit on the deck. It is a beautiful sunny day, the type of day that Brian and I used to enjoy with long walks in the fields with our dogs. I open each card slowly and savour every word that is printed and written. I can tell that the cards were picked with care and were so meaningful. Reading the personalized words brings tears that stream down my face. I wipe them away with the back of my hand.

My mother had taught us the importance of purchasing greeting cards. She would stand in the card store and read card after card until she found one with exactly the sentiment she was looking for. Not every card would do. To my mother there was no point of sending a card if you hadn't taken the time to find the right card. She never understood people who just grabbed any card. She enjoyed hunting through the stacks of cards at a Hallmark store. All my siblings have been on card shopping trips with Mom, and we all follow in her footsteps and ensure every card sent whether for a birthday, to say thank you or to express sympathy is a card picked specifically for the intended recipient and is being sent from the heart.

I think of all the cards Brian and I have exchanged over the years and I am grateful that I have saved them. I think back to one year when money was tight and we had foregone Christmas presents for each other. Brian hand made me a card and that has always been a treasure to me. I have kept it in my top drawer for almost twenty years. I walk into our bedroom and pull open my drawer. There at the bottom, in a plastic sleeve is the card. I pull it out and sit on the edge of the bed before I pull it from the protective sleeve. I read the words slowly and savour the moment. Then I gently put the card back in the plastic sleeve and tuck it under my underwear in the drawer. I will never again get a card from Brian.

I walk from the bedroom and stare at the hospital bed that still sits in our dining room. I trace my finger along the mattress. It is forest green in colour and plastic, of course, for ease of cleaning. Then I lie down on it. I look up at the ceiling and think of all the days that the ceiling was Brian's view when he opened his eyes. I jump off and incline the bed. I get back on and see the view as Brian would have when he was sitting up. I could see the living room and out the dining room window. I could even see the horses moving in the corral. I knew, however, that Brian's sight would not allow him to see such distances. I expected that he probably only saw a blur beyond the window. I let a few minutes pass before I get up. I decide to call the home care company, again, to see when they will pick up the bed. It is hard to look at it each day – empty. It is a constant reminder.

I sit down and check emails. There are so many messages of sympathy from long distance friends and work colleagues. I am surprised at some messages from people I had worked with more than five years previous. Many emails expressed surprise as the senders had not known of Brian's illness. As I scroll down the unread emails I see messages from my staff in Panama. I start to cry as I read their messages and heartfelt words of sincerity. I count and there are six emails from staff who did not know English, yet they had translated their message into English for me. Their words were compassionate and caring. I immediately feel comforted.

I pick up the phone and call my friend Victoria in Panama. Hearing her voice is comforting. She is the person I leaned on in Panama when Brian was undergoing treatment. She is someone I can talk to. I share my sorrow and we both cry. I wish I was there to get a hug from her. I must cut the conversation short as emotion overtakes me.

FORTY ONE

espite how detached I feel, I know that I must start planning a celebration of Brian's life, of our life really because I had not just lost Brian; I had lost the life we had. Nothing would ever be the same again.

As I look at the calendar to determine a date for the service, I see the next two appointments that Brian has at the hospital; for blood work and an MRI. I call the hospital to cancel the appointments and get bumped to three departments before I am able to get off the phone. I must explain to each person that answers the phone why Brian will not be keeping the appointment. It is all I can do to not cry while I talk. I am glad when I finally get off the phone and stroke out the appointments on the calendar.

I have decided to have Brian's service in Calgary, a city three hours away. I do this as most of our family lives there, so it will make it easier on them. It is also a more central city for family and friends to fly or drive to. For me, unfortunately, it meant that I needed to meet with two separate funeral homes.

As I think about who will want to give remembrances, I start to go through our photo albums to select the photographs that will be in the video at the service. I am grateful that I have always printed our photos and they are all held in photo albums and are easy to access. I start with the most recent photo album and flip through the pages, selecting photos that include family and friends. It is a big task as there are twenty-eight photo albums. I pull photos and scan them so that I can hold on to the originals. They are all I have now, and I am scared to part with them to the funeral home. Within an hour I realize scanning is just too time consuming so I stop.

I sit at the computer and eventually tears take over and I am no longer able to look at the albums. I get up and walk from the room.

Later that day I take all the photo albums to the dining room. With a drink in hand, I start with the most recent album and select photos and put them in piles on the spare bed. I stack them by family. I want to ensure that I do not overlook a family member or friend. Once I am through half of the albums I take a break, proud of what I have accomplished.

I go outside and stand on the deck. It is a clear crisp night and the sky is lit up with stars. I wish Brian could be out here to stare up with me. I look at the constellations and make a wish that I know will not be granted. All I want is to have my Brian back. I look up and smile, knowing he is in heaven smiling back at me.

The next morning, I select more photos and write on the back of each photo which album it came from. By midmorning I realize I have way too many photos, so I stop selecting more and start to go through the individual family piles. It takes me a couple of days, but eventually I am satisfied I have done a good job. In the end I trim the photos back to just one hundred. I could easily have selected two hundred. I think of all the memories created on vacations or at our home, and now Brian will never be a part of a photo again.

I have just finished selecting the photos when Brian's sister Katie calls. She is working on a verse for the memorial card. She reads me what she has written, and even though it is not complete it is a good start, and I like it.

Today I must travel three hours to Calgary to plan the celebration of Brian's life. Tears run down my face as I realize I have no one to drive with me. I wonder how I got to such a lonely place.

Close friends live only fifteen minutes away. They knew I had to travel to Calgary to make arrangements. They also knew that I had two dogs and a cat that needed to be cared for in my absence. I wonder why they do not offer to help. It is easy to blame them, but just as easy to blame myself as I am too stubborn to ask for help. Should I have asked or should they have offered? Thinking about it makes me sad and I cry. I should have realized then that our friendship had centered on Brian and that I was unimportant to them. It would take me several more months until I come to this conclusion.

I know my brothers would help me but they live in the city that I need to travel to, so it makes no sense for them to drive three hours to pick me up just to turn around and drive back the three hours.

I start to pack and break down in tears. It is a reflection of my lonely life. I sit on the end of the bed. I have trouble thinking of what I will need for the next few days. I wish that with all that I have on my mind that I didn't have to add a trip on the highway to all the thoughts bumping around in my head.

Heather, the Home Care Aide, has offered to feed the pets in my absence. Thank God for her.

I think back to all the people who have told me I am strong and will get through this. I need that strength now as I pull the vehicle from the garage. I concentrate as I drive on secondary roads until I reach the main highway between Edmonton and Calgary. I am glad that it is a divided highway and I no longer have to worry about approaching traffic, but I keep wondering if I really should be driving. Truly! I am sure that I would be considered a hazard as I was looking through eyes flooded with water like the windshield in a bad rain storm, except there were no wipers that cleared my blurred vision every few seconds. I am thankful when I finally arrive safely.

My brother Wayne will go with me to the funeral home. I bite my lip as we make the drive from Wayne's house. I want to stay focussed on what we need to do, and I know if I get emotional I will forget something. I have picked a funeral home that will allow us to have beer at the reception following the service. Brian was never a tea and cookies man, and I knew that if we only had coffee and tea at the reception he would be looking down from heaven saying *'Hey guys, where's the Budweiser?'* I was glad now that I was very organized and I had made notes as to what needed to be discussed.

The Funeral Director is a pleasant man, and it is easy to talk with him. We sit down at a large oval table in a nicely decorated meeting room. He recommends someone who is a Celebrant, and we decided this is a good option to preside over the service. It would not be religious, because again, that was not Brian. I left the photos with the Funeral Director. The photos will bounce back and forth through the years rather than reflect the timeline of Brian's life. I have picked photos of just Brian with family and friends. I have selected very few with me as I want the focus to be on everyone else. I know the good times that we had. I don't need to be reminded at the service.

Wayne and I leave after the meeting with a list of things we need to do in the next few days. At the top of the list was the music for the service as well as for the video. I have organized the pictures and numbered them so now we need to select music and match it to the pictures. I also have a folder of information which I can review and deal with in the following weeks.

That evening family members gathered at my brother Rod's house. We discussed the music that would be played during the video, prior to the service and at the reception. Rod and Brian loved music, and on weekends when we were all together they would stay up late into the night listening to music at a decibel level that disturbed the rest of us, but they thoroughly enjoyed. Rod knows best some of the music that Brian loved. I was content to watch my niece Crystal and nephews Cameron and Blair select songs on iTunes and then play them aloud so that we could all vote whether the song would be included or not. When we agree, then we decide where to place it on the CD we are preparing to give to the funeral home. The songs bring to mind many stories, and we laugh and cry recounting times with Brian. At one point Melissa was even dancing on the couch which brought lots of laughter. I know Brian would have been happy to know that so many of the family contributed to the music that would be played at the celebration of his life. I was happy to share this evening, and it took a big burden off my shoulders.

In addition to the music we discuss the food, beer and of course, the need for candy at the reception. Crystal is in charge of selecting the type of sour candy Brian loved best, which we would have in dishes at the reception. Those closest to Brian knew that sour candy and beer just went together.

When we get all that organized, we turn our attention to the memorial card that will be given out at Brian's service. I have selected the photos that will be used, and Wayne and I have already agreed with the funeral home on the interior content relating to the service itself. We start with the verse that Brian's sister Katie had started. It will be recorded on the back of the card. Reading the verse brought to mind other words which would more align with Brian, so we all sit down and read, reread, alter, sing the words, rhyme and un-rhyme the lines for a couple of hours until we agree on the final version. We keep the opening and closing lines Katie had written. She is not with us at Rod's as she is busy making two dried flower arrangements which will be displayed at the funeral home. Instead of vases she is using a pair of Brian's cowboy boots.

As we sit together we decide that all of us should wear our colourful shirts that we wore on beach vacations to the service. That will be a true tribute to Brian. I decide that I will wear one of Brian's favourite beach shirts under my suit. It is a red shirt, a color Brian had rarely liked prior to moving to Panama. Blue had always been his favourite colour and red was mine. He had bought the red shirt on a whim, not quite sure if he would like it, and yet it became his favourite.

In the end, the music, the verse, and the service are a combination of the efforts of those closest to Brian. It was a tremendous comfort to me.

The next day we return to the funeral home to drop off the music, discuss the final version of the memorial card and the last minute details.

A winter snow storm is in the forecast, so I decide that I should try to travel the three hours home today. I can't risk waiting until tomorrow in case the storm hits. When I leave Calgary it is sunny and the highway is dry. Good start I think. By the time I have driven less than an hour the skies are grey and the sun is gone. I look out the windshield and can see that the weather in all directions is getting worse. With each kilometre I drive I am grateful that there is no snow, hopeful that I will get home in good conditions. Then things change, and change quickly. The wind seems to have come from nowhere and snow is lightly drifting across the highway. Within fifteen minutes the highway is getting snow packed and I grip the wheel with both hands. I watch the tail lights of the vehicles ahead of me and concentrate to see if the road is icy. A truck passes me and as he goes over the brow of the hill I see him start to skid. Luckily he gets control of it and averts an accident. I have already slowed down from one-hundred-twenty kilometres to ninety. The weather progressively gets worse as I drive north, an indication that the storm is coming from that direction and had yet to hit Calgary when I left this morning. I am grateful that I have experience driving in icy and snowy conditions after having lived in Saskatchewan. Roads were not always plowed clear for a few days, so I needed to have fortitude to venture out some days. The blowing snow is creating icy conditions that can be treacherous because one driver that hit the brakes unexpectedly can create a pile up of vehicles. I know how to control the vehicle in a skid and just hope I do not need to use those skills today. I keep a safe distance between me and other vehicles. I listen to the radio as it updates about the highway and hear that sections north of where I am travelling have already been closed to avert further accidents. I have been counting the vehicles in the ditch as I drive. There have been fifteen. Some are snow covered, so I assume they hit the ditch yesterday. Those that are clear of snow I know went in the ditch today. That makes my heart rate quicken.

It is a nerve wracking trip, but eventually I get home safely. The three hour trip has taken me close to six hours. Hayley and Danny greet me as I pull the vehicle into the garage. I walk into the house and bring them in for company. Then I pour myself a stiff drink to calm my nerves. I have a hot bath and then crawl under the covers and sleep.

I wake up with Hayley staring into my eyes. She whines, letting me know they want to go outside. As I walk from the bedroom I realize the storm has stopped and the sun is shining brightly. I open the door and let them out, but they just stand on the deck and stare at me. I feel like I have neglected them these past few weeks, so I go and get bundled up in a winter jacket, toque, gloves and boots and join them outside.

I walk through the corral to the fields but realize the snow is too deep to get far. They run at my side, sniffing and enjoying the freedom of the field. Danny lays down and rolls and I wonder what she is rolling in. Horse poop I assume, and I make a mental note to check her before I let her back in the house.

I stop and look around. The tears start to flow. I cry over the life I now have. I want so much to have Brian at my side. I walk along the corral fence giving Hayley and Danny a good run. Danny wanders a long way from me, but Hayley only goes a few feet and then comes back to my side. She is a rescue dog and has always had separation anxiety. She needs to keep me in her sight. Eventually I turn around and head back to the house. I leave Hayley and Danny outside. As I bend down to take off my boots I hear the beep of the answering machine. I walk over and click the message button. It was such a simple message, but the words shook me.

Brian's remains are ready to be picked up at the crematorium.

I do not have the strength to deal with that today.

FORTY TWO

*B*rian's funeral service will be in two days. Like a robot I get into my vehicle and start the three-hour drive back down to Calgary. The drive gives me time to reflect. I play music that reminds me of Brian and I let myself be sad. I have done all I can now to prepare for a celebration of his life. Now all I need to do is get through it without falling apart. Never in my wildest dreams did I think I would be in this position at the age of fifty-nine. This day was something I had always thought was a long way into the future.

I drive directly to Brian's mother's and will stay with her. Maggie has flown from Vancouver Island and is there already. We sit up this evening and enjoy beer and wine and talk of all the good times over the years. There are tears of joy and sadness. The following day I talk with my brothers and Brian's sister and make the final adjustments to what we have planned for Brian's Celebration of Life. It will be a fitting tribute.

The day has come. It is November 9th and today everyone will say goodbye to Brian. I did not sleep well last night, however, I never expected I would. I start the day with coffee. Brian's mother wants me to have some breakfast, but Maggie and I both opt for coffee only. We take turns showering and getting dressed.

Brian's cousins, Ricky and Debbie are dropped off as they will ride in the car with us. We all hug trying to pull strength from each other.

"I could use a beer," Ricky says.

"Me too," I answer and move to the fridge. Ricky and I toast Brian while drinking our Budweisers, and Maggie joins us with her glass of wine. I look at the clock. It is 10:30 am, but I don't care. I know the beer will take the edge off and settle my nerves.

Brian's sister Katie and her husband Reggie are next to arrive. We all try to avert our attention to mundane talk so that we do not break down. Ricky and I are on the edge, and our tears are not easy to conceal. We all pace, waiting for the funeral car to arrive.

My thoughts turn to my father. Tomorrow is the anniversary of his passing, three years ago. I think about what an emotional few days it will be for my siblings.

"It's here," Katie says, turning to her mother.

I look out and see the long black limousine pulling to the curb. Ricky and I finish our beers and set the cans on the counter. Maggie tips back her wine glass and sets the empty glass beside our beer cans. Katie takes her mother by the arm and they walk out the door together. The driver has all the limo doors open when we step outside which makes it easy for us to crawl inside. Ricky carries a bag with more beers for the trip across the city.

Even though I have tissues folded in my purse I grab another couple from the box on the table. Maggie gives me a hug as we close the door to the house. We make small talk to keep the tears in check. Ricky and I have another beer on the drive. When we arrive we are shown into the reception hall to protect us from the crowd that is gathering and to give us a minute to calm our nerves before the service begins. The room is empty except for employees who are quietly organizing the room. I look over and see Myles. He is standing alone with his hands in his pockets. He does not move when we enter, but when I make eye contact the tears start streaming down his face. He bends his head and wipes at his eyes. I walk over to him and put my arms around him. We both cry. Myles has always had a special connection to Brian. When he was a teenager he would come out to our farm on weekends and spend the day working with Brian. At the time, he was at the age where Brian made a big impression on him. Now he was a grown man.

I always thought that Brian should have been a teacher. Children of our friends and even neighbour kids would migrate to him, and he has influenced so many young people. I like to think they carry with them Brian–ism's. He believed strongly in the importance of character. He would say that you need to be able to be happy and proud of the face that looks back at you in the mirror each morning. Myles was one of the young people that Brian had an impact on.

Myles squeezes me tight and I feel his sorrow. I know how much Brian meant to him. My thoughts drift.

It was on a weekend visit and Myles was driving the farm truck to take us back to the house. We had been out in the woods cutting fire wood for the day. The back of the half ton was stacked with the wood that, for the most part, Myles had stacked after Brian had cut it with the chain saw. Brian had jumped onto the tailgate after loading the chainsaw and both dogs onto the pile of wood. I jumped in the cab with Myles. I knew Myles was excited about being able to drive, and he wanted to show Brian that he could do it. He got the truck in motion after stalling it a couple of times. He steered over some dirt piles created by the moles. He had slowed down so I told him to give the truck some gas so it wouldn't stall. Myles stepped on the gas and before we knew it Brian went flying off the tailgate. Both dogs jumped off to be with him.

"Myles, what the hell are you doing?" Brian hollered.

Myles turned to me. "What should I do?"

"Just keep driving to the house. Brian will have calmed down by the time he walks there. We will start unloading the wood and that will help make him happier,"
I said with a laugh.

Myles looked out the rear window and then gave the truck gas and we bounced merrily over the field and back to the house. Brian finally arrived at the house and as was his nature, he had forgotten about falling out of the truck.

Inside I am smiling as I think of this story, and it gives me a moment of reprieve from the overwhelming grief.

The Funeral Director comes over. "It is time to go in now, if you will all follow me."

We fall into step behind him, linked arm in arm. We need to exit this building and walk outdoors to get to the main chapel. As we walk I keep my head down, as I don't want to make eye contact with the people who are crossing the parking lot to enter the chapel. It is taking all the strength I have to not completely fall apart. I know I do not have the strength to look into the eyes of family or friends. The music we had selected was playing melodically as we entered – 'Hallelujah'.

We are ushered to the front of the chapel and take our seats. The Celebrant stands and welcomes everyone. He speaks only briefly and then calls Larry to the podium.

I had picked Larry to give the Eulogy. He was Brian's closest friend. He reads the eulogy that I have prepared, interspersed with his thoughts and memories of Brian. Larry shares stories about how Brian always beat him at Trivial Pursuit, all the beers they had shared, all the vacations and visits to our farm. He talks about Brian's gentle manner and the hugs that made everyone warm to his presence. But most of all he describes the unique and special bond that he had built with Brian over many years. I can see the pain on his face and in his eyes.

Sophie, our niece steps up to the podium. She sniffles and wipes at her tears as she starts to speak. She tells everyone how Uncle Brian had nicknamed her 'Chip Dip'. She talks about how much she loved to visit us at the farm, playing on the hay bales, riding the tractor with Brian, the cow named Sarah, eating candy and giant Mr. Freezes. She talks about the fun that had created such happy memories.

Her pain is not masked as she tells how Uncle Brian entertained her and her brother on visits and how he always treated them as if they were his own children.

Tears run down my cheeks as Sophie tells how close she felt to her Uncle, how he always encouraged her, how she knew he was always there for her and the huge impact he had on her life. In closing she reads a poem she has written about her Uncle that I'm sure brings tears to many.

My bothers Wayne and Rod have to follow the emotional comments of both Larry and Sophie. Wayne starts to speak and pauses. He takes a sip of water before he speaks again. He makes a joke that he wishes the water was beer to give him strength. He talks of not just his brother-in-law, but his friend. He tells of vacations spent together, of all the laughter, and all the beer and he makes everyone laugh as he mentions beer several times. He wipes at his eyes before he carries on. He talks about how much he enjoyed being around Brian as he was always sure to have a fun time. I know Wayne's pain is coming from deep inside. He has always been close to Brian.

Wayne tells a couple of funny stories which gets everyone laughing before he turns serious again. He hesitates before recounting time spent alone with Brian at the Hard Rock Hotel in Panama before the three of us flew back to Canada. This was very personal time between just the two of them. They had sat together and talked about the old days.

In closing, Wayne asks everyone to close their eyes and picture Brian on his horse riding through the fields at his Uncle Johnny's ranch. I was able to picture it as Wayne spoke.

Rod stood at the podium rocking back and forth and giving words of encouragement as Wayne spoke. Now it is his turn. He steps up to the podium but then moves to the side where he can move while he talks. I know that is how he is keeping his emotions under control. He tries to be uplifting with stories and has the gathering laughing. He talks about a time when he and Brian went horseback riding and Brian's horse was acting up and started to spin to buck Brian off. Rod just sat on his horse and watched it all from a safe distance. In the end the horse won out and Brian was thrown, but he only cared about not spilling his beer in the process. Rod is animated telling the story and has everyone laughing.

He talks next about visiting us in Panama and what a great time we all had. Then he turns somber as he talks about when his son Cameron and Brian went tandem parasailing in Panama. It is a funny story about the weight imbalance and the angle the parasail tilted. He can no longer hold in his grief and tears overcome him.

When Wayne and Rod returned to their seats, I could hear sobs and an outburst of grief and knew that it was my youngest brother Rod. He had tried to be strong, but now he no longer needed to hold in his pain.

Wayne and Rod's comments were sometimes serious, but other stories were light-hearted, bringing joy and laughter to the gathering. Brian was a big brother to both of them and always brought excitement and laughter into their homes. Now all they felt was pain.

I think back to when Rod's son Cameron was young and he decided to emulate Brian by dressing as a cowboy. He wore his jeans, blue jean shirt and cowboy hat everywhere. We have a picture of Cameron on Brian's lap and they look like father and son dressed identically.

Wayne's son had been named after Brian.

Next it is Crystal's turn. Through her tears she tells everyone that she joined our family when her mother met my brother Wayne. She tells how Uncle Brian welcomed her with open arms and made her feel she was welcome and that she belonged. That was the type of man he was. She talks about how Brian lived in the moment, how he was always present, how he enjoyed every day. She shares a story from a vacation in Mexico when she sat on the bow of a boat with her uncle as they watched dolphins frolic. She says she always thought of her uncle as a superhero – an Avenger.

Like all our nieces and nephews, Crystal had a close and special relationship with Brian. As I listen to her I think back about the impact Brian had on her.

When Crystal was set to graduate grade 12, she invited Brian to the graduation ceremony. I don't remember being invited. It was a bond between the two of them. We were living in Panama at the time. It was easy for Brian to tell Crystal he couldn't afford the time away from work, and also it was expensive as the plane ticket was over one thousand dollars. Crystal was disappointed when he told her he couldn't travel back to Canada, but she understood. Secretly Brian was plotting with Crystal's mother, Melissa to attend. It was a secret that got more and more difficult to keep as the weeks passed. When Brian finally walked through the front door of their home, the look on Crystal's face was hard to describe. I think of it now, remembering the photo Melissa had taken.

Brian's cousin Ricky is called next to the lectern. He stands and walks forward with his head down. He is shaking as he places his hands on either side of the podium. He stares down.

"I don't know where to start," he says pausing. "I have lost my brother. I can't express what he meant to me."

He talks of horseback riding, of storytelling, of hours passed drinking beers and the bond since childhood that no one else would ever fill. He talks about unique passages in time and how we can't relive those moments. Ricky's comments reflect the raw emotion that he is still struggling to deal with in accepting that Brian is gone. I feel sorry for him as I know that he will struggle for months to deal with the loss. I wish now that Ricky would have had the opportunity to visit us in Panama. He and Brian would have had such a tremendous time talking, drinking beers and walking on the beaches. I think it would have created memories that would bring Ricky comfort now and in the months ahead. Instead he was in pain thinking of days gone by.

Cindy and Lauren step forward together. Cindy speaks first about the amazing man they called their uncle. She talks about how much he meant to them. She shares stories of visits to the farm and of fun Christmases exchanging gifts. She talks about Boxing Day shopping with her uncle. Then Lauren speaks about visiting us in Panama and going on a fishing trip. Their stories are happy memories and bring laughter to the crowd.

As Cindy and Lauren return to their seats I reflect on all that was said about Brian. I am so proud of everyone who spoke. Their stories were heartfelt and brought tears, but also laughter, telling of a man who was loved more than their words could convey.

Next the video of more than one-hundred photos was played to the music that we had so carefully selected. The words from each song bring specific memories to mind, and I watch the video as if my life is flashing before me. The video is a true reflection and celebration of Brian's life, of our life, really.

Since the service was two days before Remembrance Day, poppies had been handed out as guests entered the chapel. Remembrance Day was important to both Brian and me. Brian had been in the Canadian Navy, and both our fathers had been in World War II. Growing up we had always attended Remembrance Day services. I remember shining my father's medals that he wore proudly as he marched with the other veterans. Brian and I had always tried to attend a Remembrance Day service wherever we lived. Brian loved retreating to the local Legion or Anavets Club following a Remembrance Day service when drinks flowed and stories were told by the veterans, and we could pay our respects to them in person.

At the conclusion of Brian's Celebration Service, guests are asked to place their poppies on a pillow at the front of the chapel. After I leave with Brian's mother and Katie, one by one the guests walk forward and place their poppies down. Some choose to place their poppies on Brian's cowboy hat.

I am emotionally drained but I need to muster the strength to walk from the chapel to the reception hall. I keep my head down, staring at the carpet rather than making eye contact with people as we proceed out. I know that I do not have the strength to look into the eyes of our family and friends and see the pain, the tears, their loss. I just can't do it. I have no more inner strength to draw on. I have used it all up and I am now operating on fumes.

I hold tight to Brian's mother, trying to give her strength as we walked. I do not want to bury my husband, but even more than that, no mother should have to bury her child.

The reception is held in another building which affords everyone the opportunity to walk across the parking lot and reflect, and in my case, the chance to catch my breath. In addition to a lunch and refreshments we included Budweiser beer and sour candies, which everyone knew were so Brian.

I stand in the center of the room and people line up to pay their respects. One by one people tell me how sorry they are, what a great guy Brian was and how much they will miss him. I feel like I am frozen in time as I listen, smile, and thank them for coming, hug them and wait for the next person to speak. I do not cry. I am not sure why, as the comments were so touching. I see my oldest sister in the line. She had distanced herself from me when our mother became ill. Through the settlement of my parents' estates she was remote and cold towards me. I am not sure why. I never understood what I had done. I know now it is probably difficult for her to have to face me. I know she had always liked Brian, and she had sent him a couple of letters while he was ill. I was also fairly certain that she had not liked me for many years and it just did not come to a head until the death of our mother. Today I am numb, so no matter what she says, I don't care anymore.

When the line ends I walk over and sit with our friends to thank them for coming. I know it will give me a chance to sit and catch my breath. Dudley jumps up and gets me a small lunch which I nibble on.

Music plays throughout the reception hall, and every once in a while I catch a phrase and smile as it reminds me so much of Brian.

I walk around to each table and thank people for coming and listen as they tell me a remembrance of Brian. I have spent my life with an amazing man that so many people loved and respected.

Brian was a son, a brother, a cousin, an uncle, a loyal friend and someone you could count on. He was a story teller. He had the ability to make everyone feel welcome and accepted. He was a mentor, and a teacher of sorts. He was someone that our young friends and relatives looked up to. He was a voracious reader and had a memory that made him a wizard at Trivial Pursuit. He had an entrepreneurial spirit and engaged in many business ventures. He had the gift of gab. He could engage anyone in a conversation and keep their attention. He was a community supporter and volunteered at countless charity events, Food Banks, homeless shelters and service organizations. He was a caring man who once took his horse to search through dense brush for a young girl lost in northern Saskatchewan. He had a brilliant mind that was now silenced.

But above all this, Brian was my life.

FORTY THREE

*T*wo days after Brian's Celebration of Life service I was back at home on our acreage. Brian's mother had come with me so that we could be together and reflect. I stood looking out to the fields. It was November, and while there was only a skiff of snow on the ground, I knew that winter was upon us. I had not been in Canada for the past three winters and wished I was not here now.

I have lost everything that meant anything to me. I wonder where you turn when your world has been turned upside down. What do you do when all that you have known is gone? The road map for my life has ended. There are no directions to follow. I wonder what compass I will follow. It is hard to know. No one makes a plan to be alone, so there is no resource that I can go to that will give me the steps to my new life. Together we lived a life that was planned and we had goals and dreams. I feel like I have lost a part of me, like an appendage amputated. I am no longer whole. Will I be able to function again? Will the pain ever end?

I sit with Brian's mom and we talk over coffee, each of us shedding our grief through tears. It all seems so senseless. We do not shelter our pain from one another. I have lost the man who meant everything to me, and she has lost her only son. We talk about Brian growing up and the man he became. She shares with me a story I have heard many times in the past. It is about a photo that hangs in our kitchen. Brian was just three at the time. He is dressed in typical western attire to attend the Calgary Stampede. He has on a cowboy hat, and a play holster and gun strapped around his waist. Everyone that saw the picture had always commented on Brian's stance and the smile on his face. It was a favourite photo to both of us. At Brian's service my brother Wayne had referred to Ruby's little cowboy, and this is the picture he was talking about.

We continued to talk about fun times when Brian's mom had lived close to us and all the places and celebrations we had shared. We both talk from the heart and share our inner feelings. It is good for both of us to share our pain.

In just a few short days Brian's mother returns to her home to be alone and I, as well, would now be alone.

I sit by myself and weep. I am mad that God has taken Brian from me. Why did he have to go? I can accept a stroke or even cancer. That I could deal with, but losing Brian was never in the cards. The tears are uncontrollable and I shudder. I talk to Brian and ask him why he left. Why did he go? We had so many plans. We have an unfinished life. I know I cannot carry on without him. I need him so. There is a pain deep inside and I think it is my heart breaking in two.

I walk into the bathroom and open the vanity. I stare at Brian's cologne still sitting on the shelf. I reach for it and remove the lid. I place it to my nose and breathe in. The scent is so distinctive. I close my eyes and imagine that he is standing next to me. I see that we are all dressed up and going out somewhere special. The smell lingers and I savour the comfort it provides. Then I place the bottle back on the shelf and close the vanity. I see my reflection in the vanity mirror. My eyes are bloodshot and my eyelids are red and look as sore as they feel.

Our photo albums have always brought me comfort. I sit down and open one, allowing myself to digress to a simpler, happier time.

The year is 1985 when we travelled to the Dominican Republic to celebrate our tenth wedding anniversary. It was our first experience at an all-inclusive resort. I look at the photos and my heart skips a beat. We look so young. We are laughing in the photos, and it brings warmth to my heart. I sit and think of how many vacations we have taken. Brian and I were fortunate to have enjoyed similar vacations in the Caribbean and throughout Mexico. In recent years, while in Panama, we travelled to many Central and South American countries. The photo albums are keepsakes and are all I have now, and I cling to them for comfort. I know we were fortunate to have travelled so much. Now when I sit here alone I am so grateful for all those memories. It takes the pain away for a few short minutes.

Grief for me is all consuming. I search my soul for peace, but there is none. *I am in the ocean – alone. I remember so many vacations when we went out deep sea fishing with family and friends. Now everyone on the boat has left and I am alone in the sea – forgotten and left behind. I feel myself slip under the water and sink deeper and deeper. The sunlight does not glisten through the water. It is dark and getting darker as I slip even further into the depths of the ocean. I don't know how, but I return to the surface and gasp for air. I look for the boat and a rescue but there is nothing on the horizon. I am alone with no one to care about me.*

I worry that one day I will not return to the surface. I will allow the weight of the grief to take me. I should not be alone. I know that. I do not know how to live a life alone.

Brian and I had arranged our lives so that anytime we weren't at work, we were together. We were each other's strength and support. He was the sail on my ship and I was his. We were happiest when the weekend came and we spent every minute of it together, without the need for outside contact. I remember going to work after a weekend and my co-workers would ask what we did for the weekend and I would reply, '*Nothing. We just stayed home together.*' Their reply was generally always the same. '*We could never do that,*' referencing their own relationships.

Even when Brian and I were separated by travel due to work commitments, I never felt alone. We would talk every day by phone and share in each other's lives.

Now that is gone. There is no one who understands. There is no one to call. There is no one who has my back. I need a big bear hug like Brian would give. A hug that allows you to slump as you know his arms will hold you up. Brian was my grounding rod. Like the lighting rod secured to metal buildings on our farm to keep them safe in a storm, Brian kept me safe. When the pressure of work was too much and the stress was making me wonder what I was doing being separated from him for my career, he would always comfort me. He was my confidant. He was the voice of reason when I could not be. But now there is no one to comfort me. There is no one to give me a big bear hug. No one seems to care.

Days slowly tick by. The silence is deafening. It has been five days since the phone has rung, and it just reinforces my feeling of abandonment. Brian and I never cared if anyone called. We were fulfilled just being with each other. But now I long for someone to call, to ask how I am doing, to give me the opportunity to talk and get my feelings out. I long for the house to be alive again. I want someone to care. I wonder how I became unimportant. I wipe the tears away with the back of my hand.

I realize that I don't know how to cope alone. I have never been alone. Many people may enjoy the solitude of being alone, of being able to do what they want to do but for me it was crippling. I thought back to my childhood. My parents lived in a one-bedroom house when I was born. My two older sisters and my parents were already sharing that bedroom. My bed was the bottom drawer of the dresser. My dad told me that he put wood supports in place so that no one could shut the drawer with me in it. It sounds funny now, but it was the truth. When I was two we all moved into a new three-bedroom home. My parents lived there for more than fifty years, and it was always the place I called 'home'. When we moved in, my oldest sister Kimberley got her own room and I shared with Janice. After Penny was born, Janice moved in with Kimberley and Penny and I shared a room. Later my brothers arrived and I went back to sharing with Janice as my parents shifted us all again. After I left home there were only a few months when I lived alone until I met Brian. I realize now that I never learned how to live alone and lacked the internal mechanism to be comfortable. I wonder if at my age I have the ability to ever become comfortable with just being 'with me'.

My attention is distracted when I look at all the cards still on the mantle. I decide it is time to put them away. I carefully take all the sympathy cards and place them in plastic sleeves for protection and then into a binder. I place the binder in the box where everything from the funeral home still is.

When I finish that job I walk into our bedroom and open the closet door. I look and see all Brian's clothes. I reach out and touch his blue jeans that are folded on the shelf. I look at all of his shirts. I wonder why we have so many clothes. I look at his favourite shirts and wonder what will become of them. It is painful to know that he will never again where these clothes. I thought I could deal with this, but I realize I am not strong enough to do this today. I step out of the closet and shut the door. Maybe tomorrow it will be easier.

I walk to the back door where Brian's outdoor clothes are hanging. These jackets were mostly used when Brian was out working with the horses or walking in the fields. They are less personal to me, so I decide to wash all the jackets, toques, scarves and hooded sweatshirts. Winter is upon us and I know that there are many homeless in the city that can benefit from these warm clothes. This motivates me, and for the next two days I wash and fold everything and take it to the homeless shelter. I feel good when I drive away knowing that someone will keep warm this winter because of these clothes.

I am struggling to get through the day. It has been a month since Brian passed away, and tomorrow would have been our thirty-ninth wedding anniversary. I look at his picture and cry. I think back on our life and want to be happy for what I had, but I cannot. I am not ready to live a life alone, but that is where I find myself. I try to change my mood by looking through the photo albums. Within an hour a smile has returned to my face as I see us enjoying Christmas and beach vacations with friends and family at our side. I have much to be grateful for. Deep down I know that, but it is difficult to be grateful for the situation I am in.

To change my mood and break the silence I decide to go shopping. As I walk into the mall the sound of Christmas music shakes me. I walk through the stores and blankly look at Christmas decorations. Brian loved Christmas. He would string up Christmas lights on everything he could. When we lived in Saskatchewan he even put Christmas lights on the barn. This was no small feat and it took him a couple of weeks. Then he strung lights down the hedge that lined our driveway. There were lights in his office, around the mirror in the bathroom, above doorways and anywhere that tape or a nail would secure them.

Holidays are a difficult time once you are widowed. Holidays are supposed to be a time to be happy and together. For me it is now an empty time where my sadness is magnified. I watch people buying Christmas presents and decorations and see the joy on their faces. I have always loved Christmas, but now all I feel is the loneliness inside. I think of all the Christmas parties Brian and I would have gone to. People were celebrating and attending parties that I no longer got invited too. As a couple you get invites, but for me, now alone, there are few invites. It has been seven weeks of pain. I know that I need to change it, but I don't know how. I pick up some chocolates and leave the store, walking quietly back to my vehicle. I wish there was someone to call and meet for lunch or a drink to celebrate the season. Instead I go home to an empty house.

My brother Wayne calls tonight. He tells me that his family, and my other brother Rod's family would be coming to spend Christmas with me. I am so happy that I cry. He has thrown me a life raft, something that I can cling to that gives me the lift I need to start thinking of someone other than myself. When I get off the phone, I call my mother-in-law and invite her to celebrate Christmas with us as well.

Brian and I have always done something to give back at Christmas. We have volunteered or purchased food and gifts for Secret Santa programs. Once again I think of the homeless shelter I was at last week dropping off Brian's clothes. I decide to also bring some Christmas cheer to the less fortunate in our city. I check the shelter website and make a list of items that are always in high demand. The next day I go back to the mall, but this time I am in high spirits and the Christmas music makes me happy, not sad. I fill my shopping cart with items from the list. I also purchase lots of candy canes because they are individually wrapped and easy to hand out. I picture someone smiling as they savour the minty taste. I add chocolates to the cart on my way through the checkout lane.

Two days later I arrive at the shelter with two large bags. As I turn and walk from the building I notice a man leaning against the building, one leg bent at the knee and his shoe resting on the brick. He is hunched over against the cold. He looks up at me and with a quiet voice said, "Merry Christmas to you."

I look over my shoulder. "Merry Christmas to you as well."

The next morning, I decide to start decorating the house. For me I never considered not putting up the tree as Brian and I always had, but now I have added incentive. Also I feel I will be honouring Brian by decorating the house. I know that I can't put up all the lights that Brian would have, but I can put up the tree. We had purchased an artificial tree a few years ago so I go to the basement and stare at the box. It looks larger than I remembered. I open the box and pull out a section realizing I will have to carry each section up the stairs separately. After three trips up the stairs I have all the sections laid out on the floor. I smile to myself once I have all the pieces put together. The tree stands in the same corner of the living room where we had decorated it for seven years before we moved to Panama.

I find the bin with lights. As I pull off the lid I see the plastic bags that are holding individual string of lights. Brian had packaged them this way when the tree was taken down last Christmas in Panama. I wonder how a year could have passed already.

Next I start to bring up the bins that hold our Xmas decorations. I am looking forward to decorating the tree, even though I know that it will be hard to look at some of our ornaments that hold special memories. I sit on the floor next to a box and unwrap the tissue paper which has kept my treasures safe. It is a brass ornament from my mother. Engraved on it is *Brandy 1986*. I think of my mother who always bought us Christmas ornaments engraved with the names of our pets. For my siblings, of course, the names were those of their children. Mom always wanted to treat all her children the same, so for us she had no alternative but to use the pet names. I stand and hang the ornament, thinking of the pet that has long since gone to heaven.

A few days later I have the tree decorated. I know that it will not be a normal Christmas, but I want to make the best of it. I sit this evening with only the tree lights on and sip a rum and Coke. The lights are all red as that is what Brian liked. I preferred multi coloured lights as it reminded me of Christmas when I was growing up. For now though, the lights are a reflection of Brian. As I stare at the tree I think of past Christmases. Brian and I would be sitting together on the floor by our tree with our dogs surrounding us, enjoying the warmth of the fireplace. Christmas was a time of giving, and the dogs would lie peacefully on their blankets with their new toys. Now I talk to the dogs, Hayley and Danny, and tell them about all the pets that have come and gone before them. I let them know that in only a few days we won't be alone.

My mother-in-law is arriving today, December 18th. This will give us a few days together before my brothers and their families arrive on Christmas Eve. It will be difficult to celebrate without Brian, but I think we both know that we must. The days together are healing as we talk about past Christmases when we lived at the farm in Saskatchewan. We laugh about the fun we had and the times when something would inevitably go wrong. At the farm when we were raising cattle, on more than one occasion Christmas dinner was interrupted by a cow or calf getting out of the fence and us chasing it down the highway. Or the water lines would freeze or the power would go out and we would be running around searching for candles. One year the hot turkey supper ended up being cold turkey sandwiches. Something we could look back on now and laugh, but both of us remember that things were not funny at the time. We agree that one thing we never worried about was keeping warm. Brian would always have the fireplace a blaze.

Over the few days together we go out to the mall and to dinner. On Christmas Eve we cook a ham as is our tradition. The aroma of cloves fills the air as we wait for everyone to arrive. I have lit the fireplace and the crackle of the logs is nostalgic to happier days. I get up and down and stare out the window, eager to see their trucks appear on the road. They will be travelling together, following each other.

"They're here," I say to my mother-in-law.

I slip on my boots and even though it is cold I walk out on the deck without a coat. It is only a couple of minutes until Rod's truck comes around the drive, then Wayne's. I am so excited to have company. Within minutes everyone is in the house – Wayne, Melissa, Crystal, Blair, Rod, Linda and Cameron.

The house is full and ringing with laughter. After dinner we play games and open one present tonight before we crash into bed. I sleep peacefully. I thought I would be troubled, but I am not. I think of Brian and all the Christmas Eve's that we had company and it brings me joy not tears.

In the morning there is considerable noise as we all talk at the same time and yell to be heard over the person sitting next to us. There are six kids in our family and growing up we always acted this way, and now it is just a part of who we are. Brian and I had a tradition of having champagne and strawberries on Christmas morning. We would sip champagne at the same time as a cup of coffee and eat oranges and candy from our stockings. Today I appreciate that everyone is open to keeping the tradition alive. As we take photos, tears run down my cheeks. I am both happy and sad. I recover quickly for the sake of my family, but inside I am thinking of Brian. I should be grateful for all the wonderful Christmases we have shared, but I am selfish and want Brian here to keep enjoying Christmas with me. I do not want to be alone, but no one asked me. They just took Brian. I did not get a say in my future.

On Boxing Day everyone leaves, including my mother-in-law and I am alone again. I hug and kiss them one by one and wave as the vehicles pull out of the driveway. I cry, but I have always cried when family leaves. It reminds me of all the visits in the past, but then when I felt sad to see family leave, I had Brian to comfort me. Now I stand alone on the deck. I walk inside the house and listen, but there is no noise. There are no voices. Toes, the cat, meows. I look down at her. I feel myself slipping back into the darkness of grief. I walk into the bedroom and lie down on the bed. I grip a pillow to my chest.

When people are around I put on a brave face. People tell me I am strong and will get through this. In time you will feel better, they say. But no one sees through the façade to know that I am crumbling on the inside. They don't see the dreams and nightmares that replay the last days in my mind. I wish to have more time. The pain in my heart cannot be repaired with time.

No one knows the sleepless nights. The gut wrenching loneliness. There are no words to describe my pain. The death of a loved one leaves us with a permanent scar. It is the simplest of daily routines that are painful. I miss the simple conversations we had over coffee. I miss having someone to plan and cook supper with and someone to watch television or a movie with at the end of the day. I miss our long conversations walking with our dogs across the fields, smelling the freshly cut alfalfa or freshly baled hay. I miss sitting on our deck and enjoying a cold beer on a hot summer's day. But most of all I miss Brian's hugs, the way he wiped away my tears with his thumb, the feel of his hand in the small of my back and the warmth of his body next to mine.

I wake up to the sound of the wind howling. I get up and look out the windows. It is dark, but I can see heavy snow falling in the glow of the barn light. Snow makes me worry now, as I have no way to clear the driveway alone. I never knew how to use the snow blower that we have, and now it does not function anyway. It is just one more thing I worry about that never used to enter my mind. Brian would always clear the snow, but this is just a reminder that I don't have him to take care of me anymore. I have no one to take care of me. I must figure it out alone.

It is only December, so we still have four months of winter left. Up until now the snow has not been too heavy, so I have been able to make a path up and down the driveway with my vehicle. I know as winter moves on that this will no longer work. A few weeks earlier I had called Trent and asked if he could come and feed the horses. He knows how to drive the farm tractor that is required to move the 1200 pound bales. When he was here, I got him to drive the tractor up and down the driveway and track down some of the snow in front of the garage. As the tractor has spears attached to move the bales, it is not possible to clear snow like when the bucket is on the tractor. He does the best job he can.

Now I worry as I listen to the wind and imagine the snow drifting in front of the garage. I worry that I won't be able to get the car out. I wish I was somewhere warm, walking on a beach and leaving the snow behind, if only for a short while. I think of all the vacations Brian and I took in the winter months to get away from the cold. We would walk on beaches and talk endlessly. Now even if I go somewhere warm I have no one to talk to, no one to plan with. It all seems pointless.

FORTY FOUR

I plan to spend New Year's Eve alone. During the day I walk out to feed Jesse and Dustin horse treats, and I let Hayley and Danny run around in the corral as the snow is too deep to venture out in the field. I stop at the barn and gather fire wood for this evening. I eat turkey soup for supper. Once I have the fire started I light some candles. Hayley lies at my feet as I sit in front of the fire, and Danny goes to lie down at the front door where she is cooler. Her thick winter coat protects her from the cold outdoors, but it also means she gets too warm in the house. Hayley, being a German Shepherd, has short hair and while it thickens in winter she is happy to be indoors, and lies quietly.

I struggle to open a bottle of champagne and remember the tradition Brian and I had. I look at the glasses resting side by side. They are hand painted wine glasses, not champagne flutes. Brian purchased the glasses years before and we had used them every Christmas and New Year's since. Today, alone, I pour champagne into a glass for him as well. At Christmas with family present I did not pour champagne for Brian, but now alone I can. I talk to him and let my tears comfort me.

Bri, do you remember last New Year's? We were in Panama. We golfed on New Year's Eve and stayed overnight at the Summit Resort. Remember all the fireworks. Then we golfed again on New Year's day before going back home. I took that really good picture of you in the golf cart, and you look like you are in the jungle but it was just one of the pathways on the golf course.

I do not hold in the emotion for fear that I will explode. I look down at my hand. I have been wearing Brian's wedding band on my right index finger. I spin the ring on my finger. Tomorrow will be the start of a new year, and I will forge ahead alone.

Like marbles dropped on the floor, people have rolled away. They have gone back to their jobs, their kids, and to the business of living their lives. I wonder if people think about me. Do they think that I have gone back to living my life as well?

How do I carry on when my life has ended? I have no job, no kids and nothing to make me want to carry on with life. I have no plans, no promises, no will to live. All our hopes and dreams are gone. All I have is a broken heart and loneliness. Hours drag by and I dread having to crawl into bed by myself. I lie on the bed and stare out the window. I see chickadees flitting from tree to tree and try to remember when I last filled the bird feeders. I think about it, but I don't really care. Let them find food for themselves.

As I lie there I realize that this is not me. I have always enjoyed filling the bird and squirrel feeders and listening to the chirping of the chickadees, the mountain jays, the sparrows, the meadowlarks and the siskins. Losing Brian has even robbed me of that.

Tears run down my cheeks and fall on the pillow. I eventually grab the sheet and wipe at my eyes. I see the mascara stain on the sheet and wish I had used a tissue instead.

Today is the day when many people start on their New Year's resolutions. They will have talked and planned something to make a change. I have no plan. I can't even think of anything I want other than Brian, and that is not possible.

I am tired. My body, my mind, and my heart are just worn out. I am emotionally drained. I can't remember the last time I slept through the night. Nothing makes sense to me. I cannot focus. The television is on but I just stare at the screen. I do not relate to the words being spoken. Time has no meaning.

I stand and walk to the living room. I sit down on the couch and pick up the remote control. I flip channels and stop on the comedy channel. The show 'Two and a Half Men' is on. Charlie and Alan can always make me laugh.

I remember how my mother also loved Two and a Half Men. At the time it was only a weekly show, not like the five days a week it airs now. Without fail, after each episode our phone would ring, and as I picked up the receiver I could hear my mother's laughter. She would recount the antics of Charlie, Alan and even Berta. Even though I had just watched the same episode, mom would tell me all about it and we would both laugh. I want to thank Charlie Sheen and Jon Cryer for the joy they brought into our lives.

I wish I could call my mother now and hear her voice. I know she would have comforting words. In 1988 Brian and I moved to Saskatchewan for a greater career opportunity. We left behind all our family in Calgary, more than seven hours away. Up until then I saw my parents every Sunday. After we moved I phoned my mother every Sunday. She would tell me about the happenings of my siblings and their families and I would tell her about our life on the farm. When I was done talking I would pass the phone to Brian, and he would talk to her and they would laugh. Lastly I would get back on the phone to talk with my father. Dad and I would talk about our livestock, about the crops, and about the weather that was such an important part of life on a farm. Dad would always tell me a story about growing up and the farms he had worked on as a young man in Quebec.

I had always felt close to my father. When I was young he would take me with him to the golf course. I remember walking the course and pulling or pushing his golf cart down the fairway each weekend as he enjoyed some much needed time on the course. I also spent time with dad in the winter when he would curl. I would sit and watch game after game, being happy just to be with him. He taught me to paint in the pantry at our grandmother's house. From that early age I learned how to properly use a paint brush, and I had always been the one who painted the walls in our homes.

In 2003 Brian and I moved back to Alberta to be close to family. We would now be just three hours away. We were close enough that weekend visits were frequent, and everyone could still get enough of the country life on our forty-acre property.

I think about my parents now and wonder how life is for them in Heaven. Do they see Brian? Do they see me?

My father had undergone heart surgery, and for years we had always expected that mom would out live him. He was stubborn and rarely followed the doctor's orders, so my siblings and I just accepted the fact that Dad would succumb to heart failure at some point.

We were in shock and denial when Mom was diagnosed with terminal cancer. Time slipped away so quickly. In her final weeks she was moved to a hospice. It was a nice facility with caring staff, and my siblings and I were allowed to stay overnight with our mother on a pull out couch. We made up a schedule so that each of us six kids could have time alone with Mom.

My siblings and I were like a loose thread on a sweater when pulled. We were unravelling under the stress of knowing that our time with Mom was coming to an end. Mom had dedicated her life to caring for us six kids and our father, yet no amount of care from us would change the outcome. I remember that last visit.

I arrived at the hospice and carried my bag with clothes to stay overnight. I sat down beside Mom's bed and chatted as she dozed on and off. I turned on the TV. Flipping through the channels, I stopped at 'Two and a Half Men.' Even though Mom was not awake I believe she could hear me as I told her what Charlie, Alan and Berta were up to. I tried to laugh. On that night laughter was difficult.

By morning I needed emotional support and called my two brothers. They arrived and we stood silent and looked down at our mother. As I had not eaten supper from the night before nor breakfast that morning, I talked my brothers into going out to lunch.

Over a drink we were able to relax and talk. We went back to Mom's room and then called our other siblings. By dinner time five of us were with our mother. Our parents were approaching sixty-one years of marriage, and we all agreed it would be too difficult on our father to bring him to be with our mother at this point. It was a difficult decision, but we did it with the best of intentions. I still to this day question it.

As we stood at her bedside we knew that Mom was in her final hours. A nurse would come into the room each hour and see if there was any change. The staff allowed us the privacy to be alone without their interference, but we knew the nurses were there if we needed them. In the most caring act, the nursing staff had changed Mom into a pink and green nightgown, which matched a pink and green fleece blanket that covered her bed. The blanket had been made by my mother-in-law.

We tried to talk amongst ourselves and tell stories as the arms on the wall clock ticked by. It was a painful time and we were all struggling. The tears were unstoppable and we went through boxes of tissues. We wiped away the tears, blew our noses and within minutes we started the cycle over again. We talked continually to Mom knowing that hearing is the last sense to go, so Mom was probably hearing everything we said. Anyone who has stood by in the final minutes of a life will understand how depleting it is. You want them to be free from pain, but when that last breath comes you want so much to have more time. You want to cling to those last minutes as you know that you will never again be standing by your loved one.

Minutes ticked away as we waited for the attendants to come and take Mom away. None of us but my brother Wayne was strong enough to stay with her. He stood at her side as the shroud was placed over her. I stood with my other siblings outside the room and we all telephoned our spouses to advise them. When all was done we decided that we would go together to tell our father. We followed each other in our vehicles to the house that our parents had lived in for fifty-four years, the house we had all been raised in. As we walked up to the front door, I breathed in to steady myself. Dad had sensed something was wrong and was distraught when we arrived. Maybe being married to someone for sixty-one year's gives you a sixth sense. For the second time in my life I saw my father weep. The first time was on the death of my mom's sister, Jean. We comforted Dad as best we could.

Mom had dedicated her life to raising us six kids. She always taught us to be close and to care for one another. Unfortunately, we were letting Mom's death separate us. We were all unprepared emotionally to lose her, and the pain was just too much.

Mom was the glue that held our family together, and losing her broke the binding of our family book. Like a book that has dried out, the pages of our lives started to pull apart.

Losing a parent is never easy. I now miss the comfort of her voice, her nurturing nature and knowing that she is there for me. I miss being able to talk with my father. Now I knew the pain of a greater loss - the pain of losing a spouse.

FORTY FIVE

I am drowning in a sea of despair. I feel like I am drifting on a raft, and there is no life vest and no one coming to save me. I close my eyes and see Brian and me walking hand in hand on the beach. I do not recognize where we are, and I do not try to focus on this. I just listen as Brian talks and we make plans for the year ahead. He talks of the cattle and our home and we reminisce about all the good times we have shared this year. The sand is warm and I skip my feet through the shallow water as we walk. I feel his hand slip from mine and I grasp for him but he is gone. I feel the ache within me and tears roll down my face. I cry for lost dreams, lost hopes, lost love. I cry for the hopelessness that is encircling me. I think of what will never be.

I feel powerless to change. I no longer feel in control. I have always been a type 'A' personality. I am a take charge person, driven to results and accomplishments both in my personal life and my career. Now my world has crumbled. I feel empty and unmotivated.

I know that I cannot succumb to the hands of depression. They are reaching out and pulling me into a dark hole. I try to resist, but it would be so much easier to just give in. I close my eyes and envision what I'd gain if I departed this world. I would be able to feel Brian again, his hugs, his lips, his body next to mine.

In heaven I would be able to see my parents, a cousin, aunts, uncles, and my grandmother. Also there is Brian's uncle and grandparents. The faces flash before me. I reach out and try to touch their faces. I realize just how many have left that I long to see. I want to wrap my arms around my tiny mother, to hear her voice, to see her smile. I want to have a conversation with my dad. Thoughts race through my mind and I know I will feel warm and safe once I am with them in heaven. I will be free from my grief, free from the pain of being alone.

I am so focused on being with Brian. The longing for him is overriding any logical thought. I do not think of who will need to deal with my death. I don't think of the impact on their lives or any pain that my passing will cause. The need to be with Brian again is all that I can think of.

The last photo I took of Brian before he had the stroke was taken on vacation in Panama. He was tipping a Balboa beer, giving a thumb's-up and sporting a huge smile. This is the photo I used on the memorial cards at the celebration of Brian's life. The photo now sits on the mantle. Every day I look into his eyes and tell him what he means to me. Today I pick up the photo and clutch it to my chest. I ache to be with him just one more time. I want to feel his arms around me, his body next to mine. Tears stream down my face as I feel the weight of what has been lost.

I get in my vehicle and drive down the road. I stop a few car lengths from the intersection of this rural road and the main highway. I shut off the engine. I know how easy it would be to drive my vehicle in front of a transport truck and end my pain. This for me seems like an easy option. I count the semi transport trucks that pass. The speed limit is one-hundred-ten kilometres per hour, so I know there would not be time for the transport truck to slow down before my vehicle would be struck.

I look down on the passenger seat to the photo of Brian. I touch my finger to my lips and then to his. I love him so. I don't know how to carry on. I need him. Tears stream down my face. A vehicle approaching the intersection beeps and startles me as it passes.

I think of my brother-in-law as he investigated accident scenes. I realize I don't want him to be dispatched to measure the brake skid marks, the torn carnage, the end of my life. It would not be fair to him. Next I think of my brother, Wayne, who I think would feel my loss the most. My conscience also thinks of the semi driver. It would not be fair to the driver emotionally as he would feel some guilt at my death.

I start the engine and turn the vehicle around and head home. I tell myself that God would punish me if I took my life, and God would not let me see Brian so it would all be for not. The only reason to leave this world is to be with Brian, so this reasoning works. I am happy for logical thought and the gloom lifts as I drive back home.

I know that I need to find help. I need to break the cycle of feeling hopeless. I search on-line for grief support groups or a widow support group but I find nothing. I call and make an appointment with my doctor.

The following week I get an appointment with a grief counsellor. I am excited. Finally I will have someone to talk with. I am anxious as I wait in the office. There is no one else waiting. Within ten minutes a plump woman steps from a door and invites me into a small room. She introduces herself and tells me she provides counselling for various situations, grief being one. She starts by asking me questions and I talk freely, baring my soul in the hopes of finding some comfort and understanding together with support and direction in dealing with my grief.

The counsellor can't relate to my situation and her suggestions are text book. Get up every day, get dressed, go for a walk, get out and meet new people, blah, blah, blah. It is of no value. She has no idea what I need.

Nothing she suggests is going to take away the pain of waking up every day alone and crawling into bed every night still alone. No amount of going out for coffee and lunch was going to fix my loneliness. I left feeling worse than when I had arrived. I went to the appointment with high hopes but I left full of disappointment.

I know I need to talk with people who understand the pain of losing a spouse, people who can relate to the ache when you wake up in the morning, the loneliness when you go to bed at night, and the longing for someone to hold you once again.

It has been four days since I have left the house. I know that each day I stay home alone is contributing to my current state. I decide to go to the library if even to read magazines. At least I would be amongst people. On my way to the library I think of books on grief. When I walk through the doors I immediately go to the computer and research about grief. I find a large collection and go home with four books.

For the next week I read books on grieving and loss. Reading stories of loss helps me to understand that what I am feeling is normal, and part of the process of grieving. I find that there are actually steps in the grieving process. I also learned that as part of the healing process it is important to be able to talk about my feelings in order to progress through the grief steps.

Brian's loss is overwhelming. I realize as I sit here that I am still grieving my parents as well. Not being able to call my mother just adds to my sorrow. Mothers are the glue that holds most families together, and our family was no exception. When we got the diagnosis that mom was sick with cancer, it was already too late for treatment. She was gone less than three months later. On her death our family shattered like a china tea cup dropped. Me, and my five siblings were struggling to come to terms with her loss, but not as much as our father who had lost his partner of sixty-one years. We all dealt with the loss differently, but the closeness between us was gone. There was no one now who kept all the extended family members in contact. Fourteen months after we lost mom, our father passed away. Less than three years later I lose Brian.

I sit down at the computer and key in the word *grief*. So many searches popped up that I was almost overwhelmed, wondering which link to pursue. As I scrolled down the page I stumbled on a website site called Widowed Village, a program of Soaring Spirits International. I sat for more than two hours and clicked on the various links within this site and was excited to read comments posted by other widows. This was a community of widowed people from all corners of the world. I immediately felt like I had an outlet for my grief.

For a week I go into the site daily and then feel comfortable enough to register on the site. This site becomes a life line to people who are also struggling to come to terms with their loss. There are numerous groups and I connect with people who, like myself, had been widowed in 2013. I read the questions asked by widows and the replies from those who had already dealt with the same matters. Seeing numerous comments to particular queries gave me a new perspective.

As I read today I see so many comments posted from widows talking about the strength and support they had from friends. Close 'girlfriends' had been invaluable as the widows walked the grief journey. As I read today I think of the person I called my best friend.

I stand and go to the room that holds our photo albums. I sit down and look through the albums and I see photos of us, of our families together, at our farm, at Christmas, on vacations. I could not turn more than a few pages without seeing photos of us together – a friend for over thirty years.

I wonder now where that person is. It was a friendship built over many years, but has dissolved like a sugar cube put in hot coffee. I wonder why. I think of all the times we have spent together, all the events, all the holidays and I am sad.

I remember her emails and the caring words. *'We are here for you, we love you, you have lots of support, we will do anything…'*.

Where I thought I would garner support there was none. For so many months caring for Brian I had needed help, and yet there was none. Her words were shallow and meaningless.

I wonder if she thinks of me as I think of her. Why did she throw me away when I needed her most, in my darkest hour. Had I done something?

I wanted to call her, to talk, to share my sorrow, to cry together, but I do not.

I think that our friendship had broken down years before, and I just never realized it. I had clung to something that was not real. I just couldn't bear it anymore. I had cried a thousand tears over the past months wondering what had happened. I could shed no more tears over it. In the end I add the loss of this friendship to the long list of my grief. I lost my mother, then my father, then my Brian, and now without any warning, my closest friend.

I look out the window at the large snowflakes that are slowly filtering down. It has been snowing most of the day, and I wonder how long it will last. The sun shimmers as if it is bouncing off crystals. It is magical. Images like today are when postcards are produced to trick people into seeing the beauty and not the cold.

I sit down at the computer and go to the Soaring Spirits International site. I read the comments posted on the Widowed Village link. I see that I had knowledge in particular matters that other widows did not, and that gave me the strength to share my thoughts online as well. Getting replies and sharing gives me comfort from knowing I am not alone.

Afterwards I get dressed and go out to the barn and bring in wood to start the fireplace. Once I get the fire roaring I call Hayley and Danny to come in and lie by the fire.

As I sit by the fire it stirs up memories of all the fires Brian and I have sat in front of, and I decide to write a letter to him to document what life is like without him. I walk to the office, open the desk drawer and pull out a lined pad of paper. I walk back and sit down next to the fire. I start by writing - *The 1st Year.*

FORTY SIX

I have come to believe that we get signs from our loved ones. I need to believe this. It gives me comfort to think that events that happen are being sent to me by Brian so that I will be comforted. It is his only way to communicate with me.

Today as I look over at the television a flash of a program about Panama pops up. I turn up the volume. I know it is a message from Brian. I can feel his presence today as I sit here. Looking at the beautiful Panama countryside brings me comfort thinking of all the wonderful days we shared there.

I also see Brian in the things that I do, the places I go. In Walmart I stand in the candy aisle and look at so many brand names. I want to reach out and place items in my basket, but I know that now there is no one at home to be surprised and tear open the packages. A simple gift of candy could put a smile on Brian's face. So many holidays have special candy – Valentine's Day, Easter, Halloween and Christmas, and now with marketing in stores it seems like each season extends into the next. Christmas candy is either on the shelves or being discounted on the store shelves right up until the Valentine's day product arrives and so on.

In all our homes Brian dedicated one or two shelves in the pantry to his candy. Jelly beans, jelly bellies, ribbon candy, dinosours and sugared jelly rings were all amongst the regulars that were stacked on the shelves. In addition, he had a glass candy jar on a pedestal in his office. It required that you put money in the slot and turn the handle to get a few jelly beans to slide down the spout. Brian loved to get the kids to put nickels and dimes in it.

When our nieces and nephews visited they would run to Uncle Brian and I would hear *'Can we have some candy, please.'* Brian would go with them to the pantry. For the kids it must have felt like they had found candy heaven. There was so much to pick from that I remember sometimes they would just stand and stare, uncertain what to select. Brian did monitor how much they ate over their visit, but then again he was using his internal monitor, so they all ate more than they should have. Sugar intake was always high during their visits, and so was their energy level.

Our niece Sophie talked at Brian's service about the gigantic Mr. Freeze Brian would give them. They would all get brain freeze and laugh, but they couldn't resist eating the whole thing anyways.

Everyone has always included candy in gifts to Brian. My mother always bought him ribbon candy from Olivier's Candy in Calgary. It required a special trip to the store, and one of my brothers would need to drive her. She was always so happy as she knew it was something that Brian appreciated. Brian was fortunate that his body processed sugar and his high intake never caused a health problem. When we were in Panama, Brian would always ask visitors from Canada to bring some of his favourite candies down with them.

At Brian's Celebration of Life, we had a container of sour candies that meant so much to everyone who knew how much candy Brian ate. I still have the remainder of that container in the pantry.

Today looking at the candy in Walmart has made me sad once more, and I start to cry. I must walk away until I can gain control of my emotions. Most of the time going to the frozen food aisle will do it. There is nothing I want, so I can just stare at the freezers until the sadness passes. Before I leave the store I buy some chocolate marshmallow hearts.

As I walk through the mall I notice the people and everyone has someone. Couples walk hand in hand. I see girlfriends laughing and chattering together. I have no one.

In part I know that our lifestyle impacted the situation I now find myself in. We had moved away from friends for new opportunities, and in some cases friends had moved away from us for their own opportunities. Over the years Brian and I became closer and relied on each other to fill the void that had been filled by close friendships. As our lives moved on we were separated by distance from daily contact with friends, but we remained linked by phone, email and vacations spent together. We were linked by the bond that made us friends in the first place. But now when I needed it most, I did not have those close alliances to lean on day to day. I no longer have that lifelong friend to go to coffee with, to cry with, to care about me. Where did that person go?

FORTY SEVEN

*B*rian has now been gone three and a half months. This weekend will be Valentine's Day. The following day Brian would have turned 61. I have two events to deal with.

My brothers Wayne and Rod and their families are visiting bringing Brian's mother along as well so I won't be alone. My sister Penny and her husband, Mark, will also be travelling up. I try hard to be strong when they are here as I don't want them to know how close to the edge I am. I have always been the tough sister, the one who can handle anything, so I can't let them see inside me now. I listen as they update me on everything that is happening in their lives and what other family members are up to.

I know they are trying to make me feel a part of it. I pull up my façade and face each day while they are here and only crumble once they have retreated to their busy lives. I go back to my sorrow, to my lack of interest in living. What is the point of caring when there is no one to share my life with? There is no one to dream with. There is no direction to my life.

A week later I wake up even more dark and gloomy. I know that I have dreamt thoughts of being with Brian. I don't care about life without him. I know that what I am feeling is depression, and I want to shake the feeling. I do not want to fall into the hole of constant darkness. I fear that I will never return. I try to shake the feeling as thoughts of suicide pop into my head. I want to go drive my vehicle in front of a semi transport that will surely mean the end of me. I feel unloved and unwanted. I wish there was someone I could share my feelings with, someone who would take away my fears.

I make coffee and put on layers of clothes to fend off the cold winter air. Hayley and Danny come running when I step from the house. I plan to walk as far as I can in the fields following the path made in the snow by Jesse and Dustin. They have several paths packed down winding through the trees. I hope that the fresh air will bring happiness to my heart. I try to focus on the birds singing, on the blue sky and all that I have to live for, but it does not help. I stop and sit on a fallen tree trunk. The sadness is overwhelming and I start to cry. Danny is off running and sniffing in the field looking for mice, but Hayley returns to my side. She knocks me with her nose and I know she understands my sadness. I close my eyes and try to block out the feelings of doom. *Who would come and feed the dogs if I was not here? How many days would pass before someone knew I was dead?* These thoughts contribute to my feeling worse. I realize that it may take days, at least until the weekend. Somebody will call on Sunday I thought. Today is Tuesday. I stand and continue walking and talk aloud to Brian. I ask him and God to help me get through this.

My mood does not improve. I am frightened by the hopeless feelings that grip me. I feel like there are arms pulling me across an imaginary line that will take me from a place of recovery into a dark hole of sadness. I want to stay on the right side of that line, but today it is hard. I feel like there is no one that cares. I tell myself once again that God will punish me if I take my life. He will punish me by not allowing me to see Brian. This is enough to keep me in the here and now.

I go in the house and open the dresser drawer. I look down at Brian's photo on the plastic case of the DVD. I open the case and slide the DVD into the machine. I take a breath before I hit play. For the next ninety minutes I watch Brian's Celebration of Life. Then I place in the other DVD that contains the video of photographs. I listen to the music and cry. When it is finished I play it again and again. I want to touch the television screen. I want to have back what is gone.

I crawl into bed and pull the comforter over my head, blocking out the sun coming through the window. I try to change my thoughts to happy times with Brian. I picture him on vacation with a beer in his hand and his ever present smile. It warms my heart and I drift off to sleep.

When I wake I feel brighter. I think that my dreams have given me new energy. I lift my arms over my head and have a big stretch.

I sit down and make a list of things that I need to get done. I have always been a 'list maker'. Brian used to laugh as I always had a, *To Do* list on the go. When we lived on the ranch I had two lists. One list included all the work that needed to be completed outdoors, like fixing the barbed wire fences, painting the corral, trimming hedges, cutting wood for winter, and on and on. I also had a list of things I wanted to get completed indoors, like cleaning the basement, donating old clothes, painting the bedroom, cleaning the closet, and more. I found that working full time, plus travelling for work meant that I would think of chores I wanted to complete but wasn't home to tackle, so a list always kept me on track mentally. Also I felt a sense of accomplishment from stroking items off the list when they were completed. Brian got to where he would write a task on the list after it was done, if it had not been on the original list, just so that he could stroke it off. Anyone who has run a ranch knows that there is a never ending list of tasks that must get completed. We never got to the end of the list until we sold the ranch, and I think even then there were things left undone.

When I finish the list there are fifteen tasks recorded in no order of importance. I surprise myself as I feel focused, not overwhelmed by what needs to get done.

I decide to start by sorting through Brian's clothes. I make a cup of coffee and rest it on the dresser before I open the closet door. I stare at all the shirts, jeans and tee shirts. Brian was a big guy, and most everything in the closet is a large or extra-large size. Nothing in here will fit my brothers. Next I think of our nephews and again nothing probably will fit, but I select some of Brian's new hooded sweatshirts that I think the boys will like. I go to the basement and bring up a plastic tub. I fold the sweatshirts and place them in the tub. I pile the clothes hangers on the bed. I feel like I have accomplished something when I go make another cup of coffee. I work for the next two hours going through Brian's clothes that I don't feel an emotional attachment to, keeping his favourite shirts hanging in the closet to be dealt with later. When I am done I have two tubs of clothes for family to look through and a bag that can be donated. I smile as I stand and look at the closet. A good start.

I take a break and go outside for a quick walk. When I return I sit down and log into the Soaring Spirits International website, and then the program called Widowed Village. I click on a new link and find information about conferences that are held called Camp Widow®. I look at the photos from past conferences and I get excited as I read through the information. The next conference in the United States coincides with our goddaughter's wedding in Cancun. I am disappointed, but decide I will try to attend a conference on a different date.

Thinking of the time frame brings to mind that the wedding is just a couple of weeks away, and I can feel anxiety building as I think about going alone.

FORTY EIGHT

*T*oday I am going to start packing to attend Lauren and Trent's wedding. I pull out the suitcase Brian and I have used so many times in the past. I look at the luggage tag with his name on it and cut it off.

I have packed many times for beach vacations, so I am almost robotic as I select items from the dresser drawers. Once I have packed all my clothes I select a favourite shirt of Brian's to take with me. As I slip the shirt off the hanger I notice the shirt that Brian had purchased to wear to the wedding, months before he became ill. I slip it off the hanger and decide to call Brian's best friend Larry and offer it to him.

Thinking of going away without Brian is almost inconceivable for me, but I know I must. I reflect that Lauren had talked for years about her desire to walk down the aisle with her father Larry on one side and her Uncle Brian on the other side. It was so hard to believe those plans were made and tickets were purchased, and now Brian was no longer with us.

I am sad for all our nieces and nephews, who will miss out on having Uncle Brian in their lives, to celebrate their accomplishments and to attend their weddings. I am sad for his mother who has lost her little cowboy. I am sad for our family members who have enjoyed Brian's presence for thirty-nine years. I am sad for our friends who say Brian enriched their lives.

I know that family and friends are grieving, but their pain is different than mine. Their lives would go on, albeit changed with Brian no longer a part of their world. My life had stopped.

Attending the wedding is more difficult than I had expected. Every day when I go to meals I miss having Brian at my side. As I fill my dish at the buffet I look for people from the wedding group that I can sit and eat with. Too many times I sit alone. I walk on the beach alone and talk to Brian, remembering the years that we had walked hand in hand on a beach.

The pain of being alone seems to be magnified. I think the last night is the worst. Some of the group flew home last week and everyone else will fly home tomorrow. I get dressed up thinking I would be spending tonight with our good friends, Larry and Sally. I assume we will eat together and spend the last night drinking like when we had vacationed together in the past. We met and ordered drinks, but before we had finished drinking them, they left as they had made dinner reservations. I was left sitting alone in the lounge with my half drank beer. I watched them as they walked away. Inside I said, 'what about me?' I need my friends and I know if Brian would have been there we would have all gone to dinner, but without Brian I just get left behind. I am cut to the core. I want to run down to the ocean and not stop.

I wish I could get on a plane at that moment and return to Canada. I am afraid as I no longer fit in. I wonder how I will ever gain control over my life.

I finish my beer and then go up to the bartender and order two rum and Coke. I carry them, one in each hand, back to my room. I sit on the balcony and drink letting the tears run off my chin. The pain is indescribable.

FORTY NINE

*T*oday I feel like my sorrow is consuming me. I am no longer myself. I am like a turtle who has pulled into the shell. I want to shelter myself from the outside world. I miss driving in the car with Brian when we had no plan or place to be. We would just drive up and down the gravel country roads and talk. We would try to take alternate routes just to see where the road would take us. We were out to discover new places.

I feel like I am invisible to everyone. I walk into a restaurant or up to a customer service counter in a store and no one acknowledges me. I wonder if that is because I am alone or I am just not noticeable. I never paid attention to such mundane things when I was with Brian. Brian was the gregarious one, the one everyone remembered, who everyone wanted to talk to. He was the beer drinker and challenged everyone to keep up with him. On holidays we made new friends because people were attracted to Brian. I was his sidekick, but not noticeable in any way. Now I just fade into the background.

I hate coming home to an empty house. I put the key in the lock and turn the knob. There is no one for me to call out to, no one to greet me and welcome me home. The house echoes with my footsteps. My only comfort comes from Hayley and Danny who run into the garage when I arrive. You can always count on pets to make you feel needed. I am glad now that I have them.

I look back and realize I was in a fog, going about the motions that it took to plan a celebration of Brian's life. Some weeks I feel like the fog has lifted ever so slightly, but days like today I feel the fog is engulfing me and there is no light to look out to. I am in a dark tunnel called loneliness.

I know I must start to make some changes. I need to get out of the hole that I have fallen into. It has been a long, cold winter and even more difficult being alone. Living on the acreage has meant isolation. I talk to the pets just to hear a voice.

Brian passed away five months ago now. I spend every day alone. I have not gone out to lunch, to coffee or to a movie. It is not that I have declined invitations, there have been none. My circle of friends is broken. I think about the situation I am in.

I had a career for thirty-six years. I was a boss, a coach, a mentor, a friend, a colleague and a shoulder to lean on. I miss my work. I miss being needed. I miss having to make decisions. I miss the pressure and stress of the work environment. I miss the satisfaction that comes from accomplishing goals. Now I am not needed. No one calls me for my opinion or to garner my support for a work project. I no longer have goals or targets to achieve. There is nowhere that I need to be each day. There is no direction to my life. I wonder what my purpose is now. I am no longer a wife. I am no longer a boss. I am no longer a daughter.

I look out to the snow that is blowing across the deck. I can see snow drifts clinging against the tree trunks. There are no birds at the feeder. I turn on the television and see the temperature has dipped below minus thirty. I shiver even though the house is warm.

Being unable to clear the snow from the yard and driveway by myself worries me. On some days I am unable to get the car out of the garage due to the snow that has drifted against the doors. Every time it happens it reminds me that I can no longer rely on Brian to handle the snow. Being unable to leave, and too lonely to stay, has made me feel trapped on many days. The walls feel like they are closing in on me, and the isolation of living in the country is just too much for me to handle. I know it is contributing to my depressed feeling.

I listen to the news channel reporting we have had above average snowfalls reported with more snow on the way. Temperatures have also been below average. It is just my luck that it is one of the worst winters in recent years. As I listen to the news I watch more snow fall. The phone breaks my thoughts. It is a neighbour who has found someone who will come and clear the driveway. All I need to do is call when the snow is too much for me to handle. This is a good option. It makes me feel somewhat better. I thank him for caring about me.

As winter moves forward I have lots of time to think. After considerable thought I make the hard decision to sell our forty-acre property and move into the closest city. I hope that this will be my last winter in isolation. Once I have made this decision I move forward and get the acreage listed for sale.

As I walk around the property I wonder how I will deal with everything alone. The house is four thousand square feet, developed, and full of furniture on three levels. I walk around the buildings outside and try to assess what it will take to empty everything. My eyes scan the attached garage, which has tools on three shelves, some attached to the wall rack and more littering the floor. I wonder as I pull open the tool drawer why Brian needed so many screwdrivers. There must be more than one hundred of varying sizes and shapes. I move on to the detached garage. I look at the farm tractor that I know will have to be sold with the property. Then I look at all the wood that Brian had stored on shelves. Some boards were sixteen feet long, too much to handle on my own. There were sheets of plywood against the wall, fence posts, extension cords, tires and several gas cans. I shut the door and move on. Next I open the door of the potting shed. The shelves are lined with flower pots that I store in there during the winter. There are more pots than I will ever fill with plants. Next I walk over to the barn. It is relatively clean, with all the horse tack and saddles on stands against the wall. I hope to be able to sell the tack without too much problem. I am starting to feel overwhelmed and am not confident I will be able to deal with selling everything without help, and I wonder if an auction is a better option. Next I look in the wood shed. It is full of metal fencing panels, metal corral gates, barbed wire, wood fence posts, fence rails and rolls of page wire fencing materials. All items needed when you live in the country and have livestock. It is necessary to be prepared at all times to repair fences, build new fences, or patch, patch, patch the fence or corrals together. As my eyes scan the space I realize there are more items behind what I can see. This will be a lot of work. Before I return to the house, I walk into the largest building. Here is the riding mower, more lumber, cattle handling equipment and tools, countless buckets of nails, staples and bolts. There are doghouses, old and new lawn furniture and numerous items that have just been put in here as there is nowhere else for them to go. Outside I walk past the truck we use to drive into the field and I add it to my mental list. In addition, we still own two horses.

I wish I had someone to bounce ideas off. Walking through all the buildings has left me feeling like I have an impossible task ahead of me. I sit down with a drink and weigh my options. When I go to sleep that night I haven't resolved a thing.

When I wake up, however, I feel clearer thinking. When I worked I would often solve problems in my sleep and I always kept a notebook on my night stand as I would wake up in the night with answers to issues that had been problems during the day. When I wrote down the thoughts in my head, I was able to sleep better. I was happy now to see that I was thinking like my old self.

I continue to rely on the Soaring Spirits International website for support. Over the past couple of months, I have connected with a small group of 'friends'. I see a post about an upcoming conference titled Camp Widow®. I am overjoyed when I see the conference is going to be hosted in Toronto, Canada. I can't control my excitement and register quickly to attend. I know this is a positive step to deal with my grief.

I am on a high and decide to start searching for a new home right away before the acreage sells. I know that a forty-acre property may take a few months to sell, and if I can find a suitable new home then I can slowly declutter the acreage and deal with some of Brian's tools before the acreage sells and I am forced to act quicker.

This ends up being the best decision. I find the perfect home that is vacant, so I can get a quick possession date. Daily I pack items into boxes and place them into my vehicle. Once it is full I make a trip to the new house and unpack everything so that I can reuse the boxes. This becomes a pattern that consumes my time over the next two months.

I am excited about a new house to decorate and hopeful that I will meet some new people. My emotions some days are on a roller coaster. I feel elated when I am at the new house unpacking, and then I feel sad when I return to the acreage and pack up possessions that had such special memories.

I am terrified to let go completely of Brian and his stuff. The material things like his book collection, his golf clubs, his favourite clothes and other personal items surround me. Some days I cling to his things like a lifeline. I wonder if I let it all go will the memories go as well. Because I cannot bear to part with everything, I pack it into boxes and plastic tubs and move it all to the new house.

After a successful day of packing I went alone to the golf course. I made a tee off time at Elk Island National Park that was only fifteen minutes from the acreage. Brian and I golfed there often. As I ride around the course I think of so many golf games when Brian and I would go alone, not needing anyone else to make it fun. Now I have flashes that make me sad as I go around the course. I talk to Brian, telling him about my good shots and skipping the shots that weren't so good.

Once the acreage sells I contact friends and ask for their help as they also live in the country. Fred and Dorothy had lived in the area for more than twenty years, so I was hoping they would know people who I could sell items to without having to advertise. I am scared to advertise in the paper or online and have people come to the acreage to purchase items when I am alone there. I would rather give it away than risk my security by having strangers show up. Fred and Dorothy immediately offer to help me. Fred got the truck sold for me and also found people interested in some other items.

Then I contact a friend who is a cattle rancher, hoping he will be interested in buying the gates and fencing materials. Lyle comes over within a few days and we are able to negotiate a deal that benefits both of us.

Wayne drives up from Calgary to help me sort through tools and other items that could be given to family or kept for me to use. On the following weekend Penny and Mark drive up from Calgary and help move items that need an extra set of hands to move. I also got help from Lauren, Trent, Cindy and Carl. At the end, Wayne was there again to help sort through everything that was left.

I plan a final celebration at the acreage. Wayne, Melissa, Penny, Mark, Larry, Sally, Trent and I all go golfing at Elk Island Park. Brian's mother rides along in the cart with me. We share some laughs as she drives the golf cart and we take photos. Afterwards we go back to the acreage to eat and enjoy drinks on the deck.

FIFTY

t is the first week of June and just over seven months has passed since I lost Brian. Today is my last day at the acreage. Sadness is overwhelming me. Yesterday I walked into the field and spread some of Brian's ashes allowing them to blow in the wind. He will always be a part of this land, I think. Then I open a Budweiser, take a sip, and pour some on the field for Brian. The tears make it almost impossible for me to see as I walk back to the house. Then I walk down the driveway and took down the name sign that was nailed to the rail fence. It had been a gift from Penny and Mark. When I am done, I took the last photos of the property. Last week I had dug some perennials and moved them to my new flower beds. The plants had been transplanted from my parent's yard years before when we bought this property. I just could not leave them all behind. I have already moved many decorations that adorned the yard and flower beds.

I look over to the corral to our horses and walk out to feed them for the last time. They will remain on the acreage which has been their home for the past eleven years. Tears run down my cheek. I reach out and stroke Jesse's muzzle. It feels like velvet as he twitches smelling my hand. I wrap my arms around his neck and bury my head in his mane. I breathe in the familiar scent. I talk to him and tell him that I have no choice but to leave him and Dustin. I feel guilt at my decision. I reach into my pocket and feed him the horses treats which he gobbles up, leaving a green smear on my hand. Danny and Hayley are at my side, and they are both nervous that they will be left behind as well.

I do not try to hold back my sadness. I walk Danny and Hayley for the last time in the fields and think of all the times that Brian and I walked the dogs out here. I look at the barbed wire fences and think of all the times Brian and I walked the fence line and repaired it. I look back at the barn and equipment shed and how nice they look now from when we purchased the property. The old worn wood has been covered with metal, and now the buildings will be sturdy for fifty more years protected from the elements of wind, snow and rain. I look at the corrals that we built together. I remember holding the long wood rails as Brian nailed the end to the posts. I remember painting the corral after it was built and how proud we were when it was finished. I know I will miss being able to walk in the yard and think of Brian walking beside me. I think of the sunrises and sunsets that I have seen here and all the photos I have taken. I know that the sun will not shine into the windows in my new home like it does here in the country.

I walk back to the house and stand on the deck, remembering when it was built. I think of all the beers we have shared with family and friends on this deck. I wonder if I will have the same feeling at my new house.

I finally say goodbye to the inanimate objects and load Danny and Hayley into the truck. I have already moved Toes, our cat, to the new house. I slowly inch down the driveway and onto the highway. There is no traffic behind me so I move slowly past our property, and then when I'm past our fence I step on the gas and drive to the new house. I try to reassure myself that I had no choice but to move, as living alone in the country was not helping me deal with my grief.

I purchased a newer home so that I wouldn't have to deal with major repairs for a few years. It is in a new district with walking paths and green spaces, which is good as I will need to walk Hayley and Danny. First, I thought, I will need to teach them to wear a collar and walk on a leash. On the farm they never had collars on and walked freely with us. For today they have the fenced-in yard.

I walk into the garage and look at all the items I have brought from the farm that now litter the floor of the garage. At the farm we had tool shelves which kept everything organized. There were also a lot more buildings so things did not seem so overwhelming. Now as I look at it all I wonder where it will fit. There are no shelves in this garage, no hooks to hang anything up.

I feel that I can hang shelves by myself. I have seen Brian use a drill hundreds of times. I know I will feel better having organized some of the garage. I get out the appropriate drill head I need to fit in the screw and adjust it in the end of the drill. I look for an electrical plug and realize there is not one close. I swear at the previous owner of the house for not having put more electrical plugs in the garage. I find the extension cord and finally get the drill plugged in. All's good so far. I locate the studs behind the drywall. Next I place the support against the wall and using a level I put a small mark on the wall where each screw should go to ensure that when finished the support will be level. Again these are things I have watched Brian do. I place the support against the wall and line the end of the drill into the screw. When I squeeze the trigger on the drill, the power forces the drill bit to jump off the screw. The screw and support fall to the ground. I pick them up and try again. This time I get the screw part way in, and then it strips and will no longer rotate. I can feel my frustration building.

I try several more times, and I finally get the second screw into the wall. I start to cry. This would have been so easy for Brian. He would have had all the supports up by now. I look and realize I need to put up two supports for each shelf and that requires eight screws. I had envisioned putting up three shelves today. That means twenty-four screws. I have now spent more than thirty minutes, and I have only two screws partially in the wall. I feel defeated.

I wish there was someone close who could help me. Everyday there are reminders that Brian is no longer here. Putting up shelves is just such a simple task that Brian would have dealt with, but for me it is frustrating and I feel like a failure that I cannot accomplish this task. I put down the drill and leave the garage feeling overwhelmed.

I walk back into the house and decide to unpack items and organize the basement. This is something I can do alone.

I haven't heard from anyone since I moved in two weeks ago. There is no offer of help from friends. I guess that people expect that if I need something I will call, but it is difficult because some days I just need someone to sit with me while I cry. To me it seems like no one cares. I feel hopeless and it frightens me. I wanted so much to change my attitude by moving to a new house, but it has not happened. I still feel just as lonely.

I sit down on the stairs and look at all the boxes. I know that as this house is smaller I will not have room for everything, so I systematically select boxes that can be unpacked easily and not add to the clutter. After two hours of working in the basement I come back upstairs with a sense of satisfaction.

I have always gotten up early in the morning. My alarm was set for 5:00 am or earlier for so many years that my body clock is set for an early start. Retirement has not changed that. Most days I am up and dressed making coffee by 6:30 am. I walk Hayley and return home. I have my second cup of coffee and look at the clock. It is 8:15. I wonder how I will fill my day.

FIFTY ONE

*I*t is the end of June and I fly to Vancouver Island to attend our niece Sophie's wedding. It is a perfectly planned ceremony on the side of a lake. When we sit down to the dinner I feel the pain of being alone. I look at the name plates, and Brian's name is not next to mine. I keep my pain to myself and hide my feelings. When the music starts I think of dancing in Brian's arms and close my eyes envisioning him next to me. I step outside to get fresh air and distance myself from those dancing. It only takes me a couple of minutes and I return, happy to be with everyone enjoying this celebration. Brian's little '*Chip Dip*' (his nick name for Sophie) is now a married woman. I smile thinking of Brian as I take photos of her and Colin dancing, laughing and enjoying their day. I know that Brian and my parents are looking down from heaven on all of us.

After the wedding I drive two hours down Vancouver Island and visit with Debbie. As always she makes me laugh, and we enjoy a good visit over wine and beer. Then I go spend a couple of days with Maggie. I have flown one way as Maggie and I will be driving her vehicle back to Alberta. It is a leisurely trip and gives us lots of time to talk which I need.

I feel stronger emotionally after spending time with Maggie. She has walked in my shoes, being widowed twice. She understands the pain I am living with every day.

We stop in Calgary and pick up Brian's mother before driving up to my home. Now that Maggie has arrived I feel more stable. Talking with her allows me to bare my soul. Together we sort through Brian's tee shirts. We select all the ones from vacation destinations and Mary will put them together in a quilt. The logos of the resorts and bars, together with graphics like iguanas, toucans, turtles and such will blend together to make a colourful collage of vacation memories.

It is a big task to go through Brian's clothes, and I am glad that Maggie is here. We also select four shirts to send to a relative in England. Finally, I feel like I am headed in the right direction.

Less than a week later I watch Maggie and my mother-in-law pull out of the driveway, and I get the gnawing feeling in my gut. I am alone once more. After all the chatter of having company, the silence in the house now is crippling. I leave the television on just to hear voices.

As has become my routine I talk to Hayley and Toes so that I do not lose my mind. I have also come to get comfort from the song 'Happy'. I turn on the CD player in the kitchen and advance it to the song. I clap my hands, sing and dance across the kitchen floor as Hayley lies on her pillow and watches me. By the end of the song a smile has returned to my face. No matter where I am, every time I hear this song it brings a smile to my face.

When I am done dancing I check emails. Once again there is an invitation to visit Dale and Bonnie in the Maritimes. I have also received invitations from Scott and Belinda to visit in Saskatchewan, and from Dudley and Lauretta to visit in British Columbia. I appreciate their support so much, and I need their constant emails to make me feel that I matter. I decline the invitations to visit, however, as I am afraid that I will be a burden on them. Emotionally I am not ready to see friends without Brian. I think I would just cry, and I am afraid to show how vulnerable I am. I make promises that I may come at a later time when I am stronger.

To meet new people, I start to attend the free meetings that are advertised at the local library. This puts me in touch with a group that meets monthly to talk about travelling. Each month there is a speaker from the group who shares photos from a recent trip. They share tips on where they have travelled and I find it an interesting afternoon. Most of the group are couples, so to feel like I fit in I talk as 'we'. It is my way to shelter myself. I cannot bring myself to say 'I' because I get a stab in the gut at the reality. I keep the fact I am a widow a secret from these new people and keep referring to my husband. I know that one day I will have to face the fact that I am a widow, but for now I can't face that. I have spoken of my life for thirty-nine years as 'we' so I don't know how to speak in the first person singular.

I had hoped that moving from the acreage that held so many memories would make my recovery from grief less painful, but I feel just as lonely in a different space. So many things are different living in the city from the acreage.

I realize how much I miss watching the sun peaking over the trees on our acreage. The brilliant oranges, pinks and even purples were striking. The sunrise in a city cannot compare to the country. I also miss the sound of coyotes yipping in the early evening. Coyotes would call to one another, and sometimes it would seem like they were in our front yard when they were actually across the fields in their dens.

There are positive changes, however, to living in the city. I am closer to the stores and the library. I live in a new district with walking paths and a wetland area where I can watch the ducks and geese swimming in the pond and raising their young.

Today as I walk with Hayley through the wetlands, I notice a park bench that bears a plaque in memory of two people. Each day I pass this bench, and finally one day the idea pops into my head to investigate whether it is possible to purchase a bench in memory of Brian. I am surprised when I go on the City website and see a link which puts me in contact with the right department. I talk with a pleasant girl who immediately tells me this is possible, and she asks if I have made a decision about where I would like to see the bench erected. This is not something I had even thought about. I assumed they would tell me where it could be erected. Over the next few days, before my meeting with her, I looked for a spot while Hayley and I walked around the pond and pathways. I select a spot by the dock as there is no bench in the area. Also from this spot you can see the sun rise each day, which reminds me of the farm.

Within a week I have made arrangements for the bench and the wording for the plaque to be affixed. I feel an inner peace. I am so excited that I hit play on the CD player and dance my way across the kitchen listening to 'Happy'. I play it once again and sing even louder.

When I am done dancing I sit down to check emails. I open an email from the funeral home. It is a notice about the annual tree planting ceremony which will be in September. A tree would be planted in memory of Brian. I realize the date coincides with the passing of my mother, which makes me feel anxious.

It is the weekend of the memorial tree planting. I get in my vehicle and start the three hour drive down to Calgary. I arrive at Wayne and Melissa's. Both my brothers and families are going with me. When we arrive at the event I realize I am unprepared. I imagined I would receive a name stake that I would put beside the tree for Brian. That is not the process. Trees are planted in bulk in the memorial gardens. Together we look at families with balloons and mementos in their hands. I think to myself *'They've done this before'*.

We walk amongst the trees and select a small foot-tall pine tree. It stands at the top of the planting rows. We stand beside it and listen to the other families. I text my sister, Penny, and tell her to bring blue ribbon or wool that we can tie to our tree and a felt marker. When she arrives we tie the ribbon on the tree. Then we write Brian's name on a rock and add it to other rocks at the base. We walk around and pick up some flat rocks and put them in our pockets to take home with us. We take photos with all of us by the tree before we leave.

That night Melissa, Crystal and I decorate rocks with decals – a saddle, a cowboy hat, spurs and a horse shoe. Then we shellac the rock in an attempt to keep the decals affixed. The next day we return and place the decorated rocks under Brian's tree. As we walk away I feel peaceful, having left a fitting tribute.

FIFTY TWO

have highly anticipated the upcoming weekend. At eleven months out (the widow's term for timeline following the loss), I am travelling to Toronto to attend a conference called Camp Widow®, a program of Soaring Spirits International. After checking into the hotel I go in search of the registration desk. I receive a name badge and a coloured notation as to how long I had been widowed. Next I attend the orientation session where I meet my first friend – Bailey. After only thirty minutes I feel uplifted. Here there were people who were also dealing with the loss of a spouse, and there was an immediate connection.

There was a commonality among us – the loss that hovered over us. Some participants had been widowed for many years, and then there were the widow's, like me, who had not yet hit the first anniversary of the passing of their spouse.

The conference was a series of workshops, and I never felt alone. Even at coffee breaks I found people who wanted to talk and share their experiences. There was a special bond between not only the participants but the presenters too. All the presenters had also experienced the loss of a spouse. I was inspired by the leaders who spoke from their hearts and truly understood the pain of loss. We all learned from each other.

I am grateful for having had a career, for understanding financial matters and for my experience travelling. I realize that handling financial affairs is one of the most challenging aspects for some widows whose spouse had always handled everything. They were left with no experience or knowledge of how to handle day to day affairs. This contributed to their anxiety. Listening to their stories I feel fortunate to have had a career as a banker. I also met widows who had never travelled, so getting on a plane to attend the conference had been a big challenge for them. I had considerable experience travelling in my career, so I never think twice about jumping on a plane or going through a large airport.

On the reverse, I realized that I lacked the support network that so many widows had relied on. They told stories of friends who had come with meals weekly, who had helped with yard work, who were there to lean on. I had no such support. My on line friends were there for me, and their emails gave me comfort, but I realized how much I could have progressed with that friend at my side. I never once was invited for coffee or lunch. I listened to these widows and the strength they garnered from friends.

I have always been an independent person, and my circle of friends has always been small. I do not have a gregarious personality and I keep things close to my chest. I do not share in idle chit chat. I had no children, through which many widows had made neighbourhood friends. I know that I have not always reached out to create new friends, but I never expected that in losing Brian I would also lose friends. I went to bed that night determined to make a change.

I meet Kim at the first workshop I attend. She and I seem to have an instant connection. We had been married close to the same number of years, neither of us had children, we both had careers, we had travelled, and we both were wearing our husband's wedding band on the index finger of our right hand. We chat at coffee time and dinner. The next day we are in the same workshop together again and spend most of the rest of the weekend supporting each other. I knew right away that when I'd leave the conference I would have a new friend, and that made me feel stronger.

I met widows whose husbands had also succumbed to GBM (glioblastoma multiforme), the most aggressive malignant brain tumor. They told me of the personality changes their husbands underwent, which created even more strain on their families. I realized I was fortunate because Brian was as pleasant his last week as he had been his whole life. The Brian I knew and loved was there until the end, and for that I am truly grateful. While our family lost Brian we were spared the pain of his changing into someone none of us had known.

It was a healing weekend attending the workshops and sharing stories amongst other widows/widowers. We even had a party to celebrate. Everyone got dressed up and we took photos as we laughed and cried.

At the end of the weekend I got on a plane and prepared to return home. I thought I was equipped to go forward and heal. In some of the discussions at Camp Widow® we heard from widow's who had struggled in year two, three and beyond. I wanted to believe that I was past the bad days and that I was going to start to feel better.

After Camp Widow® I had planned a trip to Arizona to a location we had been to many times. Brian and I had shared the drive numerous times, but now I would be driving alone. Instead of arriving in two days I spread out the distance over three days so that I would not drive in the evenings alone. I researched solo woman travel tips before I left and incorporated a few. Firstly, I reclined the passenger seat so that when on the highway it would look like someone was sleeping in that seat. Secondly, I always stopped at large gas stations. I would use the washroom and get gas. I never let the gas tank get less than half full. When I went up to pay for gas I would buy two drinks as if I were with someone. Sometimes when the gas station was full of men I would walk up to counter and ask *'Did my husband already pay for the gas?'* again giving the impression I was with someone. I stayed two nights in hotels and made the reservations in advance in both our names. Maybe none of these things make a difference, but for me mentally I felt better and that was all that mattered. In the end I found the drive very meditative.

Once I arrived I found things more difficult. No matter where I went, I had flashback memories of being there with Brian. Just sitting at the pool, which I hoped would be relaxing, made me sad and wish for Brian to be with me. I talk to him constantly.

Today I am sitting at an IHop restaurant in Arizona having breakfast. The 60's and 70's music makes me melancholy. It is all I can do not to cry. I look across the restaurant and remember the booth where we last sat. Brian and I were with Wayne and Melissa. We were laughing and kidding each other. Now I sit in silence. Even breakfast isn't the same.

My desire in coming on this trip was to deal with some of my sadness and find a way to look back without tears, to let memories bring me happiness. Today that isn't working, so I decide to go for a drive to the next town and go shopping. I find a Swap Meet along the highway so I stop, and that redirects my attention for the next couple of hours while I walk amongst the booths and talk with the merchants.

I find nights lonely, so I go on the water taxi across the Colorado River from Arizona to Laughlin, Nevada. There I can walk up and down the boardwalk along the river and pop in and out of the casinos. There are lots of people milling about, so it helps to make me feel better. I have a nice dinner, and when my legs are tired of walking I jump back on the water taxi to get back to Arizona.

Four days later both my brothers and their wives arrive. They have flown down from Canada and together we are going to celebrate Rod's 50th birthday. As his birthday generally coincides with the Canadian Thanksgiving weekend, we had celebrated his birthday together numerous years. I buy him a cake and decorate the condo with birthday signs to surprise him when they arrived. Rod is the baby in the family and was naturally spoiled by our mother. She made him a chocolate birthday cake every year, even long after he and Linda got married, so I knew a cake was important to him. We joke and laugh as we celebrate.

The next few days I am able to enjoy having company and put aside my loneliness. We spend time together enjoying the casinos in Laughlin and walking the boardwalk. We have drinks, enjoy good meals, and there is lots of talking, laughter and sharing of memories. We toast Brian on a few occasions.

Rod, Linda and Melissa fly back to Canada, and Wayne stays behind extending his vacation to drive back to Calgary with me. Wayne, Brian and I had shared the drive to Arizona in the past, so for me this was going to be a chance to move forward from those days.

I have spent months sheltering my real feelings when talking with family, as I am worried about baring my soul. Now that I am alone with Wayne, I share my true inner self and the pain of being alone that I cannot shake. Just being with Wayne I am feeling stronger, and I reflect on everything I have taken away from the experience at Camp Widow®.

As part of my journey to recovery, I had purchased tickets for Wayne and me to attend the RISE Lantern Festival in Jean, Nevada. I had seen it online and knew it was a magical event. I was totally unprepared for the magnitude of it however. I expected one thousand people and the event drew several thousand. We are transported to a dry lake bed in the desert and walk across the sand to the location of the event. Once we find the area that relates to the level of ticket I had purchased, we find yoga mats to sit on in the open desert floor. There are torches every few feet to provide light as the sky darkens.

Everyone is given three lanterns as part of the ticket price. The lanterns are four feet tall, made of biodegradable materials. We are also given a black felt pen. I had researched the RISE Lantern Festivals in other countries, so I had arrived prepared with my messages already composed on a sheet of paper. I transpose my messages onto different sides of the lantern. Wayne does the same. We do not share our messages. They are deeply personal, to not only Brian but also our parents, other relatives, and friends.

Over the loud speaker music is playing. When the night sky has finally darkened we get instructions on how to light the lantern and hold them, allowing the heat to build up which will enable the lantern to lift off. With precision, the crowd lets go on cue and we look up towards the sky, which is magnified by the number of lanterns lifting off.

It is an emotional and spiritual experience that is hard to describe in words. Only pictures will do. Wayne and I stand in awe, along with everyone else, as almost ten thousand lanterns are released in one synchronized motion, travelling to heaven with messages for our loved ones. This process is repeated with our remaining lanterns. We take lots of pictures to capture the evening.

Within a day Wayne and I start the drive back up to Canada. I am on a high after Camp Widow® and the lantern festival, and I am looking forward to being back home with a renewed vision for my future. Little did I know that I was going to crash once again.

FIFTY THREE

*W*ayne and I arrived back in Calgary. The anniversary of Brian's passing is just days away, and my plan is to spend the day in reflection with family in Calgary and not return to my home for another week. That all changes when I get a message that my fourteen-year-old Border Collie has been in failing health for a few days. The friends taking care of Danny had not wanted to alarm me before I drove back from Arizona, so knowing I was on my way home they postponed telling me until I was safely back in Canada. I must put aside my plans to stay in Calgary. I pick up Brian's mother and we drive the three hours to my new home. When we arrive, Danny is in grave condition, so I load her into the vehicle and we go directly to the vet. It is all over in less than two hours. Danny was always Brian's dog, so now she has gone to be with him. It is October 25th, two days before the anniversary of Brian's passing. We cry together today for a whole new reason.

I am anxious to see the memorial bench I purchased for Brian. It was erected while I was in Arizona. We go for a walk, and I am thrilled at how wonderful the bench and plaque look. His mother and I take turns sitting on the bench and looking out at the ducks and geese swimming in the pond. We take photos to capture the day. The next day I walk Hayley towards the bench and sit down to watch the sun rise. I know Brian will enjoy the view from here as well. The sun glimmers off the pond and rises above the house tops. After several minutes Hayley is restless to get walking, so I stand, say goodbye to Brian and walk back home.

The following day is the first anniversary of Brian's passing, and his mother and I spend the day in reflection. We support each other throughout the day when family and friends call and bring our raw emotion to the surface. Danny will also be cremated today, fitting as she was always Brian's favourite dog. Later in the day Brian's mother and I go to Brian's bench and I talk silently to him as we sit there. Then we go out to supper at one of Brian's favourite restaurants. Once we are back from supper we drink a Budweiser beer and toast to Brian. I sleep restlessly, thinking of all that has happened since Brian has been gone.

Brian's mother returns to Calgary and I am alone once again. I sit down and reflect. It is November 1st. I have now experienced the "FIRST's". The first wedding anniversary alone, the first Christmas, the first New Year's, the first Valentine's Day, Brian's birthday, Easter, my birthday, Thanksgiving and now the first anniversary of Brian's passing. Holidays and events are the most difficult time after you are widowed. Those are occasions which always have special memories, so it is hard to celebrate without your loved one.

I need support, so I call my friend Kim who I met at Camp Widow®. I update her on everything that has happened and she comforts me with words. I really need a hug, but Kim is across Canada so words were all we could share. Words and understanding each other's pain.

I have also finished my letter to Brian documenting the 1st year without him. I read the letter out loud as if he is with me listening. I don't know why, but it brings me comfort to read it aloud.

I tell him how I miss him every hour, every day. I tell him how different life is without him, and all the pleasures I used to enjoy that now only bring me pain. I tell him about his Celebration of Life and how proud I was of everyone who spoke. I describe to him the music we played and the photos in the video. I tell him about our wedding anniversary, Christmas and New Year's that so quickly followed his passing. I tell him about his birthday and Valentine's Day. Then I tell him about attending Lauren and Trent's wedding in Cancun. I tell him how proud he would have been of me as I rapelled into a cenote. Being afraid of heights, I almost chickened out standing on the platform, but I knew it was something I needed to do to show you that I could do it. I tell him how lonely it was when I walked on the beach and every day wished he was with me. I think of all the beaches we have walked on, hand in hand. Then I tell him about my need to move off the acreage and start somewhere new. I tell him about the new house. I go on to tell him about Sophie and Colin's wedding, visiting with everyone on Vancouver Island and Maggie's trip back with me. I tell him about the memorial tree planting and all the rocks we decorated. Then I go on to tell him about attending the conference for widows, the trip to Arizona and all that happened at the lantern festival. I tell him about Danny passing away. I tell him about the memorial bench and the plaque that is affixed. Lastly I tell him all the places where I have spread his ashes. Now when I visit those places Bri, you will be there with me.

As I read the letter I realize all the feelings that I have captured as events unfolded throughout the year. The emptiness of being alone every day, the pain of looking at photos and knowing we will never be captured together again, and guilt for enjoying celebrations.

I keep reading aloud to Brian the memorial announcement that I have posted in the newspaper. It read:

The moment that you died,
My heart was torn in two
One side filled with heartache
The other died with you.
I have lost my soul's companion
A life linked with my own
And day by day I miss you more
As I walk through life alone.

Then I read him the announcement that Wayne and Melissa posted in the newspaper. I cry as I read aloud.

Lastly I tell him about a sign I bought as it reminded me of him. I have hung it above the photo collages that hang in the hallway.

We cannot discover new oceans,
Unless we have the courage to lose sight of the shore.

It has snowed lightly all night. I walk down to talk with Brian at his bench. When I approach the bench I notice two snow angels made in the snow. I stop in my tracks. There are no footsteps up to the angels. I look around and wonder how these appeared. There is no one else in the park. The snow angels are side by side just a couple of feet from Brian's bench. There are no snow angels anywhere else. There is untouched snow all around and no reason for someone to lie down here so close to the bench where it would have been more difficult to make the angels. I smile and know it is a sign from Brian.

Whenever we would get a fresh dump of snow, Brian would want to go out and make snow angels. We had done it hundreds of times living in the country. I close my eyes and picture Brian lying in the snow with our dogs eager to get on top of him as he moved his arms and legs.

I gain strength from this message Brian has sent. I walk back home for my camera and return to take photos of the angels. Once I have the photos I feel an inner calm as I return home, excited to send emails and share this moment.

After making fresh coffee I sit down to read our local newspaper. I see a notice about an information session about getting through the holidays following the loss of a loved one. I am excited. The second Christmas without Brian is approaching. I call and register to attend the following week.

As I continue reading I see a notice for volunteer opportunities at a Long Term Care facility. Even though I still struggle with emotions, I know deep down that it is time to get involved in community service once again. I had been a member of the International service organization Kiwanis for ten years when we lived in Saskatchewan. I found satisfaction in the community projects we were involved in and felt like we were making a difference in the lives of kids at risk. I had always felt a need to give back, and now I felt this was a chance to give back in a different way. The care facility is located close to my house. The following day I go and apply to be a friendly visitor as well as assist with activity programs. The schedule is flexible, and I can do as much or as little as I want.

I feel a sense of accomplishment at taking this step to get back out in the community. I go shopping on my way home. As I walk in the mall I run into an old acquaintance. As we chat she says "You should be over it by now. After all, you knew it was coming."

I was stunned and resisted reaching out and slapping her. As if knowing that Brian was going to succumb to a cancerous brain tumor should shorten the grieving process. It was actually a more painful process, watching him lose a little of himself day by day. I held my composure as I replied.

"Well, I'm trying to heal. Nice to see you. Keep well." With that I walked away as I could feel tears welling up.

I was angry at the person that spoke these words. I know that people think that time heals all wounds but it does not heal grief. It does not erase thirty-nine years of memories. It does not erase love.

FIFTY FOUR

$\mathcal{T}$onight is the meeting for the support group called W2W (widow to widow). The group was started by Jessica who is not a widow herself. She started the group after her father passed as a way of helping her mother deal with her grief. Jessica knew there were widows attending the same church and her idea was to connect them. It is a tremendously supportive group that has grown to over one-hundred widows.

I do not regularly attend a church, so it feels unusual as I pull into the parking lot. I am spiritual, but not religious. I walk into the Sherwood Park Alliance Church for that first meeting and feel a sense of calm envelop me. I am welcomed into the group like an old friend that hadn't been seen for awhile.

I learn that the group meets monthly to hear guest speakers like tonight, or just for a social outing and fashion show. Everyone is welcome. I am encouraged to join a small group of five other widows to meet more regularly to support one another. I take notes as the speaker talks, and I am given a handout of tips on how to best manage emotions during the holiday seasons. I leave that evening knowing that this is a group I can get support from going forward.

Our wedding anniversary passes and I am the only one who remembers the day, and of course I can't expect other people to say anything. It is bitterly cold outside, thirty-five degrees below zero with the wind chill. I want to be somewhere warm, walking on a beach with Brian. Instead I make more coffee, take out the photo albums and look back on our wedding. It was nothing extravagant, just a small gathering of family and friends. I smile, looking at my hair and thinking of all the styles and colours I have fashioned over the years. Right now my hair is back at a long length like the day we were married. I tried having short hair many times, but Brian never liked any style, so I would let it grow, then get frustrated, cut it short, and then let it grow long again. Now I realize I have not cut it since he passed away. It is unruly without any style. I get up and phone the salon to get an appointment before Christmas.

Over the next two weeks I volunteer four times at the Long Term Care facility. I enjoy visiting residents and assisting with activities. I find engaging with the seniors rewarding as they talk about their lives and days gone by. Today a youth group is here, singing and visiting. I think what a great school program this is to show young people the value of giving back.

Christmas is just a month away so I start to think about where I will put the tree in this new house. I drag out boxes and start to string some lights outside on the veranda. I am happy when night falls and I am able to turn on the outdoor lights and view them. I get the tree set up in the corner by the fireplace. In the morning, while I am sitting on Brian's memorial bench, I think about a decoration for him as well. I want something that will stand up to the wind and snow and decide on a Christmas tie. I go buy a bright new tie and wrap it through the railing on Brian's bench. I smile as I think of all the crazy ties Brian wore at Christmas, and so with this gesture I feel him with me in this moment.

It takes me a couple of nights to finish decorating the house. I sit alone with just the Christmas tree lit and embrace the glory of it. My attention is broken when the phone rings. It is a woman from the Widow to Widow group who is just calling to check in on me. We chat for a few minutes, and when I hang up I feel a little less lonely.

The second Christmas without Brian is days away and it looms over me. I have made the hard decision to not celebrate with family. I do not want my family to travel three hours in the snow and unpredictable conditions just to be with me. I tell my brother Wayne that I need to make my own way, but I inwardly wonder if I can. I accept an invitation to spend Christmas dinner with five other widows from the W2W support group who also feel lost and uncomfortable with the holidays.

Today, Christmas Eve, I will volunteer at the Long Term Care facility. I think of all the years that Brian and I volunteered or gave to charitable organizations at Christmas as our way of giving back. Last year I took gifts to the homeless shelter.

It is late afternoon when I arrive at the Care facility. I walk the hallways and talk to those residents who recognize me. There is a one-man band setting up in the main area outside of the dining room, so I wheel some of the residents from their rooms so that they can listen to the music. It is a festive atmosphere with many family members visiting.

As the music starts, I walk around the residents sitting in wheel chairs. I outstretch my hands and look into their eyes. Some are anxious for the touch, others do not move. On my right a man recognizes me and reaches out to me. I take his hands in mine and as I sway to the music, his eyes light up and he starts to move his arms and legs. He sings loudly to the carols. When the song is finished I move on to another resident. Finally, I come around to a resident whose body has let him down. His lips move, but he cannot speak. I see the sparkle in his eyes and gently take his hands in mind. I slowly swing my arms and move my feet as I sing. His gaze meets mine. As he tries to speak some spit forms at the corner of his mouth. His wife reaches over and wipes at it with a napkin. I look down at her and see the pain in her eyes. She has lost her husband who was trapped in his body. In some ways she is worse off than me.

As I let go of his hands, he smiles and it warms my heart. I am making a difference today, and that helps to put a smile on my face as well.

It is dark outside by the time I drive home. I bundle up and take Hayley for a walk to Brian's bench. I sit for a few minutes and talk to him about past Christmas Eve's. Before I leave, as always, I tell him I love and miss him. As I walk home I think about the uncertainty that looms ahead of me. I decide to just focus on getting through the holidays. That's enough for now.

Once I get home I turn on the gas fireplace. It is not like the real fire I had at the acreage, but the glow does add to the atmosphere. I mix a drink and sit with no lights but the tree lights. The lights sparkle in the darkness. I look around my new house and feel relief as I do not see Brian in every corner. I watch two Christmas movies and realize there is nowhere else I want to be at this moment.

On Christmas morning I open a small bottle of champagne and pour myself a glass. It was our tradition, and I don't want to change that. I put on festive music and sit on the floor by the tree. I have on my Santa hat and Christmas pyjamas. Hayley comes and lies beside me. I look under the tree at the one lonely present I bought myself. Even though I know what it is, I wrapped it and placed it under the tree as the thought of nothing under the tree was just too much to handle. I have also put candy in my stocking. Brian's stocking lies next to mine on the couch. I laugh when I look at the two stockings that we have had for so many years. We never hung the stockings up on a mantle, because at the farm we didn't have a mantle. We always just sat the stockings in the corners of the couch. For me, that was the way my parents did it as well.

I go for a walk with Hayley and stop by Brian's bench. I straighten the tie that has flipped backwards in the wind. I feel him with me this morning in a way I cannot describe. I am not sad.

Early afternoon I get dressed up with my Christmas sweater and earrings and drive to Yvette's house for dinner. All the women bring food, and we end up with a wonderful array of dishes with lots of leftovers. We share stories about our spouses and the families that we are not with today. We all work hard to make it a happy time and not somber. After dinner we play some games and laugh out loud.

The answering machine is blinking when I get home. It is a message from my brother Wayne to advise they will be up to visit me tomorrow, Boxing Day. I sit by the tree, just as I did last night, sipping a rum and Coke. I feel a warmth radiating through me. I am happy that I will see my family.

I get up early the next day to check the weather reports. Everything is clear between our two cities, and highway travel is safe. I know my brothers and their families will be able to drive up today. When they arrive the house is alive. Even Hayley is excited. Wayne, Melissa, Crystal, Blair, Rod, Linda, Cameron and me gather around the table. It is a short visit, just a few hours, but we enjoy our time together and have a small celebration. They have brought along small gag gifts and we play a gift exchange game as we joke with each other. My brother Rod, as always, has us in stitches over the simplest of things.

When they return home, I reflect. It has now been fourteen months since Brian left us. The beginning of a new year is just days away. I look at my wedding band and slip it off my finger. I plan to go to the jewellery store tomorrow and have the band enlarged so that it will fit the index finger on my right hand. I have worn Brian's wedding band on my index finger since his passing, and now my band will cling to it.

On New Year's Eve I return to the Long Term Care facility. As I did on Christmas Eve, I walk from resident to resident and engage them by taking their hands in mine as I sway to the music. Today the music is old time songs. Many residents sing along, and I am amazed at how well they remember the words. Just like at Christmas it brings joy to my heart to see a smile on the faces of those residents I interact with.

When I return home I once again follow the traditions Brian and I created. I sip champagne and sit by the tree. We always would talk about all that had been achieved in the year that had passed and what lay ahead. We would make plans for what we wanted to accomplish in the next year. Sometimes they were just dreams of wonder and not realistic, but we discussed them anyways. We never wanted to stop looking forward.

Now as I sit here I think only of the past.

FIFTY FIVE

Today the house sitter arrives who will take care of Hayley and Toes while I go away with Maggie. We had planned a trip to Panama several months ago. Now as the date draws near, I feel my anxiety building. For Maggie it will be her chance to see Panama and all the places Brian and I visited. For me it is my opportunity to reconnect with friends and work colleagues.

Maggie and I are leaving from different cities, so the first leg of both our flights will be to Denver. From Denver we will board together the plane directly to Panama. It is freezing cold when I board the plane in Edmonton. For Maggie it is pouring rain and foggy when she boards on Vancouver Island. Both weather conditions lead to our flights being late, which of course is worrisome because we had a connecting flight to board. In the end it all worked out, and we were on our way. Over the next ten days I show Maggie the Panama we loved. We enjoy a gathering with my work colleagues and I feel at home, like I never left.

During our trip I sprinkle Brian's ashes in places he loved. Today I stand with Maggie at the ocean shore near where Brian and I had lived. As we stand there I think of all the times Brian and I were in the same spot walking our dog Kona. We both walk along the beach and I bend over to pick up some sea glass.

Maggie sees something white and bends down to find a domino. She hollered over to me. "This is unusual. I found a domino washed up here."

"Strange. Must have come in from one of the cruise ships," I reply.

"Do you want to keep it?" As I am thinking, Maggie continues, "Do the numbers five and three mean anything?"

I looked at her stunned. "Brian was born in 1953."

Maggie walks over and hands me the domino. I know Brian is with us on the beach. Tears stream down my cheeks as I watch the ashes wash out to sea. Maggie gives me a reassuring hug and we walk away, back to our hotel.

Maggie and I are great travelling companions, being of like mind. We enjoy a cocktail at the end of the day and drinks in our hotel room while we sit in our pyjamas and talk. It is refreshing for me to have her to discuss my inner most pain after losing Brian. I search for answers from Maggie's journey along the widow path, hoping that I will return home stronger.

Today we go our separate ways, on separate planes back to our homes. I cry as I hug her goodbye. While I am with Maggie I am able to function. I can laugh and cry without falling apart. I can control my inner sadness so that it doesn't overwhelm me. Now as I sit on the plane I feel alone once again. I need that crutch to lean on. I need someone to be with so that I do not fall back into the black hole. There will be no one to greet me at the airport. I stare out the window as hopelessness wedges into my thoughts. I know it will engulf me if I cannot change my mood. I close my eyes and lean my head back.

We are in the depths of winter when I get back home, which contributes to a gloomy mood even without all my emotional baggage. I was gone for eleven days, yet there are no messages on my house phone. I wonder why I pay for a land line that no one ever calls. Then again there were no messages on my cell phone while I was gone either. I search emails and am happy to at least have some messages to reply to.

I reconnect with my widow friends. When I talk with Kim, I tell her how I struggle to move forward. I wonder what is wrong that I am able to function and hide my sorrow when I am away from my home, yet when I return it is like a kick in the gut and I regress to the shallow feeling of being alone. Kim also shares some of the same feelings. We talk for a long time by phone and both wish we were closer in distance to be able to support one another.

I fall back into my daily routine of walking Hayley and stopping by Brian's bench and talking. I know as I sit here now that Brian and I were fortunate. We loved each other deeply. We supported each other with career choices, we lived life simply, and we gave back to our communities. We were friends and lovers. We shared laughter and tears. I am also grateful that Brian and I had openly talked, long before he became ill, about what to do in the event one of us died. We had drawn up wills years earlier and our financial affairs were in order. Those decisions made my life easier now.

I accept an invitation to go on a week vacation to Cuba with my sister Penny, her husband Mark and my sister-in-law Linda. I am packing today. It is Valentine's Day, and of course I think of Brian. Tomorrow he would have turned 62. There is a brisk wind outside making it too cold to walk to Brian's bench, so I talk to him as I pack. When I am done packing I drive into Edmonton to pick up Crystal who will be taking care of Hayley and Toes for me. We chat the evening away with memories of Brian. It is good for both of us. Crystal shares pictures that are on her laptop. A favourite is when we were in Huatulco, Mexico and we chat about that vacation.

We were with Wayne, Melissa, Crystal, Rod, Linda, Cameron, Larry and Sally. We had planned a deep sea fishing trip. Once we got out to sea, Brian, Crystal and Cameron moved up to sit on the bow of the boat. All of a sudden the boat was surrounded by dolphins frolicking in the water. Within less than half an hour we realized that the dolphins were following us, which would scare away the yellow fin tuna, so our plans for fishing were replaced with watching the spectacular dolphin display.

I know as we talk that going to Cuba will be difficult for me as Brian and I vacationed in Cuba four times. I am glad that we are going to Varadero, as Brian and I have not vacationed there, so I will not get those flashback memories of being there with him.

The next day I board the plane in Edmonton. It stops in Calgary and Penny, Mark and Linda join me. I am excited to be going on this vacation with them. The four of us spend most of our time together, and that helps me. With people around I am able to hide my sadness. Today Penny, Linda and I arrange to go out for a ride on a small catamaran. It is a beautiful, calm afternoon. We crawl on to the canvas as the catamaran rocks with the waves. We crawl up to a comfortable spot, hanging on to the ropes as we are pushed off from the shore. The captain jumps on and adjusts the sail so that we advance out to sea. When we are just drifting with the tide, I release some of Brian's ashes. The captain sees my action and stops the catamaran completely, so that we can take a moment. We are silent as we watch the ashes drift out to sea. I shed a tear. Then I nod to the captain that we can start to move again. I try not to look at Penny or Linda as it will start a flood of tears. Instead I focus on the waves and know that Brian will be happy to be at sea.

The following day as we walk on the beach I feel the weight of my loneliness as I watch couples walk hand in hand. I wonder whether I will ever find that happiness again. Without warning I start to cry and turn my back.

"I wish I could make it better," Linda said and draped her arms around me. These were some of the kindest words ever said to me. I continued to cry, but at that moment I realized that no one could take the pain away, no one could take the loneliness away, only I, could make it better. I need to find a way to make it better, for myself, for who I am. I need to get well. I make a silent vow to myself.

When I board the plane for home I already feel the tension of returning to an empty house. Penny, Mark and Linda get off the plane in Calgary, and I stay on the plane until it lands in Edmonton. By that time, I have a tension headache. When I walk from the garage Hayley is happy to see me and follows me in the house where Toes greets me with a meow. I read the note on the table from Crystal who left this morning to get back to university.

I had just enjoyed a week long holiday yet I feel overwhelmed now that I am home. I try to relax by taking Hayley for a walk. I stop and sit on Brian's bench and talk to him about my fears.

I feel defeated. Every time I was positive about progress I was making, the talons of depression grip me with such pain that I succumb back to the comfort of darkness. Was this my destiny?

FIFTY SIX

*T*he hands of time keep turning as I search for meaning to my life. There is no timetable to follow. I am unmotivated. There is no magic date by which I will feel better. I feel like I matter to no one. Everyone has returned to their lives. When they do call, they talk of their lives and what they are doing, but they avoid asking how I am doing or speaking of Brian. I wonder if they don't ask as they are tired of hearing me cry about losing Brian. Do they think they are helping me by not mentioning Brian? I don't know, but I need to talk about him.

I feel isolated from everyone, not just by distance but by the connections that have broken over time. I feel sometimes like I am on one side of the bridge and everyone else is on the other side, and I cannot get across the bridge to join them.

Things that used to bring me comfort are now painful. Driving past our acreage makes me sad. I remember walking in the fields with Brian, hours spent on our deck with family and friends. The happy memories are still there, hidden deep inside, but the immediate reaction is sadness for what was lost. Driving down the country roads used to bring me comfort as I thought of Brian, and I could laugh at getting lost, but now I avoid the same roads.

I wonder if I call my doctor and explain my condition if she will diagnose me as having 'loneliness'. I'm sure she won't, but to me it is a real condition that I cannot shake.

I have tried to work towards being less lonely, but there is no difference in my inner self. I no longer sit home alone like I did for months after Brian passed. Now I am out almost every day. I am interacting with people when I volunteer at the Long Term Care facility, I am with people when I attend the seminars at the library, I have gone to the widow support group meetings and have gone out to coffee with some of the ladies. I have gone on trips with family. Still I suffer from loneliness. Severe loneliness, and isolation.

As soon as I walk into the house there is a weight and cloud that overshadows me. I am crippled by the emptiness. It is not that I have never spent time alone, because I have. I have travelled for my career for many years and would be in a hotel room alone at night. But I never felt alone in those days as I always had Brian. He was always at home waiting for me. He was my link.

I know I must help myself to get better. I want to be able to feel happiness when memories sweep over me rather than sadness. I want to turn things around so that I am happy and grateful for what I had, rather than sad for what I lost.

I sit down and think about how I handled situations in the past and the thought of a Vision Board comes to mind. I decide that this will be a good way for me to materialize my thoughts. I go to the store and purchase construction paper and a twenty-four by thirty-six inch foam board. I pull out old magazines and start searching for words that will give me strength and a focus for the future. I cut out words of inspiration with different colours and different fonts and glue them to the board. I have old travel magazines in the cupboard and flip through and cut out pictures of beaches in Cuba and Mexico, plus popular places we had visited in Panama like the Panama Canal, and Gamboa Rainforest. I flip through more pages until I find the Galapagos Islands. All of these places remind me of my travels with Brian. Then I select pictures that represent destinations I would like to visit. I include pictures of vineyards, mountains, and volcanoes as well as structures like castles and churches. Pasted on top of the pictures are names of countries that Brian and I had vacationed in. Then I add countries like Spain, Ireland, Iceland, Australia, Switzerland, England and Portugal that represented my future dreams. This process took me more than two weeks. I felt a new energy as I looked through travel magazines and started to think of travelling to a new destination.

I am pleased when it is finally finished. The pictures are enhanced by the words and sayings that overlap. As I glance over the board certain words bring up thoughts of Brian and the past, but at the same time I could see a reflection into the future. Some of these words are: *Love, Happiness, Dreams, Health, Family, Memories, It's what you make it, From the heart,* and *No regrets.*

I look at the words *'No regrets'* and I immediately think of Brian. That is how we lived life. We never wanted to look back with regrets. Brian's life was cut short, but I know that he had accomplished more in his time than many people will ever have the opportunity to.

Then there were words aimed only to give me direction going forward like *Reinventing, Carrying On, Life after death, It's time, Moving forward* and *Imagine a better life.*

The Vision Board is the last thing I look at in the evening and the first thing I see when I open my eyes in the morning. I have positioned it in the bedroom for this purpose, so that I can use it as a positive influence over my thoughts for the day. There are names of countries where Brian and I had planned to travel to, so now I look at those countries and try to envision myself there without him.

I am proof that year two is more difficult. I realize now that the first anniversary of events following Brian's death: our wedding anniversary, Christmas, New Year's, Valentine's Day and Brian's birthday all fell within four months of his passing, so I was in a fog. The second anniversary of these occasions is when I truly feel the pain of his loss. My new reality is walking through life alone, and on many days I am crushed beneath the depth of my sorrow.

Simple things are getting more difficult, not easier, as time goes on. Now that I have sold the acreage we lived on, I feel like I have no roots. The new house is nice, but it holds no special memories. There is an emptiness in the house which I cannot fill without Brian. I don't know if I will stay here, in this house, more than three hours from my family, or whether I will wake up one day and move. I know I am in search of somewhere that I can call home again.

March has passed and it is now April. I receive an email advertising a quick four-day charter trip to Arizona. It is a trip Brian and I have taken in the past. I think about it and make the quick decision to go. I sit by the pool where Brian and I have sat many times. I was here in this same location six months ago with Wayne and Melissa. We have all been at this condo many times together. Today I smile. I do not let sadness overtake my feelings.

When I return home, I register to attend a weekend writing workshop. There I meet many interesting people and have something to talk about. I find a friend in Rachel. She invites me to lunch and I accept. We get together several times to talk and share our writing projects.

For my sister Penny, the highly anticipated first grandchild has arrived. Our niece Sophie has given birth to a beautiful baby girl. A few weeks later I fly out to Vancouver Island to meet my new great-niece. I am ecstatic to spend this time with Sophie, Colin and little Nicki. With every day that passed we watched this new little bundle grow and change. I have thoughts of Brian while I am there in moments of silence, but it does not make me sad as I am witnessing the start of a new life.

FIFTY SEVEN

*P*eople say that I have changed, and that is probably true. In four years I had lost my mom, my dad and Brian. I thought of all the plans for the future, when I expected to be with Brian, and now I would no longer fulfill. I had left behind my job and a country we had grown to love – Panama. I left behind the friends and colleagues from a long career. I have grown to realize that I have lived away from family for so many years that I was no longer missed at family events. My family loved me but they had become accustomed to my absence. I read emails which told about how the family had all got together, and I felt like I was outside of the family circle looking in. The way Brian and I had lived our life, needing only each other, coupled with travelling on behalf of my employer, had resulted in too many missed celebrations which now left me with few support channels.

In my career I was driven to achieve success, confident, decisive and goal oriented. Now I have no direction. I have lost my zest for living. I have lost me. Perhaps losing Brian has stripped me of the one person who always believed in me and encouraged me. Now I have no one that cares about what I do. I have no one to build me up and encourage me forward.

I look at things differently now. I know too well how precious life is. My siblings and I had learnt that lesson when our mother and father passed away. Now I was reliving it with the loss of Brian. I now appreciate every day with family in a way I never have. When we depart I always hug them and can't help but wonder when we will see each other again.

As I look back on my grief journey, I try to take solace in the steps that I have made to recover. I record the positive progress and reflect on the hurdles that keep me in the past. I feel proud that I have been able to carry out Brian's wishes to have his remains sprinkled at sea. Brian had loved the sea since he joined the Navy at the age of seventeen, and now he was resting in places he enjoyed.

It has now been twenty two months since Brian passed. Some days I feel more lost than ever. It is not easy to move forward, away from a life, the habits, and comforts of thirty-nine years. I know it will be a long road to recovery for me, a long time until I can leave behind the grief and start every day with a positive feeling. I want so much to be happy, but it is a struggle.

I stand naked and look at myself in the mirror. My weight loss is noticeable. Skin sags around my waist yet I have no desire to exercise. I step on the scale.

As I look down I realize I now weigh less than the day I met Brian in 1974. Once again I cry.

I know that losing the weight is not a bad thing. I have been out shopping for new clothes and it felt good to select smaller sizes.

I reflect and try to understand why it is hard for me to move on. I have talked to widows who, like me, struggle to move forward for years. I have also met widows who found moving forward not as difficult. I don't know what the future holds for me. I know that my life will never be the same. I accept that. I also accept that some friends we had as a couple are now no longer in my life. I accept that I cannot change the past. I can only influence my future.

I know that my experience is unique to me, to who Brian and I were. Brian and I always were in sync with each other. We rarely had a disagreement. We lived by a code of love. We agreed to always tell each other we loved them every day, to never go to bed angry, to never sleep in separate beds, and to always care more for the other person than we did for ourselves.

I will always love Brian and the life we had. I know that I was truly blessed to have loved and been loved so deeply. I know that many people will never experience the love and life that I have had. I am truly grateful for that life, but it is also the source of my pain. I spent all my time with Brian, and Brian alone. I have never gone on 'a girls night out', or on 'a girls only weekend getaway'. I never had any desire to do so. I was content and fulfilled spending all my time, outside of my career, with Brian.

I am still on my journey through the grief tunnel. I accept that I will probably never get over losing Brian, but I will learn to live life again. I know that life must carry on. My life was intertwined with Brian and now I must create a new Wendy, one without Brian. I must learn to look back on our life and be happy to have experienced and loved so much, and not feel guilty for still wanting to live life. I am a survivor and must carry on. I know Brian would want that.

I want to experience simple things like looking at the stars at night, watching the sun rise and set, hear coyotes howl, and walk in hay fields without it making me sad anymore. I want to be able to walk on a beach, go golfing, go to a rodeo, or go to the shopping mall and not miss Brian at my side.

I have made a decision, a big leap of faith, in an attempt to heal. I am leaving behind my family, my pets – Hayley and Toes and my home. I have purchased a one-way ticket to Europe. I am going in search of a new me. I need to find a place where I fit in. A place where I am not flooded with memories of Brian that are so crippling I cannot exist. I need to visit countries that Brian and I have not explored, to create new Wendy memories.

I want to find somewhere I feel at home, even if for a short while, and along the way I hope to find love again…

PART IV

What I learned

I have compiled lists of things that I discovered as a widow. If you are grieving or know someone who is, or you know someone who is a caregiver, then the information on the following pages is intended to be helpful. My desire is that through sharing this information it will make someone else's grieving less painful.

If you are a widow, then perhaps like me you are on a journey that you did not choose to take. There is no right path for any of us. Each of us is travelling down a different road on our grief journey. I have written a list of things I learnt from being widowed, and I hope these tips will be of benefit to you.

- Give yourself time to grieve. Don't listen to all the people, and they are out there, that tell you "isn't it time your get over it". Unless they have walked a mile in your shoes they really have no business giving you advice.
- Sometimes the best advice comes from strangers. I found that the best advice I got was from people who knew neither me nor my husband. They spoke with honesty and experience, having grieved a spouse themselves.
- Cry as much as you need to. I found myself crying in a Walmart store when I walked past the candy aisles as my husband always shopped for candy first. On some shopping trips I had to enter by another door so that I could skip the candy area. I also cried in other stores and would walk to the frozen food aisles and gather myself together

before I carried on. Sometimes I would have to leave the store, and that is okay too. It is better to let your body release the emotion then to contain it because you are embarrassed to cry in public. Do what is right for YOU, not for others.

- Read books. I went to our local library and took out a variety of books on grieving. Sometimes I would read the whole book as I could relate to it, and others I just read sections of. I found some amazing websites through those books.

- Go to the website Soaring Spirits International at www.soaringspirits.org. This site connects widowed people no matter where they live. I found comfort and understanding among the online community under the banner Widowed Village, a program of Soaring Spirits International. Later I attended a weekend conference called Camp Widow® that allowed me to attend workshops and connect with other widows.

- Take time to adjust to being called a widow. It is not easy to go from being married to now classing yourself as a widow. It took me months before I introduced myself as a widow to new people. I continued to talk as 'we' leaving people to conclude I was married. I did not need pity from people I did not know. As I grew closer to new friends I revealed my widow status.

- You will make decisions that may not be popular, but you must do what you think is right. I did. I was the one that knew my husband best. You may also be faced with hurtful comments and criticism. I certainly was. I tried to make the best decision I could for my husband as he was the only one that mattered to me.

- Know that you will have friends that you can count on and friends that will disappear from your life. At least that is what happened to me. Not everyone is comfortable with your new status as a widow, so their way of dealing with it is to withdraw.

- In many books you will be advised not to make any major changes for at least a year. I know for me it was important to move and sell the forty-acre property we owned. The upkeep was too much for me alone, and the isolation of the property was contributing to my feelings of loneliness and abandonment. As I had always had a career and was knowledgeable in business affairs I was equipped to deal with a real estate transaction. I viewed it as a necessary step in my healing. I was relocating to a city only twenty minutes away, but familiar to me, and a location that would enable me to have neighbours and more security. I think you need to decide what is right for you. Not all matters can be put off until the grieving has diminished. Moving wasn't easy, but it gave me something to focus on.

- Get assistance with your financial affairs if you are feeling overwhelmed. There are many people within your inner circle, including children, that can probably provide assistance until you are thinking more clearly.

If you know someone who is grieving then the following tips are intended to help you in relating to a widow or a grieving family.

- CALL, CALL, CALL. Don't assume that the grieving person will call you if they need something. Reach out to them and don't stop calling. From my experience I found that I grieved so deeply that I fell into depths of despair and I needed so desperately to know that people cared. It was important to talk about my loss, but so many people avoided the subject. So please talk about the person who has passed away.

- Offer to help with laundry, house work, yard work or grocery shopping.

- Communicate by email or snail mail, whatever way you need to. If you have a remembrance but do not feel you can communicate it verbally, then put pen to paper or fingers to a keyboard and record your thoughts. These special memories mean so much and brought me much comfort. Even if several months has passed since the loss of the loved one, it is never too late to send a note or email to say you were thinking of them today and a description of the event that brought them to mind. Almost a year after Brian passed away, I received an email from a friend who said she had dreamt of Brian the night before. She wrote how they were on vacation with Brian and me and how real it all seemed. She thought it was a message from Brian to her. I treasured getting her email.

- As a family member or friend of the deceased you are also grieving the loss, but the pain you feel is different than the widow's. It is easy to turn away and avoid the widow. It is difficult to know what to say and you are probably feeling that no contact is the best alternative. This is only a good alternative for you, not the widow. I ask you to put aside your discomfort and contact the widow. It is so important for you to keep contact with your family member, friend or co-worker who is grieving. To lose you as a friend just adds to the widow's feeling of abandonment.

- Call and ask "How are you today?" "Is there something I can do for you?"

As a caregiver I was walking in uncharted territory. This is a list of things that would have helped me. If you know someone who is currently a caregiver, think of how you can make a difference in their life:

- Don't be slighted if you receive a group email giving you a progress update on the ailing friend/family member. As a caregiver sometimes all the time you have must be dedicated to sending a group email even though you would like to send out personalized updates. Don't be angry that you don't receive a personalized email. Consider yourself special for having been selected to receive personal updates that are difficult to communicate for the caregiver. To be included in a small circle of family/friends means you are important.
- Take over meals. Check to see what would be easiest for the family so that you don't make something that will take too much preparation.
- Don't just offer to help. Do it. Call and say that you are coming over to cut the lawn, to do the laundry, to clean the house, to shovel snow, to take the kids to the park or a movie, etc. There are so many ways that you can help and that would be so appreciated.
- Go over and just lend comfort. Listen. As a caregiver you are frustrated with the situation and sometimes you need to vent, to yell, to lash out and just let all the pent up frustration get released. Talk about the person that is ill. Let the caregiver share their fears. Silence is not golden. Talking helps more than silence.
- Offer to sit with the loved one who is ill so that the caregiver can get a break. Even a few hours for a caregiver where you don't feel that you need to look over your shoulder, to worry, to do something, is a welcome break from the everyday pressures.
- Most of all remember that the caregiver and later the widow/widower is doing the best they can at the time, so please do not judge them until you have walked in their shoes.

REFERENCES AND THANK YOU'S

1) In my search for answers and understanding I read many books on loss, grieving and recovery. I found that even when the topic was not directly related to my situation, I was able to garner comfort and improve my ability to cope. I don't know if it was because I became aware of the fact that what I was feeling was normal and experienced by other widows, or whether I just wanted so much to find answers that I made correlations that might not have been obvious. It doesn't matter why. It is just important that the words of others brought me comfort.

   One of the books that I read more than once, and referred to for months was:

On Grief and Grieving by Elisabeth Kubler-Ross
and David Kessler

2) I searched in vain to find a Widow Support Group in any city near my home. It shocked me that in a city of more than one million people I could find no Widow Support Group. Now maybe there were groups, but they were not available to me through an on line search and I really knew no other way to find such a group. I found counsellors for family therapy and child grief experts, but no one focussed just on the loss of a marriage partner.

   Eventually I found an online support group referenced in one of the books I read and that on line group became my salvation. The web page is called Widowed Village, a program of Soaring Spirits International. You will find caring, supportive widows and widowers who have all been through what you are going through, hence their words of support mean so much more. In my darkest hours I was able to go to the website and find comfort. One day while I was on the site I asked a complete stranger if I could call her. I found her because of the comments that she had posted online. I needed someone to talk to. I was desperate. I did not know if I could make it another day alone. So Cathy from Alabama was my saviour. She did not know me, but she gave me her phone number and agreed to talk to me. She listened to me one night and she provided me the support I needed to survive another day. I will never forget her caring voice, her understanding, her sharing of her own pain and grief and her encouragement. Her words directly impacted me and let me know that there were people who cared, strangers who cared.

3) A year after Brian's death I found a support group (W2W) in the city where I live. Jessica had started the group five years earlier, and since then has brought together dozens of widows. I want to thank Jessica for pushing me to attend grief counselling sessions and also to participate in social events. She stayed in contact with me and made me feel like I mattered.

4) I want to thank Dr. T as he was my life line each week when he visited us at home. He gave me the reassurance I needed to be a caregiver. He was the most compassionate person. He saw me at my worst.

5) I want to thank the Home Care Nurses that showed me true empathy. They listened to me when I did not think I could go another day and they provided encouragement and support.

6) I want to thank Heather, the Home Care Aide who became my friend and salvation. Heather would come to the house Monday through Friday, and she provided care for Brian but also a kind and caring heart for me. She laughed with me, she sat with me when I cried, and she was there as a friend long after Brian passed.

7) I want to thank my work colleagues in Panama. These people knew me and Brian fewer than three years, yet they treated us like family. They showed me such empathy and compassion, and I relied so heavily on them to get through each and every day. No words can ever repay them for their kindness.

8) At a particularly low time in my recovery, a man came into my life. I look back now and think he was brought into my life by the forces in heaven. He is exactly the type of man Brian would send for me. He is a kind, gentle and caring cowboy. He took me to a rodeo and horseback riding, two events that Brian and I also enjoyed. He left my life as quickly as he entered it, but I want to thank him. I learned to smile again and I heard myself laughing. He gave me hope that my heart will heal and that I will find happiness again.

9) I want to thank a friend who said *'you are lucky to have loved and been loved so deeply. I have never had anyone love me that much.'* I remembered those words and months later I was able to reflect and appreciate the life I had with Brian rather than looking back and being sad for what was lost.

10) I want to thank Pharrell Williams for having produced the song 'Happy.' It has brought me tremendous comfort. On days when the grief was overwhelming I would play 'Happy' really loud and sing along as I danced across the kitchen floor. This song never let me down. Every time it would put a smile on my face, sometimes only for a short while but it was appreciated. Still today when I hear this song I want to dance.

Printed in the United States
By Bookmasters